OUR DAUGHT

G000075186

OUR DAUGHTERS' LAND

Past and Present

Edited by

SANDRA BETTS

CARDIFF
UNIVERSITY OF WALES PRESS
1996

British Library Cataloguing in Publication Data

A catalogue record for this book is available from the British Library.

ISBN 0-7083-1335-3

Typeset at the University of Wales Press
Printed in Great Britain by Dinefwr Press, Llandybïe

CONTENTS

ILLUSTRATIONS

TABLES

EDITOR AND CONTRIBUTORS

SANDRA BETTS is a lecturer in Sociology at the University of Wales, Bangor. She has teaching and research interests in the sociology of childhood and in women's studies. She is co-ordinator of the Women's Studies degree course at Bangor and is a co-editor of the volume *Our Sisters' Land: The Changing Identities of Women in Wales* (University of Wales Press, 1994)

SIMONE CLARKE recently graduated with a BA Hons. in history from the University of Wales, Aberystwyth. She is currently a research student, working on a doctoral thesis which focuses upon the education, communicative activity and sociability of Welsh gentlewomen in the seventeenth and eighteenth centuries.

PATRICIA DANIEL has taught in schools and colleges in various parts of the world. Most recently she taught on the postgraduate Certificate of Education course at University College of Wales, Bangor where she worked on equal opportunities projects. She has contributed to national conferences on teacher education and gender issues. She is currently involved in evaluating educational projects overseas and is working on a book about women and development which examines links between women in Wales and women in Nicaragua.

SARA DELAMONT is Reader in the School of Social and Administrative Studies, University of Wales, Cardiff. She has published widely on the sociology of education, the sociology and social history of women, qualitative research methods and European anthropology.

BENJAMIN M. DRESSEL received his secondary education in Great Britain and the USA, and then majored in sociology at the University of Columbia, Missouri. In 1994 he obtained his M.Phil. from the University of Wales with a thesis on the sociology of education. He is Director of Central University of Iowa's Overseas Study Centre at Trinity College, Carmarthen.

W. GARETH EVANS is Reader in Education at the University of Wales, Aberystwyth. He is the author of several articles and books including *A History of Llandovery College* (1981), *Education in a Victorian Community* (1990), *Education and Female Emancipation: The Welsh Experience 1847–1914* (1990).

GRAHAM GOODE is Head Teacher at Jenner Park Primary School, Barry, South Glamorgan. He studied for his PGCE at the University of Wales, Cardiff.

SUSAN HUTSON is a Research Fellow in the Department of Sociology and Social Anthropology at the University of Wales, Swansea. She has worked, throughout Wales, on social policy issues concerning young people and children. Her areas of interest include homelessness, the labour market, local authority care and sport.

HILARY LLOYD YEWLETT was born in Bargoed, in the Rhymney Valley, and educated at Lewis Girls' School, Hengoed and the universities of Swansea and Cardiff. She has taught English and drama in schools in Cardiff and in universities in France, Sweden, Greece and Mexico. Her main publications are in these fields. She was on the staff of the Department of Education, University College, Cardiff for twenty years and transferred to Swansea University, January 1991, after closure of the teacher training courses at Cardiff. She discovered Women's Studies in middle age and has now taken on a new lease of life!

LESLEY PUGSLEY is a native of Cardiff. Having raised a family of three children, now themselves university students, she entered higher education via an access course. Her first degree in Sociology and Education was gained at the University of Wales, Cardiff where she continued her studies for an MSc in Social Science Research Methods on an ESRC Studentship. Her academic interests are located within issues of gender and education policy.

MICHAEL ROBERTS is a lecturer in the Department of History and Welsh History at the University of Wales, Aberystwyth, where he teaches (among other courses) a special subject course 'Gender in History: The Early Modern Experience'. He has published articles on the history of work, women's history and historiography.

JANE SALISBURY, formerly a sociology teacher at St David's Sixth Form College and a tutorial fellow at the School of Social and Administrative Studies, University of Wales, Cardiff, now lectures in the School of Education at the same institution. She has published papers on classroom ethnography, the teaching of adults and FE teachers. Her research interests include classroom ethnography, training, the sociology of work and the professions, and these are reflected in her doctoral thesis on the occupational socialization of further education teachers.

RICHARD STARTUP is Senior Lecturer in Sociology at the University of Wales, Swansea, where he initially held the post of Fellow in Social Statistics. He has a long-term research interest in the sociology of education and a developing interest in the integration of sociological approaches to religion and science. As well as researching Welsh education he has recently taken part in a major study of the Church in Wales.

MARGARET SUTTON came into academic work as a mature student, following a career in midwifery and health visiting. She is currently a postgraduate student in the Department of Sociology and Social Anthropology at the University of Wales, Swansea, her area of study concerning embodiment, sport and the gendering of childhood. As a research assistant in the same department, she has developed research interests in homelessness and sport.

JACQUELINE THOMAS came to higher education following a career in paediatric nursing and is employed as a tutor in the Department of Adult and Continuing Education at the University of Wales, Swansea, teaching sociology and study skills. She is also a postgraduate student at the University of Wales, Cardiff, studying Methods and Applications of Social Research.

PREFACE AND ACKNOWLEDGEMENTS

The idea for this book was born at the launch of one of its companion volumes, *Our Sisters' Land*,[1] in Cardiff in the summer of 1994. That collection of commissioned essays sought to provide an up-to-date account of the many shifts and changes in the contemporary Welsh woman's world and as such was seen as a sister volume to the earlier historical publication *Our Mothers' Land* (1991).[2] It seemed logical, if not necessarily at the time plausible, to continue the series with a volume entitled 'Our Daughters' Land'. Exploratory contacts with colleagues in colleges and educational institutions in Wales were undertaken. It became apparent that much significant and interesting work was being done in various disciplines on the gendered nature of childhood in Wales. From these initial contacts and discussions a team of contributors was formed whose areas of interest and expertise were, broadly speaking, history, education and sociology.

This book is a product of the commitment, effort and good will of that team of contributors. As editor, I would like to thank them all very warmly. I am also grateful for the support and advice of Ned Thomas and others at the University of Wales Press without whose assistance this book would not have been published. Finally I would like to offer sincere gratitude and thanks to Shirley Harris, my long-suffering secretary, and to my family who have given endless support and shown remarkable patience and to whom this book is dedicated.

Notes

1 Aaron, J., Rees, T., Betts, S. and Vincentelli, M. (eds.) (1994) *Our Sisters Land: The Changing Identity of Women in Wales* (Cardiff, University of Wales Press).
2 John, A. (ed.) (1991) *Our Mothers' Land. Chapters in Welsh Women's History 1830–1939* (Cardiff, University of Wales Press).

INTRODUCTION
Gender and generation

SANDRA L. BETTS

That Wales has for too long been characterized solely by masculine images and representations has, in recent years, rightly been challenged. Much has been done to rescue and recover Welsh women's history[1] and to record and explore the shifts and changes in the contemporary Welsh woman's world.[2] Recognition is beginning to be given to the fact that 'the land of our fathers' also included 'our mothers' and today includes 'our sisters', and that the stereotypical images of Welsh women – such as that of the Welsh 'Mam' – do great injustice to the actual involvement of women in Welsh history and to their present-day roles, identities and experiences.

If representations of women in Wales have been stereotyped and misguided, representations of children have been virtually non-existent. There are no images of Welsh children equivalent to those of the male coal-miner, slate quarrier, rugby player or choir member or the female be-costumed figure with a tall black hat and shawl. Children are relatively 'invisible' in both Welsh history and contemporary society. Historians and sociologists alike have shown only limited interest in children and childhood. Arguably this reflects the cultural assumption that children are not part of organized society. Children are marginalized and residualized – kept in a waiting position until they can be classified as 'adults', living and competing in adult society. They are viewed as 'human becomings' rather than as 'human beings'.

Against this conventional wisdom it can be argued that childhood *is* an integrated structural form in society.[3] Whilst childhood may be a transient phase of one single individual's life, it is a permanent form which never disappears, even if its members change continuously and even if it is itself historically at variance. From this perspective children are no less an active part of the 'big' society and no less influenced by major societal events and developments than any other persons or groups. Childhood is integrated in society. While it is true that the child develops into an adult, it is equally true that childhood persists as part of the social structure.

The most obvious defining characteristic of childhood is that of age. Children occupy a particular place in the generational structure of society. They are treated differently from adults and are dependent on adults. There is an asymmetrical power relationship between adulthood and childhood which is, for the most part, believed to be part of the natural order. This 'generational agenda'[4] organizes children's relations to the world in a systematic way, allocates them positions from which to act and gives them a view and knowledge about themselves and their social relations. The generational system of relations between children and adults is itself pervaded by the gender system of relations. Feminists have argued and demonstrated that all social relations are 'gendered' and this is no less true of generational relations than of any other relations. Thus the lives of children are impacted not only by the asymmetrical power relations of the 'generational agenda' but also by the patriarchal relations of the 'gender agenda'. If children as a social group are marginalized in society as a consequence of generational structures, girls are, arguably, 'doubly marginalized' as a consequence of the impact of not only generational but also gender structures.

The chapters in this book explore the effect and impact of these structures on the lives and experiences of girls in Wales from the fifteenth century to the present day. The book thus provides a picture of 'Our Daughters' in Wales to complement those of 'Our Mothers' and 'Our Sisters' provided in previous volumes in this series.[5] Taken together the chapters illustrate the strength and depth of the cultural grounding of girls' identity and how change is slowly occurring. The various contributions explore the lives and experiences of girls in Wales across time, across region and across social class boundaries. All the chapters were specifically commissioned for this volume and all break new ground by utilizing previously unused sources and documentation or recent research findings to illustrate the historical gendering of childhood and the impact of gender structures and stereotypes on the lives of girls in contemporary Wales. In keeping with the spirit and nature of much Women's Studies (and, potentially, childhood studies) research, this volume is interdisciplinary. The contributors come from a wide range of backgrounds and represent a variety of disciplines. The historical contributions in Part I provide the necessary background and framework for an understanding of the construction of gender identities. They set the scene for Parts II and III which focus the reader's attention on the lives and experiences of girls in modern-day Wales and address the areas of home, school, leisure and work from a social science perspective. In the following pages, the book's main themes are introduced section by section.

The gendering of childhood and adolescence

The chapters in Part One trace the historical grounding and formation of conceptions of gender in childhood. They provide a broad overview of the position and experiences of different groups of girls in Welsh society from the Middle Ages through to the mid-twentieth century. Whilst not claiming to provide complete coverage of such a broad time-scale, the survey provided by these chapters will hopefully stimulate further research into the historical gendering of childhood.

Michael Roberts looks at how childhood and adolescence were defined at different social levels and in different kinds of community in Wales from the later Middle Ages down to the era of Rebecca. In particular he focuses on how socialization was tackled in 'pre-industrial' conditions and how far these processes were shaped by and in turn helped to define, gender differences. The theme of 'work' is central to the discussion, thus highlighting one of the most important means of socialization in pre-industrial communities and one of the main ways of establishing an adult gender identity. The chapter draws upon a range of Welsh sources which offer great qualitative riches as well as the opportunity of reconsidering the process of socialization in terms of both its gender and its cultural dimensions. The discussion of Welsh sources is set against the background of English, and wider European, evidence and brings the distinctiveness of Welsh experiences into focus. The broad time-scale reviewed in this chapter, the data relating to the social and cultural 'framing' of pregnancy, childbirth and infancy and the emphasis on gender socialization through 'work' all serve to illustrate how thickly a girl's cultural identity was layered, how early this began and how significant was the acquisition of gendered skills required to earn a living. This contribution sets the scene for the study of the gendering of childhood and adolescence in Wales, it also complements the other chapters in the section which deal with later periods of history in which the movement for popular education figured more prominently and the experiences of work less so.

Simone Clarke focuses on the socialization of gentlewomen in seventeenth- and eighteenth-century Wales and looks in particular at the education of girls from the gentry classes.[6] The 'Welsh experience' of childhood and more specifically the socialization of the daughters of the gentry, is addressed through a comparative study of gender roles and their place in the socialization of women, in Wales and other parts of Western Europe in this period. Central to the chapter is the theme of change in socialization over the period and its relationship to changes in the position of women or the perception of women and in the fortunes of the gentry generally. This is developed through an analysis of the portrayal of women in their private papers and literary works and of girls' education – most notably a study of the female curriculum over the period. Additionally the author uses sources such as letters, diaries and household account books in order to highlight and reveal concurrent and possibly alternative forms of socialization. The suggestion is made that Welsh women active in the public domain, those running estates for example, could have provided girls in their household with a role model which was quite out of kilter with those found in educational texts and theoretical tracts of the period. Thus, from an early age, primary socialization might have inadvertently challenged forms of secondary socialization, such as education.

The chapter is based on sources which have hitherto been disregarded and thus represents something of a novelty in the present climate of historical scholarship in Wales. The gentry (or large sections of them) have been repeatedly castigated for their failure to preserve and advance the Welsh national culture (during the seventeenth century in particular) and because of this the author suggests that sources pertaining to the gentry have been utilized less imaginatively and thoroughly than might otherwise have been the case. Simone Clarke re-examines sources such as the papers, both administrative and personal, generated by prominent gentry families, in order to throw fresh light onto the experiences of this social class in the seventeenth and eighteenth centuries and to grasp the experiences of children, girls in particular, through the eyes of their better-documented adult kinsfolk.

The contribution by W. Gareth Evans moves us forward to Victorian and early twentieth-century Wales. The focus of attention is again on education and in particular on the gendering of the school curriculum. The chapter shows that the curriculum for girls in Victorian elementary schools was deliberately 'gendered'. The teaching of needlework to girls, for example, was obligatory for the receipt of government grants, and by the end of the nineteenth century laundry work, cookery and domestic economy had become recognized 'feminine' subjects. The reasons for the impact of gender on educational policy-making are discussed and the relationship between contemporary perceptions of social class and femininity is highlighted.

The secondary school curriculum of the period is also examined. Drawing on HMI and CWB reports, W. Gareth Evans shows that gendering of the secondary school curriculum played a crucial role in the debates concerning the appropriate schooling for girls and boys. The establishment of intermediate schools in late-Victorian Wales is discussed, as too are the moves towards curricular assimilation. Evidence shows that even in the early twentieth century the gender debate was prominent and a gender-differentiated curriculum continued to be urged by the Board of Education in Wales, despite strong resistance from schools. The struggle for equal educational opportunities for girls was central to this period of history.

As the twentieth century progressed, gender considerations did not disappear from the educational scene but nor did they continue to receive such a high profile. Socio-economic bias and injustices in access to secondary education became the focus of most attention and legislation. Nevertheless an underlying gender ideology, historically constructed and consolidated, remained firmly entrenched. As W. Gareth Evans argues, this was an ideology 'which recognized that there were necessary differences between boys and girls and that a degree of curricular differentiation was necessary in elementary and secondary schools to cater for girls' domestic role in the home and society as future wives and mothers'. Girls and boys were destined for different roles in adult life and therefore were regarded as needing differential amounts and types of education.

The outworking of this ideology is graphically illustrated in Chapter 4. Graham Goode and Sara Delamont focus on the experiences of a group of women who as children (in the years between 1918 and 1944) had been denied the opportunity to continue their education. These were the 'lost grammar school girls' who because of both the economic situation of their families, and indeed of Wales more generally during the Depression, and because of ideologies of gender, were unable to take up their places at grammar school, despite having the required academic entry qualifications. The chapter brings to life the experience of poverty and the gendered nature of that poverty. Education was an expensive commodity, one which the families of these respondents could ill afford no matter how highly they may have valued it for their children. But at the same time it was clearly not valued as highly for daughters as it was for sons. As one respondent says: 'It [education] wasn't important for a girl, it was important for my two brothers, but it wasn't important for me.' These women experienced the double handicap of poverty and gender which resulted in them not fulfilling their academic potential and, as the chapter shows, the bitterness and resentment this produced remained with many of them well into their adult lives.

Taken together, the chapters in this section provide ample evidence of the historical and social construction of gendered childhood in Wales. They show that the experiences of girls and boys of varying social classes and circumstances were strongly influenced by developing ideologies of femininity and masculinity. These stereotypes shaped the expectations and behaviour for both sexes in the family, in work and in education.

Gender and education

In Part I the history of women's education in Wales is discussed and recognition given to the different ways 'girls' and 'boys' schooling was deemed appropriate. It is clear that from the outset education was never intended to provide girls and boys with the same skills and abilities, and gender stereotyping in schools was formalized almost from the beginning of popular education in the early nineteenth century. Education in the early part of the twentieth century continued to provide 'an appropriate curriculum' for girls. The intentions laid down in the 1944 Education Act to address equal opportunities did little or nothing to further girls' educational chances. Irrespective of class or 'race', a girl's natural future was seen to be in domesticity. However, the development of the feminist movement in the 1960s and 1970s brought issues of inequality to the foreground and led to a wealth of research on gender discrimination in schools and on the relationship between girls' and boys' choices of school subjects and jobs. A study of 500 south Wales schoolgirls in the early 1990s, found that with the exception of middle-class girls moving in somewhat greater numbers into the professions (accountancy, medicine and law), on the whole girls' option choices and thus their higher education, training and occupational opportunities, remained remarkably gender stereotyped.[7]

In more recent years a number of initiatives and projects have been implemented in Wales in an attempt to challenge these patterns, to increase awareness of gender stereotyping and to change attitudes. The chapters in Part II of this book focus on contemporary issues of gender and education and are based upon recent research carried out in Welsh schools. They are thus able to provide up-to-date information on gender differences in education, to identify change and to evaluate initiatives.

Richard Startup and Benjamin Dressel report on a study conducted in two south Wales comprehensive schools (one rural and one urban) and provide data on the aspirations of Welsh secondary school students. In contrast to the findings of some earlier studies[8] this research suggests that girls place a higher value on education, have a more positive attitude towards school than boys and have higher educational and occupational aspirations. Girls are more likely to want to stay on at school and take GCE 'A' level, more likely to envisage entering further or higher education and more likely to aspire to professional employment. Furthermore no major class differences are discernible in girls' aspirations or attitudes. The chapter argues that these findings may be partly understood within the framework of peer group culture and within the context of the individualistic or 'contest' principles which are so much a part of the education system today. Girls find it more acceptable to be seen making academic effort, it does not go against their peer culture so much as it does for boys for whom 'sport' is a much stronger element of culture.[9] Additionally, the application and working through of individualistic principles in education, (the 'contest' nature of contemporary education) according to the authors seems to 'be serving schoolgirls well'. The evidence of this study suggests that 'our daughters' are beginning to challenge and change existing patterns of educational experience and are developing a heightened awareness of the value of education and its relationship to job opportunities.

Lesley Pugsley's chapter reminds us that education is not just about qualifications and job credentials. It is also concerned (or should be concerned) with preparing girls and boys to live in the 'real world'. According to a recent Welsh Office document,

> education isn't just about passing exams or getting qualifications – vitally important though those are . . . Education has to be about the whole person. That is why every maintained school must now provide, by law, a broad and balanced curriculum which promotes spiritual, moral, cultural, mental and physical development to prepare every child for the opportunities, responsibilities and experiences of adult life.[10]

Pugsley's chapter focuses on the delivery of sex education in Welsh schools through the Personal and Social Education curriculum. Based on a study of Year 12 pupils in three comprehensive schools in south Wales, significant gender differences are identified in respect of both the opinions of and needs for sex education. Girls are becoming increasingly aware of the importance of sex education and seek information from a range of sources. The evidence indicates a growing recognition and acknowledgement on the part of girls that it is they who are ultimately responsible for their own bodies and sexual protection and that in order to fulfil this responsibility they need to be equipped with sound information. However, such information is not easy to obtain or put into practice. Barriers exist within the context of the home, the school and most significantly within the peer culture where structures of traditional sexual attitudes and codes of behaviour remain strong. In this area of education and with respect to these stereotypes of sexuality our daughters remain at a disadvantage.

The final chapter in Part Two focuses on one of the recent educational initiatives referred to above. Jane Salisbury explores the implementation and consequences of a recent, national, positive action initiative for girls' careers education. Such positive action measures are, it is argued, particularly necessary in Wales where the situation of women in the workforce is worse than the British average and where regional variations and rural–urban divides are so prominent.[11] Taking Our Daughters To Work Day (TODTW) was first held in Wales in April 1994. The project was established by 'Our Daughters' Charitable Trust and is designed to give girls the opportunity to view at first hand the daily working of a variety of careers and to alert them to the fact that choices they make at school can have effects on their futures. The chapter discusses the background to this initiative, its take-up and implementation in one county in Wales and the responses of a sample of girls to their experiences of the day.

The main effect of the first TODTW day was to make girls more aware of the range of jobs that women are able to do. It may not have changed their preferences but it did expose them to wider career possibilities. Whilst such positive action measures are commendable because as Jane Salisbury says, 'they attempt to chip away some of the wider influences on sex role stereotyping', they nevertheless come up against structural and ideological barriers. As the chapter demonstrates, it is hard to challenge the deeply embedded views on masculine and feminine work and roles that still permeate Welsh culture and society.

Gender and socialization: the development of identity

The chapters in Part Three give a 'voice' to children and young people and to girls in particular. They enable the reader to gain an understanding of childhood in contemporary Wales from the point of view of children themselves. Each of the contributions relies heavily on transcripted material and provides insight into how girls in Wales today seek to negotiate identity and understand their situation within the structure of gendered relations.

Patricia Daniel focuses on young girls in a north Wales junior school playground. She is particularly concerned with how girls assert themselves in playground activity. How do they gain space in which to play? How do they deal with the more physical, aggressive and disruptive activities of boys? How do they cope with difficult situations? Do they see themselves as the 'second sex'? The young girls, who are the subject of study, show themselves to be possessed of a range of strategies for dealing with life in the playground: strategies which are not gender stereotyped. These girls display confidence and assertiveness and an ability to deal with problems. They are not content to be relegated to the margins of the playground, the classroom, or life more generally, and, as the author suggests, they provide us with 'grounds for optimism'.

The next two chapters trace the story through to older girls. Do the seeds of optimism noted by Patricia Daniel bear fruit in later years? Margaret Sutton, Susan Hutson and Jacqui Thomas focus on the particular issue of girls' participation in sport and seek to understand the process whereby girls progressively disengage from sport and sporting activities. Why do the 6–9 year olds, such as those in Daniels' study who were ready to engage in a wide range of activities (including sport), become young adolescents who increasingly make gendered choices in their leisure activities? The authors suggest that the answers may be found in the structural organization of sport and in cultural images of femininity. Sport, primarily defined in Wales as Rugby and Football, remains largely closed to girls and women. Both in the school and in the community there is a lack of sporting provision and encouragement for girls (noted with regret by some female respondents). This lack of provision is related to cultural and naturalistic assumptions about male and female bodies. The powerfulness of the ideologies and assumptions concerning body images are graphically illustrated by the words of both girls and boys in discussing their commitment to and participation in sport. Concern with the body is a common concern of young adolescents, but as boys become concerned to strengthen and expand their bodies in order to gain cultural acceptance and approval, girls move more towards concerns of attractiveness and diminishing their bodies. The cultural stereotypes of masculine and feminine body image, combined with the structural provision of sport in Wales, mean that gender is the overriding factor in explaining the disengagement of girls from sporting activity.

If gender divisions remain firmly in place in the world of sport are they being undermined in other areas of life? Hilary Yewlett's chapter discusses the views of older adolescent girls from south Wales on school, marriage, the family and career. These girls display an awareness of gender bias both at school and in the public world of work, but they question and challenge it. They seek an independence for themselves which their mothers and grandmothers had not done. They do not see marriage and the family as their ultimate goal or indeed as the main source of their identity. These girls have grown up in modern Wales and have witnessed at first hand the changing nature of family life.[12] They have experienced divorce, cohabitation, re-marriage and new family structures. They are acutely aware of the need for girls to be independent in adult life, both economically and personally. These attitudes are clearly expressed in their statements about boyfriends, marriage, the family and work. Their career aspirations are somewhat limited, and seem to run along traditional gendered lines (certainly compared to the girls in Startup and Dressels' study) but nevertheless there are strong signs that these girls are determined to carve out for themselves new roles in their private lives and see these roles as strongly related to their simultaneous occupancy of roles in the public world of work.

The chapters in this book provide evidence of the interrelationship of gender and generational structures in society. Children and adolescents are firmly located within the generational order. Their opportunities and experiences are largely a function of adult controlled institutions such as the family and the school, but their lives are also deeply impacted by the gender order, and by gender relations. Thus the historical and contemporary experiences of girls in Wales are at variance with those of boys. Certainly change has occurred in the construction of female identity and in the experiences and opportunities made available to Welsh girls over the last six centuries. Nevertheless many of the structures which permeate both generational and gender divisions at home, at work and at leisure remain stable. Our daughters still face structural, cultural and ideological barriers of gender divisions and gender relations. Girls are far more aware of this situation today than were previous generations and this in itself is grounds for optimism. Our daughters may be in a far better position to strengthen and speed the development of women's hard-won emancipation than were 'our mothers' or are 'our sisters', but they still face a long, hard struggle.

The chapters in this volume begin the process of rendering childhood in Wales more 'visible'. They demonstrate the gendered nature of childhood and bring the experiences of children and girls in particular to the foreground. They are intended as a stimulus to further questioning and research and it is hoped that they will lead to more informed debate and investigation into this much neglected part of Welsh history, culture and society.

Notes

1. John, A. (ed.) (1991) *Our Mothers' Land. Chapters in Welsh Women's History 1830–1939* (Cardiff, University of Wales Press).
2. Aaron, J., Rees, T., Betts, S., Vincentelli, M. (eds.) (1994) *Our Sisters' Land. The Changing Identities of Women in Wales* (Cardiff, University of Wales Press).
3. Qvortrup, J., Bardy, M., Sgritta, G., Wintersberger, H. (eds.) (1994). *Childhood Matters: Social Theory, Practice and Politics* (Aldershot, England, Avebury).
4. Alanan, L. (1994) 'Gender and Generation: Feminism and the "Child Question"' in Qvortrup, J. et al. (1994) op. cit.

5 John, A. (ed.) (1991) op. cit.; Aaron, J. et al. (eds.) (1994) op. cit.

6 Simone Clarke recognizes and addresses the problems involved with the notion of 'Welsh gentry society' and discusses these in the chapter. She is concerned with the broader category of the gentry from Wales rather than those gentry who were self-consciously 'Welsh' in outlook. Given the heterogenous nature of the gentry during this period, in terms of financial, political, social and religious status, she questions whether we can in fact think in terms of a single female role or whether there were a number of accepted stereotypes and prescribed forms of female gentility.

7 Rees, T. (1992) *Women and the Labour Market* (London, Routledge).

8 For example, see McRobbie, A. (1978) 'Working Class Girls and the Culture of Femininity', in Women's Studies Group, Centre for Contemporary Cultural Studies, *Women Take Issue: Aspects of Women's Subordination* (London, Hutchinson). Also Holland, J. (1988) 'Girls and Occupational Choice: in Search of Meaning' in Pollard, A., Purvis, J. and Walford, G. (eds.) *Education, Training and the New Vocationalism: Experience and Policy* (Milton Keynes, Open University Press).

9 See chapter by Margaret Sutton, Susan Hutson and Jacqui Thomas in this volume for further discussion on the gendered nature of sport.

10 'A Bright Future: Getting the Best for Every Pupil at School in Wales' (April 1995) (Cardiff, Welsh Office).

11 Rees, T. (1994) 'Women and Paid Work in Wales' in Aaron, J., et al. (1994) op. cit.

12 Betts, S. (1994) The Changing Family in Wales in Aaron, J. et al. (1994) op. cit.

PART ONE

The Historical Gendering of Childhood and Adolescence

1

Gender, work and socialization in Wales c.1450–c.1850[1]

MICHAEL ROBERTS

Introduction

Over the last twenty years, the exploration of women's history in Wales has understandably concentrated on the relatively recent past of the nineteenth and twentieth centuries, though not without some awareness that earlier experiences may have been very different. Even for the recent period, however, the attention paid to girls in infancy, childhood or adolescence has been small, as if these had been crowded out by the unambiguously mature figures of the Welsh Mam, the be-costumed Dame Wales, and the embodiments of piety or sexiness which Deirdre Beddoe has identified.[2] Doubts as to how much the surviving evidence might ever allow us to say about Welsh girlhood before the Industrial Revolution may have played their part in this exclusion. Now, however, the work of historians dealing with other parts of Europe has begun to suggest possibilities for exploration.[3] The recognition that women's history might be viewed as one aspect of a wider study of the historical construction of gender identities has also given a new interest and urgency to the study of the processes by which adult women and men in Wales, as elsewhere, have been created.[4]

The purpose of this chapter is therefore to survey the history of girls in Wales over the long term, by taking the historical treatment backwards from the groundwork laid in *Our Mothers' Land* (1991), and *Our Sisters' Land* (1994), to consider experiences from the later Middle Ages down to the era of Rebecca around 1840, across the so-called 'early modern' period.[5] This is a large subject, and given the present state of our knowledge what follows is necessarily a series of suggestive descriptions rather than a definitive analysis. It offers an inventory of possible themes and interpretations, and I have tried to indicate, in the footnotes, how these might be followed up. Inevitably, too, some of the discussion relates to children in general rather than to girls in particular, since our sources do not always allow the sex of a child to be identified. To give the subject focus I have chosen to concentrate on the processes by which girls came to be equipped to fend for themselves in the adult world, through the assistance of others and, once they were old enough, through their own efforts in various kinds of 'work'. This allows us to consider the widest possible range of evidence and experience. By adopting a definition of work broadened in the anthropologist's sense to embrace *all* forms of activity sustaining individual or social life, we can consider the manifold activities which girls and young women actually *did* undertake, rather than simply those 'officially' defined as work by guild authorities, employers, preachers, magistrates or, later, the census enumerators.[6]

Alongside this specific emphasis on work, we might usefully note at the outset four more general areas of debate among historians of childhood in early modern Europe. These concern the character of parent–child relationships (were these changing from indifference to affection over the fifteenth to eighteenth centuries?); the origins and direction of change (were more fond parental attitudes passed *downwards* from the upper or middling social ranks to the poorer?); the role of educational institutions in defining childhood and adolescence, and in distinguishing children from adults; and the relative weight to be placed on prevailing *attitudes* towards childhood and the state policies founded on them, as compared with particular parents', and even more importantly, children's own *experiences*.[7] Much of this debate has arisen because our evidence brings children's experiences in and out of focus largely in accord with the shifting priorities of parents, poor-law officials and other adult authorities. Similarly, we need to guard against the possibility that by tracing a girl's life cycle from infancy to adulthood, and from utter dependence to a version of self-sufficiency, we are imposing an adult's linear sense of purpose on to experiences which were probably far more protean and variegated in character.

Birth and infancy

With these reservations in mind, we can begin to explore how the identities of girls as females were shaped. If we imagine little girls posing questions to servants and female kinsfolk as they grew up and themselves became the elder sisters of new-born infants, we can see how the cultural identity of children in early modern Wales was in one sense already sealed before they were born, by an array of prescriptions and taboos which linked the biological, material and supernatural worlds together. For the women who put their faith in the efficacy of St Winifred as an aid to conception, a child's very existence might be thought to owe much to supernatural powers.[8] So all-embracing might these powers be that human agency could almost be discounted altogether, as in the assumption that a year yielding nuts in plentiful amounts would also see the birth of many children.[9] But the absence of human control could also terrify, as when the appearance of a corpse candle seemed to betoken the death of an infant.[10] Pregnancy was therefore hedged about with prohibitions. An expectant mother might be forbidden certain activities on the grounds that these might affect the unborn child: she should not step over a grave (or her child would die); nor let her hands touch dirty water (or the child's own hands would have coarse skin). Cords worn round the waist were deemed likely to bring a child bad luck, and too much attention to flowers in pregnancy could cost a child its sense of smell.[11] More positively, attempts were made to determine the sex of the child. At Ffynnon Ddier in Bodfari, the poor walked round the well nine times before offering a cockerel for a boy, a pullet for a girl.[12] The sex of a child thus clearly mattered, though the personality of a child of either sex was also of great interest, not least perhaps in influencing how that child would take up its own gender role. Attention would also be paid to the time of birth (a new moon promised eloquence, an old one good powers of reasoning; and a night birth gave the capacity to see visions, ghosts and phantom funerals); the day of the week, and the conjunction of the stars and planets.[13] Similar portents were looked for at the christening: a baby lifting its head up during the ceremony would live to an old age, one whose head fell back or rested on the arm of the person holding it faced imminent death. In a society where between 20 and 30 per cent of girls born might never reach their teens, these intimations had real meaning, intensified by the periodic bouts of high mortality brought by bad weather, poor harvests and the ravages of disease.[14]

The christening also began the admittance of the baby into the wider adult world, through the choice of a name, and of godparents whose practical and symbolic assistance might be of importance. If these came from three different parishes, for instance, the child would live to a good age.[15] At such times, when questions of inheritance and the distant future marriage of a child might be uppermost in adults' minds, the implications of gender might be quite apparent. That a daughter's birth carried lesser weight is suggested, for example, by entries in the diary of the Elizabethan Robert Parry. He notes laconically, that on 'The 7 of Aprill Luce Parry my daughter was borne' and in another: 'The 10th of Julie beinge Saterdaye 2 howres afore daye ffoulk parry my sonne was born & christned by ffoulke lloyd esqr & Ric[hard] Parry my brother & Mrs Conwaye my aunt for godmother &c'. As if this wasn't enough, Parry entered the name of his son, but not that of his daughter, as a marginal note for future reference.[16]

In late medieval Wales, godparents might be drawn from both kindred and those unrelated to the child by blood, and the extension of the child's dependence on a wider circle of people was often increased by wet-nursing and, after weaning, a period of fosterage away from the parents' home.[17] These arrangements meant that the physical nurturing of a child, its education, and even its role as inheritor of property might be determined by men and women quite other than its natural parents whilst its identity would also have been shaped less formally by other household members such as elder sisters and maidservants.[18] This is not to deny the possibility of an intense affection for their children on the part of the natural parents. Some of its range is conveyed by bardic elegies written after the deaths of children in the fourteenth and fifteenth centuries, though the subjects of most of these were boys.[19]

By the sixteenth century the formality and prominence of these arrangements seems to have been on the wane, though they continued among gentry families for some time.[20] More common perhaps were the extensive networks of poorer and distant kinsfolk whose names and entitlements to bequests festoon such accounts as those of the Myddleton family of Chirk Castle. For those without such claims to kindred, on the other hand, shortage of food might literally be a matter of life and death, as it was for two people buried in Welshpool in 1700: the 'poore girle' Anne Reynallt of Llanerchydol, and the 'poore crippled woman . . . that died at Humphrey Brown's house.' 'Her name', the parish register records, 'is not known.'[21] The vulnerability of the friendless child in what some historians have called 'the little ice age' helps to explain both the role of kinsfolk and godparents in a child's early life, and the efforts made by parish authorities to track down those responsible for the most vulnerable of all, illegitimate children. Where this could not be achieved, a substitute might be found. Thus we see the parish officials in Dolgellau after 1680 formally recording alongside the baptism of an illegitimate child, the name of the sponsors who had undertaken to relieve the parish of the responsibility for its maintenance.[22]

The ceremonies following childbirth did more than attempt to ensure the safety of the child, however; they also reaffirmed the bonds between adults. Christenings were often attended by the nurse, mid-wife and other female relatives,[23] but there may also have been a tendency for the sexes to celebrate birth independently, as though the experience had for men and women a rather different meaning, even if both shared concern for the mother and child's well-being. New-born children were, of course, spiritually as well as physically vulnerable, and the timing of baptism was often very close to the birth, occasionally on the same day itself in the Vale of Clwyd in the late seventeenth and eighteenth centuries, and frequently on the following day.[24] Once this spiritual safety-net had been secured, however, the sexes may have gone their separate ways. Lewis Morris gave money to the midwife, nurse and maidservant on attending a christening in mid-eighteenth-century Anglesey, but then he joined the baby's father, his friends and the parson at home 'to drink ye health of ye woman in ye straw'. Drinking the health of the baby itself is not mentioned, though Morris writes that he eventually returned home 'stark drunk',[25] so he may well have done so. We seem to have in Morris's account a glimpse of the male rites corresponding to those of lying in and 'churching' which were dominated by women. In south-west Wales in the seventeenth century women were said to consider churching as protection against witchcraft, as well as a reinstatement of natural fertility, believing that 'grass will hardly ever grow where they tread before they are churched'.[26] Though the ceremony was deemed by Puritan zealots to be superstitious, the Anglesey diarist Robert Bulkeley of Dronwy recorded churching as a matter of course in the 1630s,[27] as did Walter Powell in Monmouthshire even in the midst of civil war in 1643.[28] Churching took place in eighteenth-century Anglesey according to Lewis Morris 'in a week or fortnight's time at most among ye Poorer sort [;] the mother walks to ye parish church to be churchd and takes along with her her midwife & offers a 12*d*. or 6*d*. if poor'.[29]

The period of lying in, between delivery and the churching service, seems to have been understood by women themselves as a period of temporary superiority over men. It was a time in which their physical labour and sexual services were unavailable to their husbands, their individual subjection was overturned in a collective female celebration, and the meaning of this whole process was legitimated by the church ceremony to which women went, accompanied by their midwives, quite willingly.[30] Even in Civil War Monmouthshire we see signs of this occurring. Walter Powell's second wife Sibill gave birth to a son, Matthew, on 22 September 1643. A month later a 'churching dinner' was held at Powell's house, followed by Sibill's churching itself three days later.[31] Though the shorter interval between birth and churching which Morris observed among the poor on Anglesey may reflect something of the economic pressures on such women, the sums of money he mentions being offered were high compared with some elsewhere, and suggestive of the seriousness with which the occasion was regarded. At Cheswardine in Shropshire, for example, in the 1720s, the vicar received 4*d.* and the parish clerk either 2*d.* or two white loaves.[32] Most important, however, is Morris's observation that a woman walking to be churched was accompanied by her midwife, rather than her husband, and that even the poor were prepared to bear the cost of this procedure.

Nor did poverty necessarily preclude the employment of a nurse to assist the new mother whilst lying in, another of the features of childbirth reinforcing its closeted, female character.[33] This might even be sponsored by the church or poor relief authorities in the hardest circumstances. In 1748 the vagrant Hannah Barrington gave birth to an illegitimate female child inside the House of Correction at Hanmer, Flintshire, where she in effect had her lying in at the parish's expense: 6*s.* was paid for her maintenance between the 6 and 28 of January, as well as 1*s.* 6*d.* for the midwife, 1*s.* for a yard and a half of flannel and a further 1*s.* 6*d.* for 'other linens & things for ye infant'. But in Hannah's case there is no mention of a churching in the record. Instead, a total of 11*s.* was spent in paying three men to convey her the estimated twenty miles to her last place of settlement at Hawarden. More fortunate, Esther Parry of Treuddyn was allowed 13*s.* in January 1769 for the maintenance of her illegitimate child for three months; a certain Thomas Griffiths was allowed 6*s.* for accommodating her during the week of her lying in, and the midwife was to have 3*d.* for assisting at the delivery.[34] In a similar provision made at Amlwch on Anglesey in 1821, John Jones was allowed 2s. 6d. a week 'towards the present support of his daughter who is in the family way', an allowance which was to be increased to 5s. per week 'when [as the authorities put it] she becomes ill' and the clothes needed for the infant were also to be provided.[35]

Feeding the child

Besides the costs of such rites of passage, the nourishment of the infant was a matter of some consequence at all social levels. Those able to afford the services of a wet-nurse did not necessarily view the lack of mother–child bonding as a problem. Indeed, the bonds formed with strangers through nursing the infant were often highly esteemed and lasted well beyond the child's infancy. We find nurses figuring prominently among the family entourage which claimed exclusive use of certain pews in Llandygái church, Caernarfonshire in 1576,[36] and though a nurse might subsequently figure in a family's affairs on a different basis, her identity as nurse survived.[37] The high status accorded such women reflects in part the assumption that babies absorbed physical and mental characteristics from the woman feeding them, so that decent and respectable wet-nurses were sought out. Importance was placed on the avoidance of artificial substitutes such as animal milk or cereal and water pap, even where the natural mother herself did not feed the child. As the Welsh physician John Jones explained in his 1579 treatise on *The Arte and Science of Preserving Bodie and Soul in Healthe, Wisedom, and Catholick Religion*, 'It should sucke the breast rather than by anye means be brought up, unless ye meane for some singular cause to diminish the naturall growth, wisedom and strength.'[38]

Far from being a 'natural' undertaking, breast-feeding might be a source of anxiety to some mothers, perhaps not least those who were themselves not well nourished in the first place. Gwen Hughes of Penley, Flintshire, 'laborer', testified in 1657 to her experience of four years earlier when 'a suckinge childe' had fallen 'strangely sike' for a number of days, 'cryeing out skrikeing horribly and eateing nothing', after Gwen had peremptorily refused food to Anne Ellis, a woman who lived locally by 'begging and knitting of stokings'. When Anne could be persuaded to visit the child to give it her blessing 'the childe mended suddennely' and recovered perfect health. Anne Ellis, in her dependence on others' hospitality, appears to have played a dangerous game with the feelings of women like Gwen, who had their own worries about feeding their infants, and she paid for this by becoming the subject of witchcraft investigations.[39] Even where the Devil himself was not thought to be involved, popular practices testify to the sensitivity with which children's thriving was observed. Ailing children might be saved at the grave of Gwen-gu at Llanwenarth once candle-light rituals had been undertaken; and those whose health or character seemed damaged in some way might be assumed to have been substituted for a changeling by the fairies.[40]

Children's behaviour was clearly scrutinized for signs of something amiss, just as the astrological conjuncture might be observed when a child actually died, as it was by Peter Roberts, proctor in the St Asaph Consistory Court, when his eleven-year-old daughter died in 1620.[41] When in Flintshire Margaret Barnatt's little girl suffered a 'swelling in her head' and 'fell a scriking pittiful' in 1657, she explained to her mother on recovering that 'Dady the catt was uppon my backe and hath made me bleede'. The child's semi-metaphorical explanation of her pain, however, seems to have carried less weight than her actually flinching when approached by the 'witch' who had been brought to bless and cure her. This woman had been previously fed by her mother, though what she was given, her mother remembered, was 'not of the best'.[42] How many mothers must have worried that the same might be said of the food and care they gave their own children? At the same time, and at the other end of the social scale, a woman hired as wet-nurse to a gentry family might find respect and a certain long-term financial security, and in England at least it would appear that demand for such services was actually increasing through the seventeenth century.[43] Even so, those mothers sufficiently determined to breast feed were often themselves highly regarded, and when Elizabeth Myddleton of Chirk Castle died after giving birth to a son who himself lived only three days in 1675, she was to be remembered by a monument representing a mother feeding her infant in this way.[44]

Absorbing the mother's role

This particular use of the monumental medium was quite new in Wales and owed much to outside influences,[45] but women's power to give birth was already thoroughly woven into the fabric of Welsh culture at many levels, and cannot have escaped the attention of girls as they grew to be mothers themselves. Its manifestations included the

Triad of the Three Fair Womb-burdens of the Isle of Britain, preserved in fifteenth-century manuscripts, but of much earlier origin, and telling of the miraculous fertility of Nefyn, daughter of Brychan, who gave birth to twins, and whose son and daughter also each had twins. Or, to take a very different kind of example, there was Joshua Thomas's *History of the Baptists in Wales*, first published in Welsh in 1778 and translated in abridged form by Jonathan Davies in 1835, but still owing something to the medieval history of Geoffrey of Monmouth. In this appeared Ellen, daughter of Coelgodebog, Earl of Gloucester, the Welsh mother of Roman Emperor Constantine the Great; and Elen, mother of Lucius, the Welsh king who professed Christianity.[46] The mothering of Wales was an inescapable cultural theme, and a girl's destiny as the bearer both of children and of a cultural lineage was made very clear. The Henrician traveller and antiquary John Leland, visiting the commote of Edeirnion in the 1530s, recorded the genealogy of Owain Glyndŵr, indicating that Owain was the son of Helen, grandson of Eleanor, and great grandson of Catharine who was herself grand-daughter of 'Lluelin ap Irrwarth Droyndon Prince of al Wales'.[47] If Leland's principal concern was with the subsequent descent, through Owain's aunt Catharine, of Henry Tudor, father of King Henry VIII, the comprehensiveness of his account starkly revealed what Henry's descent owed to the female line.

Interest in such genealogies was by no means a solely male affair. 'All sorts of men, women and children of every parish' were said to assemble in the open air to hear recital of 'the doings of their ancestors' in north Wales around 1600.[48] By the sixteenth century this cultural inheritance was freighted with images of implicit female power, and overt subordination. These were in turn re-shaped in the process of preserving manuscripts from loss after their dispersal at the dissolution of the religious houses. One patron of such work was Catrin of Berain, grand-daughter of an illegitimate son of Henry VII, a woman whose four marriages so extended her kindred that she was called 'the Mother of Wales'.[49] Among those she employed as a copyist of texts was the bard William Cynwal,[50] who turned out a poetic defence of women, in response to a widely circulated manuscript attack on them, *Araith Ddichan ir Gwragedd*.[51] The defence of women was a literary genre whose fidelity to actual female experience might well be questioned, but the expression of a female point of view, even if by a male poet, was nevertheless an unusual contribution to the Welsh literary tradition.[52] Medieval Wales lacked sufficient courts and cloisters in which to sustain a female literary voice on the continental model.[53] A man such as Cynwal served what was in effect a craft apprenticeship as a bard, and poetry with genealogy were of course among the traditional feats expected of men of good birth and breeding. When not stressing motherhood, this masculine medium had a tendency to represent women as 'girls' which survives even translation.[54] That it might also reveal something of women's own attitudes, as through the work of Gwerful Mechain, a woman whose 'salacious' verse is conventionally written off as 'often technically lax',[55] is an interesting recent suggestion.[56] Perhaps only our own generation of historians is fully equipped to explore this aspect of the early modern world into which Welsh girls were born.[57]

Girls at play

Given the literary or poetic images of femininity which young girls encountered, how were their identities shaped by everyday life? Because our evidence underplays the usual and the unremarked, we may be glad to have the evidence of ordinary parental desperation in the custom at Ffynnon Ddier in Bodfari of dipping an infant in three corners of the well to prevent it crying at night.[58] The most desperate of all were those who killed their own children, such as Maude, wife of John Thomas, who was hanged for killing her children at Llanfoist, Monmouthshire in 1635, or Mary Morgan, the seventeen-year-old Presteigne domestic servant who, seduced by a local worthy, murdered her illegitimate child and was hanged in 1805.[59] A less drastic alternative may have been to abandon children. Such was the experience of David Morris, who was found in a basket on Penybont bridge to the west of Oswestry in 1725 and brought up at parish expense.[60]

Against these tragic cases, it is a relief to place the evidence we have of children happily at play, such as the 'kiddes' of Llansannan who used 'to play and skip from sete to sete' amongst the man-made perches in the rock on a stony hillside in Henry VIII's reign,[61] or the lively inmates of Forden workhouse, whose steward was forced to obtain a number of pegs to fix to the stair rail in 1812 'to prevent the children sliding down it'.[62] Even so, some of our best evidence for children's activities arises from the accidents they encountered during the course of them, as with the two-year-old girl at play on the banks of the Tanat who fell into the river in 1790,[63] the six-year-old son of Walter Powell scalded in the bran tub in August 1628,[64] or Richard Hughes, playing in 1649 'with other children at stoole ball' who 'as he was strikeinge the ball . . . stricked strongly and sate downe and could not rise without helpe but complaines very much of greate paine', a misfortune his parents attributed to bewitchment by the mother of the children with whom, and at whose house, he had been playing.[65]

As this last incident might indicate, some of our evidence suggests patterns of differentiation between the play of girls and boys, though it is very difficult to say at what age such differences first became apparent, and exactly how far they were fostered by adult encouragement. A child's first utterance, and its attempts to walk, might be thought to presage some significant feature of its future life,[66] and we can imagine how this process of constructive observation continued, though we as yet know little about its gendered dimension. The English diarist Elizabeth Baker, living in the Dolgellau district in 1780, observed of one pair of children that the twelve-year-old girl was 'remarkably fond of dancing', whilst the ten-year-old son enjoyed puppet shows and had recently lost a bet of one halfpenny at a cock fight.[67] Children (of what sex we are not told) were even treated to their own Ball for dancing in this vicinity, just as a century earlier the Myddletons of Chirk had paid for the dinner eaten by their children at the local cock fight.[68] At this elevated social level, at least, in the seventeenth century we see a clear tendency for daughters to be given dancing lessons, music lessons on the spinet, and to have the viol played for their amusement, whilst sons get into trouble damaging the billiard table.[69] But even with evidence surviving from such a wealthy family, the gender of any children recorded often goes unstated, so that we can only speculate as to whether both brothers and sisters were transfixed by the sight of 'the Dromedaries' which visited Chirk in 1666, or by the jester who showed his tricks there some thirty years later.[70]

What is clear, though, is that in early modern Wales adults themselves exhibited a boisterous enthusiasm for recreation of many kinds, so that the attainment of maturity did not necessarily require a turning back on the world of play. In the 1630s the Anglesey diarist Robert Bulkeley played shuffleboard, cards, bowls, football and tennis, attended cock fights, races, wakes and fairs, as well as hunting and coursing.[71] Pursuit of such sports when young may have helped boys forge a 'manly' identity through physical vigour and the mastery of animals. Work itself called for a certain everyday forcefulness, and some boys were employed specifically in this role. When the 32-year-old husbandman David ap Richard was ploughing a Flintshire field at Easter 1657 'of a sudden one of his oxen fell down upon his knees as though he would lie'. But disaster was averted when, 'being punched by the boy that drives with the goad, [it] went on and so that day they made an end of their day's work'.[72] That boys could also behave in a threatening manner to other humans is clear enough. When Anne Ellis, the Flintshire 'witch', was asked in 1657 to explain her dislike for the disabled boy Richard Hughes she asked 'Why did he pisse downe her chimley?'[73] The daughter of a poor husbandman close by Aberystwyth was reported in the previous year to have been struck by a stone, whilst fetching water at a well, 'and a boy coming toward her, she charged him, with the blow, who denyed he was so near her'. In this case, too, everyday boyish aggression spilled over into the supernatural world, the boy pointing to an apparition of the girl's father as the true source of the blow, the father then being away from home. Whatever meaning may be given this incident, which occurred in a decade of great political dislocation and religious expectation, it seems clear that the father's appearance had been imagined in terms of disturbing violence, 'and the stone was found with prints of fingers in it'.[74]

Some recreations were directly expressive of the physical exertion required by certain occupations, as with the racing and jumping amongst 10–13 year old boys which accompanied the *ffest y bugeiliaid* (the shepherds' feast) in the Llandysul area of Cardiganshire.[75] Recreations also helped mark out the appropriate areas for male and female physical activity: the naked mauling of the Pembrokeshire cnapan contest, for example, being associated with Elizabethan concepts of masculine gallantry and honour.[76] Likewise, whilst men, women and children were reported to be watching bando matches in Glamorgan in 1777, it was only 'young boys' who were being inducted into the practical mysteries of the game.[77] Games might also be expressive of the temporary freedom which servants felt during the hiring season, as with the football played in the street at Dolgellau a week following the annual April hiring fair, it being customary in many places for bargains struck at the hiring fair to be open for renegotiation at a second meeting one week later.[78] Ball playing in the churchyard or against the church wall was a regular source of friction between 'the young men of the parish' and the church authorities in many parts of Wales, fines being imposed on offenders, and iron bars and shutters were fixed to protect the church windows.[79] Occasionally boyish aggression erupted in a different direction, as with the early seventeenth-century episode involving a twelve-year-old boy quarrelling so violently over a hat which another had snatched whilst playing a game of nine holes that the disturbance came to the attention of the judicial authorities.[80] One wonders what these boys would have made of 'ye strong man' who was paid 10s. 'for showing his tricks' by the Myddletons of Chirk in 1701.[81] Or how boyish imaginations might have been cultivated by the sword worn by the 'footboy' at Chirk.[82] When the seven-year-old Edward Williams, later an Independent minister, encountered 'a company of beings' resembling dwarves he found them 'clothed in red, a dress not unlike a military uniform'.[83]

We know rather less about girls' behaviour, though it would be naïve to assume that an absence of evidence always betokened more decorous habits. Certainly, girls had ample evidence of the assertiveness of adult women, to judge from the hearings of defamation cases in the courts; and, throughout the period, local authorities continued to take measures against women deemed unruly as scolds. Whether this effectively discouraged girls from expressing their own assertiveness in words is an interesting question, not least since defamation suits so often involved disputes between women.[84] Communities also took matters into their own hands, as with the 'skymmetry' held at Wrenston in 1765 where a wife had abused her husband after a night spent dancing.[85] In a famous early nineteenth-century account of a similar ritual humiliation of a brow-beaten husband in the Vale of Glamorgan it was noted that 'the whole village was in commotion. From an early hour the children clustered in groups, and looked and talked as though something great impended'.[86] When the parading of the offending couple in effigy eventually took place on this occasion, men and boys took the leading part, the women mocking from their windows. On the procession's return to the village 'the women there had collected to scoff at them, and poured out a din of hoots and yells', suggestive of a marked gender difference in attitude to the employment of such shame sanctions against assertive women. That children witnessed these events and talked about them excitedly is particularly suggestive of the conflicting messages girls must have had about the proper character of feminine behaviour. Similarly, women and their children played a vigorous part in the protection of the local food supply, as when a crowd of 400 Holywell men, women and children seized a cart-load of wheat on the point of export at Rhuddlan in May 1740.[87] More dramatically still, women were burnt at Cowbridge for poisoning their husbands in 1562,[88] and Grace Jones of Monmouthshire was burned in 1671 for assisting her brother in the murder of their mother,[89] as was the servant Mary Saunders in 1764 for the murder of her mistress, Mrs Jones.[90] It may not have been entirely political bias which led a partisan publication during the first months of the Civil War in 1642 to represent a Royalist soldier's fear of having his throat cut whilst asleep by 'certaine Welsh and Irish Women which follow the Army'.[91]

Unfortunately it was on the whole not until girls were old enough to come under the scrutiny of employers or poor-law officials that their naughtiness becomes historically visible, and we find Frances Edwards, Sarah Davies and Elizabeth Thomas being punished in Forden workhouse in 1806 'by standing on a chair in the hall' and 'kept without dinner for quarrelling'. This was a relatively dainty punishment for that particular institution, which used a custom-made whipping frame, based on a model from the Montgomery House of Correction, to discipline adult offenders like Mary Preynolds who had stolen bread, cheese, beef and candles from the storeroom.[92]

Occasionally, however, the wrong-doings of children had a more than usual public interest. Thus Thomas Cadogan, a Brecknock alehouse keeper was fined in the early seventeenth century for harbouring his neighbours' sons and servants, and allowing them to game and spend their money. This kind of tippling was at best meant to be the prerogative of adult males. Girls might have other means of self-expression, all the more profoundly disturbing because their youth and powerlessness seemed so self-evident. One Denbighshire father discovered this in the early seventeenth century when fined £10 'for suffring his three daughters being young girles and his maidservant to go out of his house in the night tyme in superstitious manner to Wenefrides well'.[93] The appeal of this kind of religiosity to thirteen-or fourteen-year-old Elizabeth Acton of Maelor Saesneg may have been sufficient to induce her to fabricate a visionary experience of Christ, the Virgin and the pains of purgatory. She confessed to the fraud in Chester Cathedral in March 1582, but to those who had witnessed her 'counterfeited Trances' she appeared to have been 'in mighty Agonies'.[94] Ten-year-old Jane Morys of Berriew also experienced visions of Heaven, Hell and the Garden of Eden in the seventeenth century, and these became the subject of a ballad in Welsh.[95] In the eighteenth century, Gaenor Hughes of Llandderfel likewise inspired poetic admiration for her visions of such phenomena as 'The Tree of Life'. Reputed to have lived for nearly six years solely on water from a local spring, she died in her mid-thirties in 1780.[96] These were the various predecessors of the most famous 'fasting girl' of all, young Sarah Jacob, who was not yet in her teens when she died after achieving notoriety in 1869.[97] These girls and women fashioned a distinct identity and a wide reputation from the simplest of elements, and they seem to have strangely turned bodily pain, of which fallen Eve had been given the greater share, from a burden into a positive means of expression.[98] Their 'extreme' behaviour raises interesting questions about the attitudes of other girls to the laboriousness of day-to-day work in general.

Beginning to work

At what point, then, *did* girls begin to fend for themselves, to find food and drink and to undertake tasks? From their time in the womb, to their days in their mother's shawl, girls would have moved to the rhythms of work. One eighteenth-century gentlewoman described the 'long piece of woollen cloth wrapped round the waist' which was worn by Welsh women, and added that she had 'a hundred times seen a woman carrying a pitcher of water on her head and a child or a loaf in this wrapper, and knitting as she walked along'.[99] This way of carrying a child had come to be particularly associated with Wales by the eighteenth century, though we can see it in use on the continent of Europe in an earlier period.[100] Its implication seems to be that for little girls, at least, the passage from infancy to the world of work would have been quite seamless, whereas for boys there would come a time when closeness to the mother's body would no longer entail proximity to the appropriate tasks, and fathers, so far as we know, did not carry their offspring in this way.

Sometimes, the induction of children into adult responsibilities was done for symbolic effect or legal reasons at rather an early age. For example, Bridget, daughter of Arthur Pryce of Faenor in Montgomeryshire 'sold' four bushels of rye by bond in December 1630 at the age of ten, in an arrangement which enabled men without stocks to obtain corn on the promise of later payment.[101] Similarly, when he inherited land from an uncle, 'My little Master' William Myddleton, Esquire, of Chirk was admitted member of the copyholders' court at Worfield, Shropshire at the tender age of seven in 1700.[102] More usually, children of parents without substantial property must have undertaken tasks when and where it became feasible and necessary. Sometimes mothers and their children worked alongside each other at the same task, as did the wife and daughter of Jonathan Moore of Erddig, who received 10s. 'for their trouble in cleaning Erthig well' in 1694,[103] and the 'women and children' of Cardiganshire whom Walter Davies found 'industrious in collecting lichens for the dyers of the manufacturing districts'.[104] Where women were engaged in craft work, themselves processing items gathered from the countryside, their children might in effect serve an unofficial apprenticeship to this trade. It was said of girls moving to live in Newborough on Anglesey, for instance, that none over the age of fourteen could hope to compete with the speed with which those who had grown up there could turn the local marram grass into mats for sale.[105] Conversely, there were some kinds of work which may have been specifically regarded as the preserve of children, like the cleaning of shoes by boys,[106] or the tending of flocks amidst the 'bleakness' of the Cardiganshire uplands which a late eighteenth-century observer thought adults would resist 'as it has been hitherto the employment of children'.[107]

We can reconstruct something of the range of tasks which girls would have begun in imitation of those of adult women. Even when these were fully-fledged occupations, many grew directly out of household tasks, as with Katherine Perry, Wrexham innkeeper and regular supplier of speciality biscuits to the Myddletons of Chirk; Anne Evans of Denbigh, who succeeded her father as host of The Bull Inn there during the 1690s; and Mrs Spicer who had run a wine and spirit business in Caernarfon much earlier in the century.[108] Some of the most visible models may have been widows, whose experiences diverged enormously between poverty and independence. Even in the later eighteenth century, the poor widow might still lay claim to communal aid by brewing for her neighbours, whereas the widow of a tradesman might be sufficiently well placed to continue his business in her own right, as did Susan Vaughan, mercer of Wrexham in the 1680s and 1690s, and Elizabeth Lloyd, supplier of £9 worth of lead to Chirk Castle in 1686,[109] or Jennett William of Fishguard, who bought lambs at Newport fair in 1603.[110]

There are interesting signs that women and men may have engaged in the market on a different basis. An account of Anglesey written during the 1610s made the following observation:

> let a Countrey huswife upon the street sell a piece of cloth to a mercer by yard, it must be measured by the Welsh yard; And let that huswifes owne husband, or any other, follow the Mercer close by the heels to the shop, and there agree with him for the same piece of cloth, or any part thereof, and it shall be instantly measured with the English yard.[111]

Just as there were 'women's markets' in early modern England[112] we seem to see here in north Wales a gender differentiation in the choice of alternate measures which may be evocative of wider differences in access to the formal and informal sectors of the economy. Certainly, the prominence of women in occupations which were essentially an extension of household tasks, or of marketing activity, reminds us of the very limited access to formal craft training. This meant, of course, that the work they did obtain might often be very arduous or physically exerting labour rather than skill or art. Such was the life of Kath the Footpost in Wrexham, a professional messenger,[113] and of Margaret Owen, paid 1s. 6d. in 1659 'for gatheringe 4,500 slates by the leades on the top of the Castle' at Chirk.[114] We find the teenage daughter of Susan Addams of Penley at work milking the cows and carrying fuel as a matter of course in mid-seventeenth-century Flintshire, whilst flocks of sheep in upland Cardiganshire would be tended between spring and harvest time by a solitary boy or girl of some ten to fourteen years of age.[115] In the same county, women and children had been at work in the lead mining industry since at least the sixteenth century, and in 1805 Elizabeth Williams started work for her father and brothers as an ore washer at Cwmsymlog at the age of ten. A few girls appear to have started work even earlier.[116]

As these examples illustrate, some work came the way of girls through their menfolk, and in due course other work might come through marriage, its status as work sometimes compromised thereby, as for those wives of Carmarthen to whom 'the better sort and quality' gave a tip at Christmas or Easter for cleaning their seats in church.[117] Yet there are also indications that for some ordinary women at least there might be a chance of furthering opportunities through work in education. Such were the 'women and other Excommunicated persons' who were reported to be teaching in dissenters' private schools in south-west Wales for stipends of £6 or

£8 a year during the early 1670s,[118] or the wife of persecuted minister Ellis Rowlands, who maintained them both by keeping a school in Caernarfonshire before 1688,[119] and, less controversially, Anne Eyton 'the Schoolmistresse, of Llangollen' who was 'teachinge poore children' there in 1683 for the wage of £2. 8s., a year, and Jane Druett who received 16s. for teaching the children of Robert y Crydd (Robert the Shoemaker) and others.[120] How many girls were among such children, and what they were taught, is difficult to tell. Ellis Rowlands was said to have drawn patterns for the girls in his wife's school to work by, which may indicate that they were receiving a vocational rather than academic training.[121] But the charity school established in Llanyblodwel, Montgomeryshire in 1719 was being re-funded in the 1750s to accommodate up to fifteen children, 'for the teaching of such Boys and Girls to read'.[122] We can deduce something of the costs which might be involved from the 3s. which was given to the widow of the minister of Llangollen, to cover her daughter's 'schooleinge' for eighteen weeks in 1665, a cost of just 2d. per week.[123] Small though it was, even this sum was being provided for the girl as an act of charity by gentry patrons. For poorer families, whose women might earn only one penny and some morsels of food for a whole day's farm labour in north Wales at this time, the costs of a daughter's schooling would probably be prohibitive.[124] This makes all the more poignant such reports as that from the curate of Gelligaer in December 1758 of a woman aged more than eighty who, tempted to the local circulating school 'to hear the children', had gone on to begin her own education.[125] The curate of Llangïan felt sure that such children 'on Sundays at home, teach their aged parents the way to heaven'.[126]

Other doubtlessly more common forms of training were available through service and apprenticeship. There were girls apprenticed in Bristol in the 1530s who had come from as far away as Glamorgan and Pembrokeshire.[127] Generally speaking, however, the range of occupations to which girls were apprenticed was more limited than for boys, and the use of formal apprenticeship arrangements for girls also tended to be confined increasingly to 'domestic' occupations over the course of this period.[128] Work as a servant was a much more common experience for teenage girls. Work for a number of years in this way helped a girl build up her own dowry before marriage, as well as equipping her with the multifarious skills she would need when running a holding of her own. The typical age of marriage of such women, their mid-twenties, and the season at which the marriage took place, were often shaped by the rhythms of farm service. Courtship flowered through contacts with other servants and at the hiring fairs, and marriage itself followed departure from the last place of service.[129] This, however, is a very generalized picture, and we need to bear in mind the possibility that the use of servants in Wales had its distinctive features, as well as marked regional and chronological variations, especially during the last century or so of our period.

The reliance of Welsh farmers on servants living in their household would have varied from one locality to another, and with changes in the cost and availability of daily labour.[130] The practice continued to be widespread in the pastoral regions of southern Britain down to the middle of the nineteenth century, and was associated with the survival of smaller farms making relatively limited use of hired labour.[131] The number of places available to girls as servants, however, may have been limited. George Owen's extensive calculations of the costs of running a Pembrokeshire dairy farm in 1593 allowed for a resident ploughman and his wife, together with a shepherd, two ploughboys and only two 'labouring maids' to manage some thirty-six cattle, 320 sheep as well as assorted oxen, horses, pigs, ducks and geese.[132] Robert Bulkeley of Dronwy on Anglesey usually hired five male and two female servants in the 1630s, whilst his own eldest daughter Mary was herself in service, coming home to the farm for Easter visits.[133]

Larger households employed a more elaborate array of domestic servants as well as farm staff, and the subdivision of responsibilities there might give some maidservants a certain sense of status. Tips given to servants after one house visit in north Wales during 1656 included the butler, under butler, cooks, scullion, turnspit, chambermaid, groom, porter, usher, dairymaid and brewmaid. The division of labour might be so fixed as to attract extra payment for particular services, on this occasion, the 4s. given to 'the 2 maids that made clean Dishes', and on another the 2s. given by visitors to Gwydir in 1658 'to the maide that made fire in M[istress] Wynne's Chamber'.[134] Senior maidservants had responsibility for making purchases, and for handling cash,[135] whilst all maids were faced with the temptations posed by their employers' property. Some, like the maidservant of Mrs Owen, the Dolgellau milliner, succumbed: the gossip in April 1782 was that the 'poor ignorant servant' had been so taken in by Betty Johnes Morris, the fortune teller, as to have stolen many yards of ribbon from her employer. What a future Betty must have promised her.[136]

Work and sexual identity

As this case of a maidservant who may have been too eager to be told
the name of a future sweetheart suggests, when girls moved through
adolescence the significance of their work and its capacity to define
social relationships took on a new meaning.[137] This is amply
demonstrated by the evidence collected by folklorists after the end of
our period, which blossoms with the customs and rituals used by
servants to try to pin down both a competent partner for life, and that
partner's identity. Household items such as yarn, and practices such as
washing, figure alongside elements from the natural world in these
procedures, fusing 'work' as task with the cultural and psychic work
of finding a spouse.[138] Where several servants shared sleeping
accommodation these customs would be disseminated.[139]

But we should not underestimate the extent to which the
connections between work and sexuality would already have been
appreciated through aspects of popular culture before a girl ever
became a servant. Children themselves of course may experiment
with the potency of naughty words at a comparatively early age.[140] In
Wales, this was taken further in the words of rhymes prized perhaps
originally more for their testing of memory and verbal articulation
than for their encouragement of good morals. Likewise for older
children and servants, Welsh folk songs from the eighteenth century
and earlier had often recognized the sexual identity of young men and
women at work through metaphors using tools and working skills.[141]
For a time this aspect of childhood in Wales was obscured, in the
atmosphere of disquiet about sexual matters which followed the
report of the 1847 Commission on Education in Wales. When the first
complete set of Welsh nursery rhymes came to be published by John
Ceiriog Hughes in 1870 it was felt that some had to be suppressed on
moral grounds, having earlier been published in newspaper articles
amidst some controversy in the 1850s.[142] When the folk-singing father
of Dr J. Lloyd Williams joined the Calvinistic Methodists in the early
1860s, his wife burnt all the printed ballads he had collected, an
episode which so impressed his five-year-old son that he later came to
devote great energy to the recovery of that same folk tradition.[143]

Whatever its personal and sexual ramifications, however, the
significance of service should in any case not be over-emphasized.
The practice of seasonal migration between vale and upland pastures,
of migration further afield to work in other parts of Wales or in

England, and the heavy reliance of family labour to run many farms may indicate a relatively limited place for service in the economy of early modern Wales.[144] A similar situation has been identified in the Scottish Highlands in this period.[145] The custom of bidding, with its appeal to the pooling of resources across kindred, friends and neighbours on behalf of a newly-wed couple, may also indicate that service was neither as sufficient nor as widely-practised a financial basis for marriage as it may have been in England or in other parts of Europe.[146] The widespread practice of door-to-door begging may point in a similar direction.

In any case, so far as girls' experiences were concerned, formal distinctions between servants and the daughters of the house may not always have been very clearly drawn. For William Fleetwood, later Bishop of St Asaph, the obligations of daughters, maidservants and indeed of wives ran parallel to each other, and these categories of women recur in different roles in contemporary household accounts.[147] Daughters as well as maidservants appear as messengers and bearers of gifts to the Myddletons of Chirk in the seventeenth century, and the family bestowed tips on both when visiting other households. Sir Richard Myddleton, for instance, gave the following sums when staying overnight with Mr Roberts, the rector, in Denbigh in November 1691: 20s. to Mrs Roberts, 10s. to her daughter, 5s. to two servants, 2s. to two waiters, 2s. 6d. to a messenger, and 1s. to the bellman, as well as 10s. to the poor.[148] Daughters, rather than maidservants, were employed at the spinning wheel in the Dolgellau area in the eighteenth century, and we are reminded by this how much 'work' was used to inculcate habits of diligence and obedience in girls even of gentry status in this period.[149]

If the roles of daughters and maidservants were thus in some respects interchangeable, it may be easier to grasp how tensions arose between competing definitions of acceptable 'work' in this period, across Europe as a whole, and that this had particularly interesting implications for girls in Wales. The relationship between work as a servant and the process of courtship gave a shape to teenagers' realization of themselves as sexual beings which had both positive and negative aspects. Courtship which took place at the evening *cyfarfod cymorth* (assistance meeting) gave dignity and moral legitimacy to the proceedings through the spinning and knitting work the assembled maidservants undertook on behalf of some poor individual, before the arrival of their suitors for singing and dancing.[150] But the same occasion also served to reinforce the sexual division of labour between men and women, and through the sequence by which young men, by coming indoors, *joined* the women who had already been at work, it may also have confirmed the tendency for girls' and women's work to be regarded as unending. Where courtship took the form of 'bundling', the same sequence obtained, and one early nineteenth-century observer even commented on the material advantages of lying fully clothed together 'under the course expedient of a blanket' as a means of keeping warm. If employers by this period were coming to frown on such customs, he thought they did so at least as much for the threat that the hungry courting servants might pose to their larders as from 'an increased sense of propriety'.[151] For all concerned, the relationship between sexuality and material need was hard to avoid.

This being the case, it is perhaps easier to understand the ease with which sexuality informed even the children's rhymes we have already encountered. By the same token, the moral reformation of nineteenth-century Wales, as it sought to re-define acceptable notions of court-ship, came also to re-shape the meaning of work itself. Part of this process involved the redefinition of work as an activity which ought properly to exclude child labour, a process partly encouraged by the physical concentration of those at work in factories, and around mines or metal works.[152] There is a danger that the fervour of this movement and the evidence it provides may obscure the relatively limited scale of child employment which had actually prevailed in early modern Wales, as elsewhere.[153] As we have seen, it is possible to identify particular instances of very youthful work. But the evidence of the 1851 census, the first to be of practical use for this purpose,[154] indicates how limited was such early employment. In south Wales, of a population of over 36,000 girls aged between five and ten, only 176 were listed as in employment, sixty-nine of them in domestic service, a further fifty-nine in service on farms, and the rest in a scattering of occupations, including seventeen who ran messages. In north Wales the situation was similar, though there the range of occupations was even narrower. Of more than 24,000 girls aged between five and ten, only eighty-two were in employment, fifty-five of them in service.[155] Throughout Wales, the proportions of girls in service increased dramatically only after the age of fifteen, falling off again markedly after twenty-five. By contrast, some forms of work, such as launder-ing, were undertaken by adult women well into their old age.[156]

Girls' work and the image of Wales

The implications of these findings are important for our understanding of girls' social role in Wales during the latter half of our period. A limited role for service, and for the formal employment of children under the age of fifteen, implies that families in Wales had to find other means of feeding their members in years when food was scarce and money hard to come by. Among the most common were the utilization of those family members who were free to move around, either in the practice of door-to-door begging, or in migration for seasonal work elsewhere. Girls and women played a key role in both activities: this was a customary form of 'work' *par excellence*.

During the seventeenth and eighteenth centuries local authorities went some way towards establishing organized systems of relief for the poor, but it is generally assumed that these schemes were exceptional and in a sense unwarranted until the second half of the eighteenth century.[157] Court records suggest that begging fluctuated in frequency with the fortunes of the harvest, reaching a peak in north Wales, for example, in the bad dearth year of 1597.[158] There was also a sexual division of labour, as for example on Anglesey among newly married couples:

> The men go in sowing harvest abroad to begg grain and seed, and in corn harvest to gather houkes and thraves of corn all over the countrey where they can reach, and the good young wife must take an old impudent drabb with her, that can alleadge either kindred, alliance, nurserie, or some affinity or other, with all men. And in this manner you shall find them go by couples from door to door.[159]

Children were not mentioned in this particular account, whose author's prime concern was with the enormity of idleness among adults. But their possible need to beg surfaces regularly in records of charitable payments, such as the £3. 17s. 5d. given to one man in 1713 by the Holywell overseers to support three children, with an additional 4s. to provide shoes, stockings and linen cloth for the youngest daughter.[160]

There was, however, another side to the resourcefulness of the poor, contributing something quite distinctive to the image of Wales which the increasing numbers of visitors and observers absorbed after about 1740. This was the willingness to shoulder enormous burdens and to travel long distances in search of work. Girls and women engaged in this 'economy of makeshifts' even foreshadowed the stoical qualities of the later stereotypical 'Welsh Mam'.[161] Some ventured very far afield, by leaving Britain altogether for the colonies as indentured servants.[162] Women were migrating from Wales to the market gardens of south-east England from the later seventeenth century.[163] Those observed around London half a century later were said to be 'mostly only women and girls' (as compared with the men who travelled from Ireland), and to be 'all well, cleanly and very neatly clad'.[164] There is evidence of a significant proportion of unmarried girls in this workforce,[165] though the patterns and composition of migration appear to have varied between different regions of Wales.[166] In some cases, as with the 'Cardies' who usurped the customary access to gleaning in the harvest fields of early nineteenth-century Glamorgan, it was male migration which deprived local wives and daughters of their access to an income.[167]

From the outside, though, the girls and women of late eighteenth and early nineteenth-century Wales had begun to represent an object of fascination not for their variety of experiences, but through their collective presence as people hard at work, and at work when their menfolk might often be unemployed.[168] In some cases this was treated as an almost burlesque inversion of the natural order, since 'it's as common to meet a female driving the plough, as it is to see Taffy seated at the milk pail'.[169] We need to disentangle the literary conceit from the likely everyday practice in such observations. But the idea that the work of girls and women came both economically and conceptually to contribute to a distinctive Welsh identity in this period does need to be considered.[170] The rough assertiveness of the men dressed as Rebecca in the late 1830s and early 1840s drew something from its enactment of actual female strength, as well as from its disguised imitation of the officially 'weaker' sex by the stronger. For Edward Lloyd Hall, faced with the rioters, it could be almost as disturbing to encounter 'a poor idiotic girl' who, when turned away without charity from his door, 'murmured out (in Welsh) "I'll tell Becca".'[171] The proud resourcefulness with which girls in Wales were schooled gave them means of subsistence for which the term 'work' was altogether too narrow in meaning.

It would be wrong to dwell entirely on the hardships faced by girls and young women in Wales in the century or so before 1840. In the same period an expanding market economy was also encouraging parents to indulge their children with purchased luxuries. Even in 1694 a Llanfyllin shopkeeper stocked such items as satin capes for children, as well as sixteen children's necklaces.[172] Whilst these may have been of interest primarily to the better off in the vicinity, by 1759 there were probably some four thousand such shops across Wales as a whole.[173] The new tastes may have been more readily assimilated by women, and thus by their daughters and maidservants, than they were by men, to judge from the rather secretive purchases of such commodities as tea and sugar by the womenfolk who shopped at Roberts' store in Penmorfa, by Tremadoc, during the 1790s.[174] As Simone Clarke suggests elsewhere in this volume, tea drinking would in turn have sustained networks of female discussion, advice and assistance. Likewise, some, perhaps much, of the work women undertook in this period would have been directed less towards mere survival than to the acquisition of these new cultural goods. The development of interest in women's costume itself betokened the entry of Welsh womanhood into this new world.[175]

A new era?

By the time photographers were recording the everyday scene in Wales, including its costumes, after the middle of the nineteenth century, we seem to enter a new period. We can begin to see something of the awkwardness of children placed artificially by adults in an 'appropriate' position for their sex amidst the grown-up world of work, as with the placing of a little boy in the trench cut by adult men peat cutters at Parc, near Bala.[176] We also see the erosion of a 'traditional' division of labour in the awkwardness of the little girl standing some time around 1875 alongside Edward Llwyd, photographed because he was 'probably the last old man to knit stockings in Bala'.[177] The photographs of John Thomas and his like take us beyond the 'early modern' era in Wales. But the very persistence with which adults themselves posed at gender-specific tasks for the photographer, and the unsuccessful efforts they made to get children to look comfortable alongside them, vividly reflect the durability of the gender division of labour as a cultural tradition.[178] So many of the children photographed are placed in distinctive positions, in the foreground whilst adult women stone-gatherers stand behind, or seated in an upright coracle whilst adult men carry coracles on their backs.[179] These 'modern' images of children pose as many questions

1. A little girl sits with women of her parents' and grandparents' generation working *moresg* (sea reed) at Aberffraw, Anglesey, late nineteenth century (see p. 30).

2. Little girls accompany women and their buckets fetching water from the well in Well Street, Nefyn, Caernarfonshire. Boys look on from the right.

as the ostensibly more opaque sources we have examined from early modern Wales. But exploration of the very long-term continuities in the history of childhood in Wales across the nineteenth century is properly another story.

Notes

[1] I am grateful to members of the Aberystwyth Gender Studies Research Group whose vigorous discussion of a first draft of part of this paper in January 1995 encouraged me to persist with its exploration, and to Sandra Betts, Simone Clarke, Jane Rowlandson and the anonymous University of Wales Press reader for comments on its presentation.

[2] Beddoe, D. 'Images of Welsh Women', in Curtis, T. (ed.) (1986) *Wales: The Imagined Nation – Essays in Cultural and National Identity* (Bridgend, Poetry Wales Press); aspects of this stereotyping have now been further explored by Aaron, J. (1995) 'The Hoydens of Wild Wales: representations of Welsh women in Victorian and Edwardian fiction', *Welsh Writing in English* 1.

[3] See, for instance, MacCurtain, M. and O'Dowd, M. (eds.) (1991) *Women in Early Modern Ireland* (Edinburgh, Edinburgh University Press); Houston, R. A. 'Women in the economy and society of Scotland 1500–1800' in Houston, R. A. and Whyte, I. D. (eds.)(1988) *Scottish Society 1500–1800* (Cambridge , Cambridge University Press); Ben-Amos, I. K. (1994) *Adolescence & Youth in Early Modern England* (New Haven, Yale University Press); Fildes, V. (ed.) (1990) *Women as Mothers in Pre-Industrial England* (London, Routledge); Wiesner, M. E. (1993) *Women and Gender in Early Modern Europe* (Cambridge, Cambridge University Press).

[4] Riley, D. (1988) *'Am I That Name?': Feminism and the Category of 'Women' in History* (London, Macmillan); Revel, J. (1992) 'Masculine and Feminine: The Historiographical Use of Sexual Roles', in Perrot, M. (ed.), *Writing Women's History* (Oxford, Blackwell); Keeble, N. H. (ed.) (1994) *The Cultural Identity of Seventeenth-Century Woman: A Reader* (London, Routledge).

[5] John, A. V. (ed.) (1991) *Our Mothers' Land: Chapters in Welsh Women's History 1830-1939* (Cardiff, University of Wales Press); Aaron, J., Rees, T., Betts, S. and Vincentelli, M. (eds.) (1994) *Our Sisters' Land: The Changing Identities of Women in Wales* (Cardiff, University of Wales Press).

[6] Wallman, S. (ed.) (1979) *Social Anthropology of Work* (London, Academic Press); Roberts, M. (1989) 'Another letter from a Far Country: the Prehistory of Labour, or the History of Work in Preindustrial Wales', *Llafur*, Vol.5 No.2; *idem*, 'The Empty Ladder: Images of Work and Working People in Early Modern Ceredigion', (1995) *Llafur*, Vol.6, No.4;

' "Words they are Women, and Deeds they are Men": Images of Work and Gender in Early Modern England', in Charles, L. and Duffin, L. (eds.) (1985) *Women and Work in Pre-Industrial England* (London, Croom Helm).

[7] Ariès, P. (1962) *Centuries of Childhood* (Harmondsworth, Penguin); Pinchbeck, I. and Hewitt, M. (1971) *Children in English Society*, 2 vols. (London, Routledge); de Mause, L. (ed.) (1976) *The History of Childhood* (London, Souvenir Press); Shorter, E. (1976) *The Making of the Modern Family* (London, Collins); Pollock, L. A. (1983) *Forgotten Children: Parent–Child Relations from 1500 to 1900* (Cambridge, Cambridge University Press) were among the works which set the benchmarks in this field. For more, see the bibliography to Ben-Amos, I. K. (1994) op. cit. Bellingham, B. (1988) 'The History of Childhood Since the "Invention of Childhood": Some Issues in the Eighties', *Journal of Family History* Vol.13 No.2. 347–358; Cunningham, H. (1995), *Children and Childhood in Western Society Since 1500* (London, Longman).

[8] Jenkins, G. H. (1977) 'Popular Beliefs in Wales from the Restoration to Methodism', *Bulletin of the Board of Celtic Studies*, 27, 442.

[9] Davies, J. C. (1911) *Folk-Lore of West and Mid-Wales* (Aberystwyth), 221; cf. Owen, T. M. (1974) *Welsh Folk Customs* (3rd edn., Cardiff, National Museum of Wales), Ch.5. In piecing together this material I am conscious of drawing on evidence from very different periods of time, including reports of folk customs and popular attitudes recorded only in the later nineteenth and twentieth centuries. The possibility that these are not entirely representative of the attitudes of earlier centuries needs to be considered. That continuities may be identified, however, is suggested by Thomas, K. 'Children in Early Modern England', in Avery, G. and Briggs, J. (eds.) (1989) *Children and their Books: A Celebration of the Work of Iona and Peter Opie* (Oxford, Oxford University Press), 70–1; and Sutton, M. (1992) *'We Didn't Know Aught' A Study of Sexuality, Superstition and Death in Women's Lives in Lincolnshire during the 1930s, '40s and '50s.* (Stamford, Paul Watkins).

[10] Axon, W. E. A. (1908) 'Welsh Folk-Lore of the Seventeenth Century', *Y Cymmrodor*, 21, 118–120 for an instance in Cardiganshire during the 1650s.

[11] Owen, T. M. (1974) op. cit., p.144.

[12] Williams, J. G. (1973–4) 'Witchcraft in Seventeenth-Century Flintshire', *Journal of Flintshire Historical Soc.*, Vol.26, 18.

[13] Myddleton, W. M. (ed.) (1931) *Chirk Castle Accounts A.D. 1666–1753* (Manchester, Manchester University Press), 17 n.74 for the astrological context of Margaret Lloyd's birth, recorded at her baptism in Wrexham in 1663. For MS collections of astrological guidance on the birth and character of children, see Jenkins, G. H. (1977) op. cit., 454–5.

[14] Ibid., 145; Laslett, P. (1983) *The World We Have Lost – Further Explored* (London, Methuen) 112, Table 12 for female death rates; Jenkins, D.

(1990) 'The Demography of Montgomeryshire, c. 1660–1720', *Montgomeryshire Collections*, 78, 85 for the suggestion that 40 per cent of children born failed to reach the age of fifteen.

15 Owen, T. M. (1974) op. cit., 145.

16 'The Diary of Robert Parry', (1915) *Archaeologia Cambrensis*, 6th ser. 15, 119, 121.

17 Smith, L. B. (1992) 'Fosterage, Adoption and Godparenthood: Ritual and Fictive Kinship in Medieval Wales', *Welsh History Review*, Vol.16 No.1, 11–13; cf. Collins, S. (1991) 'British Stepfamily Relationships, 1500–1800', *Journal of Family History*, Vol.16 No.4.

18 For the proximity with which children and servants may have slept, see Williams, G. (ed.) (1974) *Glamorgan County History, 4 Early Modern Glamorgan* (Cardiff, Glamorgan County History Trust Ltd.) 129.

19 Johnston, D. (ed.) (1993) *Galar y Beirdd: Marwnadau Plant/Poets' Grief: Medieval Welsh Elegies for Children* (Caerdydd, Tafol).

20 The celebrated antiquary and naturalist Thomas Pennant, born in 1726, was himself put out to nurse in this way: Pennant, T. (1796) *The History of the Parishes of Whiteford and Holywell*, 100.

21 Jenkins, D. (1990) op. cit., 89.

22 Ellis, T. P. (1929) 'The Importance and Value of Local Records: The Dolgelly Parish Registers', *Y Cymmrodor* 40, 176–7.

23 Myddleton W. M. (ed) *Chirk Accounts 1666–1753* op. cit., 274; Bradney, J. A. (ed.) (1902) *The Diary of Walter Powell of Llantilio Crossenny* (Bristol, John Wright), 2.

24 Fisher, J. (1906) 'The Religious and Social Life of Former Days in the Vale of Clwyd as Illustrated by the Parish Records', *Archaeologia Cambrensis.*, 6th ser. 6, 133; the average period between birth and christening in the case of five of Walter Powell's children during 1613–43 was thirteen days: Bradney, J. (ed.) (1902) op. cit., 3–4.

25 Owen, H. *The Life and Works of Lewis Morris (1701–1765)*, 142; for the expression 'in the straw' see Wilson, A. 'The Ceremony of Childbirth and its Interpretation', in Fildes, V. (ed.) (1990) *Women as Mothers in Pre-Industrial England* (London, Routledge), 75.

26 Lhuyd, E. (1911) 'Parochialia', *Archaeologia Cambrensis*, Supplement, Pt.3. 84; cf.Thomas, K. (1971) *Religion and the Decline of Magic* (London, Weidenfeld), 38–9, 59–61.

27 Owen, H. (ed.) (1937) 'The Diary of Bulkeley of Dronwy, 1630–36, *Transactions of the Anglesey Antiquarian Society*, entries for 24 Nov. 1634, and 1 March 1634.

28 Bradney, J. (ed.) (1902) op. cit., 29.

29 Owen, H. (1951) op. cit., 142.

30 Wilson, A. (1990) op. cit., 83–93.

31 Bradney, J. (ed.) (1902) op. cit., 29.

32 Wilson, A. (1990) op. cit., 79.

33 Wilson, A. (1990) op. cit., 81.

34 Bevan-Evans, M. (1965–6) 'Local Government in Treuddyn, 1752–1821', *Flintshire Historical Soc.,* Vol.22. 34.

35 Flynn-Hughes, C. (1945) 'Aspects of the Old Poor Law Administration and Policy in Amlwch Parish 1770–1837', *Transactions of Anglesey Antiquarian Soc.* 53.

36 Jones, E. G. (1948) 'A Llandegai Pew Dispute', *Transactions of Caernarvonshire Historical Soc.,* 9.

37 For example in the record of money 'Pd to Mr Tho. Price, of Glyn, his Child's nurse for a bob periwig which her husband made for my Mr . . . 1.4.0', Myddleton, W. M. (ed.) (1931) *Chirk Accounts 1666–1753,* op. cit., 304.

38 Jones, J. (1579) *The Arte and Science of Preserving Bodie and Soul in Healthe, Wisedom, and Catholick Religion: Physically, Philosophically and Divinely Devised,* 40, quoted in Fildes, V. (1988) *Wet Nursing: A History from Antiquity to the Present* (Oxford, Blackwell), 73. For the translation of Renaissance ideas about bodily well-being into Welsh during the reign of Henry VIII see Tibbott, S. M. (ed.) (1969) *Castell Yr Iechyd gan Elis Gruffydd* (Caerdydd, Gwasg Prifysgol Cymru). For the translation of the influential educational manual by Jean Luis Vives, *De Institutione Feminae Christianae* into Welsh, see Hughes, G. H. 'Dysgeidieth Cristnoges o Ferch', in Jones, T. (ed.) (1968) *Astudiaethau Amwrywiol* (Caerdydd, Gwasg Prifysgol Cymru).

39 Williams, J. G. (1975–6), 'Witchcraft in Seventeenth-Century Flintshire, Part 2', *Journal of Flintshire Historical Soc.,* Vol.27. 33; for another instance in Wales, see Simpson, J. 'Rural Folklore', in Blum, J. (ed.) (1982) *Our Forgotten Past: Seven Centuries of Life on the Land* (London, Thames and Hudson), 159. For the centrality of such issues in continental witchcraft accusations, see Roper, L. (1994) 'Witchcraft and Fantasy in Early Modern Germany', in her *Oedipus and the Devil* (London, Routledge), 202–3.

40 Jenkins, G. H. (1977) op. cit., 442, 445; Roderick, A. (1986) *Folklore of Glamorgan* (Cwmbran, Cwmbran Community Press), 14–16; Davies, J. C. (1911) *Folk-Lore of West and Mid-Wales* (Aberystwyth), 132–4.

41 Williams, J. G. (1973–4) op. cit., 20.

42 Williams, J. G. (1975–6) op. cit., 32.

43 Fildes, V. (1988) op. cit., Ch. 6.

44 Myddleton, W. M. (ed.) *Chirk Accounts 1666–1753,* op. cit., xvi, 68, 109.

45 Fildes, V. (1988) op. cit., 85–7 citing examples from Suffolk in 1636, and Cambridgeshire in 1658. In the case of Elizabeth Myddleton, the sculptor sent a servant to her parental home 'for my ladye's picture . . . to draw a pattern to make her monument', Myddleton, W. M. (ed.) *Chirk Accounts 1666–1753,* op. cit., 119.

46 Davis, J. (1835) *History of the Welsh Baptists from the Year 63 to the Year 1770* (Pittsburg). This approach to the centrality of daughters is now poetically readdressed in Clarke, G. (1993) *The King of Britain's Daughter* (Manchester, Carcanet Press).

47 Toulmin Smith, L. (ed.) (1906) *The Itinerary in Wales of John Leland* (London, George Bell), 78.

48 British Library, Lansdowne MS 111 fo.10, quoted in Howells, B. 'The Lower Orders of Society' in Jones, J. G. (ed.) (1989) *Class, Community and Culture in Tudor Wales* (Cardiff, University of Wales Press), 248.

49 Ballinger, J. (1929) 'Katherine of Berain', *Y Cymmrodor* 11.

50 Roberts, E. 'Everyday Life in the Homes of the Gentry' in Jones (ed.) (1989) *Class, Community and Culture*, 69; cf. *idem* 'William Cynwal', *Transactions of Denbighshire Historical Soc.*, 12 (1963)

51 William Cynwal, *In Defence of Women, a Welsh Poem* translated by Williams, G. (London, Golden Cockerel Press, 1960); *Against Women: A Satire Translated from the Old Welsh (Araich Ddichan ir Gwragedd)*, translated by Williams, G. (London, Golden Cockerel Press, 1953); Williams, G. (1993) *Reformation and Renewal: Wales c.1415–1642* (Oxford, Oxford University Press), 445–9; and for the wider European context, see Blamires, A. (1992) *Woman Defamed and Defended* (Oxford, Oxford University Press).

52 Conran, A. (1992) 'The Lack of the Feminine', *New Welsh Review* Vol.5 No. 17, 30: 'nowhere in mediaeval or early modern Welsh literature is there any real attempt to present women as personalities or to be interested at all in their feelings or aspirations'; cf. Pennar, M. (1976) 'Women in Medieval Welsh Literature: An Examination of Some Literary Attitudes before 1500' (University of Oxford D.Phil. thesis); but see now Lloyd-Morgan, C. (1991) 'Oral Composition and Written Transmission: Welsh Womens' Poetry From the Middle Ages and Beyond', *Trivium* 26.

53 Conran, A. (1992) op. cit., 30–1.

54 Williams, G. (1974) *Welsh Poems, 6th Cent to 1600* (Berkeley, University of California Press) includes the 'Girls of Llanbadarn', 'To a Girl's Hair', 'Naming the Girl', 'To a Sweet-Mouthed Girl', and 'A Pretty Girl', as well as 'The Defence of Women'. Cf. the use of the language of love poetry in the fifteenth-century elegy for his daughter by Ieuan Gethin: Johnson, D. (ed.) (1993) op. cit., 27, 78–89. The translated references to 'girls' obscure the fact that the Welsh language had 'a rich traditional terminology of names for children of different ages', which survived with marked regional variations down to the twentieth century: Thomas, A. R. (1973) *The Linguistic Geography of Wales* (Cardiff, University of Wales Press), 519, 521. This would have had particular value in a period when there was a degree of imprecision even about such daughters' ages. Anne Ellis of Penley, for example, described the daughter she left to do the milking one midsummer day in 1656 as 'about 16teen years of age'. The way in which such terms might define phases of childhood in relational terms is illustrated in an early dictionary definition of the word 'merch' as 'a Daughter, also a Woman', and of 'Rhoccas, llangc' as 'a young Man in his growing years': Jones, T. (1688) *Y Gymraeg yn ei Disgleirdeb, Neu helaeth Eir-Lyfer Cymraeg a Saesneg* (London). See also Thomas, K. (1977) 'Age

and Authority in Early Modern England', *Proceedings of the British Academy*, Vol.62, 3–5.

[55] Stephens, M. (ed.) (1986) *The Oxford Companion to the Literature of Wales* (Oxford, Oxford University Press), 237–8.

[56] Johnston, D. (ed.) (1991) *Canu Maswedd yr Oesoedd Canol/Medieval Welsh Erotic Poetry* (Caerdydd, Tafol), 23. For a facetious dismissal of Mechain's work as 'occasional glimpses of what I would take to be the stuff of conversations at hen parties', see Thomas, G. (1992) in *The New Welsh Review*, Vol.16, 47. For a more serious appreciation, see Lloyd-Morgan, C. (1991) op. cit.

[57] Roper, L. (1994) op. cit. demonstrates how sixteenth- and seventeenth-century sources can be used to explore the complex relationship between mothering, nurturing, sexuality and the child's earliest bodily and emotional experiences.

[58] Williams, J. G. (1973–4) op. cit., 18.

[59] Bradney, J. (ed.) (1902) op. cit., 19; 'A Gravestone at Presteigne and its Story' *Transactions of the Radnorshires oc.* (1943); Howse, W. H. (1946) 'Story of Presteigne' *Welsh Review* (Autumn).

[60] Watkin, I. (1907) 'History of the Parish of Llanyblodwel' *Montgomeryshire Collections* 34, 152. This detail was noted in the parish register at his death in 1807.

[61] Toulmin Smith, L. (ed.) (1906) op. cit., 99. Leland clearly states that 'children . . . use to sitte and play' on the seats'; his use of the word 'kiddes' is, however, ambiguous: documented as a term for young children from the sixteenth century, the word may also refer to the goats the youngsters were herding. I am grateful to Claire Greene for prompting me to consider this possibility. That this hillside was something of an adventure playground remains clear.

[62] Morris, J. G. and Owen, M. N. (1913–15) 'Forden Union During the Napoleonic Wars', *Montgomeryshire Collections* 37, 131.

[63] Watkin, I. (1907) op. cit., 154. The use of coroners' records as a source for the study of children's history was pioneered by Hanawalt, B. (1986) in her *The Ties That Bound: Peasant Families in Medieval England* (New York), Ch. 10.

[64] Bradney, J. (ed.) (1902) op. cit., 13.

[65] Williams, J. G. (1973–4) 33.

[66] Owen, T. M. (1974) op. cit., 144.

[67] Bowen Thomas, B. (1945) *The Old Order based on The Diary of Elizabeth Baker* (Cardiff, University of Wales Press), 50.

[68] Myddleton, W. M. (ed.) *Chirk Castle Accounts AD 1605–1666* (St Albans, privately printed), 128.

[69] Myddleton, W. M. (ed.) *Chirk Accounts 1605–1666*, op. cit., 103, 123; *1666–1753*, 243, 247, 250, 321, 205.

[70] Myddleton, W. M. (ed.) *Chirk Accounts, 1605–1666*, op. cit., 130; *Chirk Accounts 1666–1753*, op. cit., 298.

71 Owen, H. (ed.) (1937) passim; for an excellent discussion of this aspect of the diary, see Morris, C. (1988) '"A Time to Keep and a Time to Cast Away": Work and Leisure on a Welsh Farm 1630–1636' (Undergraduate dissertation, University of Wales Aberystwyth, Department of History and Welsh History).

72 Williams, J. G. (1973–4) op. cit., 29: deposition of David ap Richard, 1658.

73 Williams, J. G. (1973–4) op. cit., 31: examination of Elizabeth Jeffreys, 1657.

74 Axon, W. E. A. (1908) op. cit., 117.

75 Owen, T. M. (1991) *A Pocket Guide to the Customs and Traditions of Wales* (Cardiff, University of Wales Press) 17; cf. Waddington, H. M. (1953) 'Games and Athletics in Bygone Wales', *Transactions Honourable Soc. of Cymmrodorion*, and Lloyd, H. (1960) 'Tri o Hen Chwaraeon Cymru', ibid.

76 Howells, B. (ed.) (1973) *Elizabethan Pembrokeshire: The Evidence of George Owen* (Pembrokeshire Record Series 2, Pembrokeshire Record Soc.), 62–7.

77 Williams, G. J. (1956) 'Glamorgan Customs in the Eighteenth Century', *Gwerin*, Vol.1 No.1, 103.

78 Bowen Thomas, B. (1945) op. cit., 50; Roberts, M. (1988) ' "Waiting Upon Chance": English hiring fairs and their meanings from the 14th to the 20th centuries', *Journal of Historical Sociology* 1.

79 Fisher, J. (1906) op. cit., 152–3; Owen, G. D. (1941) 'The Poor Law System in Carmarthenshire during the Eighteenth and Early Nineteenth Century', *Transactions of the Honourable Society of Cymmrodorion*, 72; cf. Thomas, 'Children in Early Modern England', 52–3 in Avery, G. and Briggs, J. (eds.) (1989) op. cit.

80 Skeel, C. A. J. (1916–17) 'Social and Economic Conditions in Wales in the Early Seventeenth Century', *Transactions Honourable Soc. of Cymmrodorion*, 141.

81 Myddleton, W. M. (ed.) *Chirk Accounts 1666–1753*, op. cit., 323.

82 Myddleton, W. M. (ed.) *Chirk Castle Accounts, A.D. 1605–1666*, op. cit., 101.

83 Jenkins, G. H. (1977) op. cit., 445.

84 Roberts, M. (1989) op. cit., 101; Price, M. (1990) *The Account Book For the Borough of Swansea, Wales 1640–1660* (Lampeter, Edwin Mellen Press) 64, 238 for repairs to the ducking stool; Myddleton, W. M. (ed.) *Chirk Accounts 1666–1753*, op. cit., 268 n.1486 for ducking stool at Wrexham in 1694; Evans, K. (1946) 'Eighteenth Century Caernarvon, Part 1', *Transactions of Caernarvonshire Historical Society*, Vol.7, 53 for 1730 order to provide 'a good Strong Douking Chair or Stool'; Morris, J. G. and Owen, M. N. (1913–15) op. cit., 96 for purchase of 'a Bridel for Scolds' in 1795. Disputes between women seem to figure less prominently among slander cases in the Great Sessions: Suggett, R. (1992) 'Slander in Early Modern Wales', *Bulletin of Board of Celtic Studies* Vol.39, 136–7.

85 Williams, G. J.(1956) op. cit., 106; for the later history of such 'ridings',

see Jones, R. A. N. 'Women, Community and Collective Action: The *Ceffyl Pren* Tradition', in John, A. (ed.) (1991) op. cit.

[86] Redwood, C. (1839) *The Vale of Glamorgan: Scenes and Tales Among the Welsh* (London), 291.

[87] Lloyd Gruffydd, K. (1975–6) 'The Vale of Clwyd Riots of 1740', *Journal of Flintshire Historical Soc.*, Vol.27, 37.

[88] Williams G. (ed.) (1974) op. cit., 105.

[89] *The Bloody Murtherer* (London, 1671); *A Most Barbarous Murther* (London, 1672) .

[90] *The Confession . . . of M. Saunders who was burnt at Monmouth on the 21st of March, 1764* (?Monmouth, 1764).

[91] *Declaration sent from Several Officers* (1 December 1642).

[92] Morris, J. G. and Owen, M. N. (1913–15) op. cit., 128, 111.

[93] Skeel, C. A. J. (1916–17) op. cit., 137, 139.

[94] Williams, J. G. (1973–4) 21.

[95] 'Gweledigaethau Geneth fechan o Ddeng mlwydd Oed' discussed in Roberts, E. (1965) *Braslun o Hen Llên Powys* (Dinbych, Gwasg Gee), 69.

[96] Stephens, M. (ed.) (1986) op. cit., 266–7.

[97] Sarah now appears in her full European context in Vandereycken, W. and van Deth, R. (1994) *From Fasting Saints to Anorexic Girls: The History of Self-Starvation* (London, The Athlone Press).

[98] The possible implications of such an approach to early modern bodily experience are brilliantly demonstrated in Roper, L. (1994) op. cit. The relationship of these factors to the emergence of a market economy is explored in Richards, B. (ed.) (1984) *Capitalism and Infancy: Essays on Psychoanalysis and Politics* (London, Free Association Books).

[99] Hutton Beale, C. (ed.) (1891) *Reminiscences of a Gentlewoman of the Last Century: Letters of Catherine Hutton*, 52.

[100] Sikes, W. (1881) *Rambles and Studies in Old South Wales* (London, Sampson Low) discussed the method of carrying babies in a shawl as one of several distinctive characteristics of Welsh women; Davies, B. R. and Jones, M. E. (1974) 'Cwtshed in a Welsh Shawl: an enquiry into the carrying of babies in the Welsh fashion' (*Health Visitor* Vol.47 c.1974) notes the decline in the practice over the preceding twenty years. Children carried in this fashion figure not infrequently in continental landscape paintings from the early modern period.

[101] Smith, D. W. (1985) 'Berriew in Stuart Times 2', *Montgomeryshire Collections* 73, 14–5.

[102] Myddleton, W. M. (ed.) *Chirk Accounts 1666–1753*, op. cit., 315.

[103] Myddleton, W. M. (ed.) *Chirk Accounts 1666–1753*, op. cit., 268.

[104] Davies, W. (1814) *A General View of the Agriculture and Domestic Economy of South Wales*, 1 (London), 473. For the gathering of lichen by brother and sister alone in north Wales, see Owen, T. (1991) op. cit., 6.

[105] Jenkins, J. G. (1991) *Life and Tradition in Rural Wales* (Stroud, Alan Sutton), 74.

106 Myddleton, W. M. (ed.) *Chirk Accounts 1605–1666*, op. cit., 59; Myddleton, W. M. (ed.) *Chirk Accounts 1666–1753*, 87.

107 Lloyd, T. and Turnor, D. (1794) *General View of the Agriculture of the County of Cardigan*, 23. Cf. the sixteenth-century instance recorded by Leland in note 61 above.

108 Myddleton, W. M. (ed.) *Chirk Accounts 1605–1666*, op. cit., 1; Myddleton, W. M. (ed.) *Chirk Accounts 1666–1753*, op. cit., 307; Jenkins, R. T. (1949) 'The County Records', *Transactions of Caernarvonshire Historical Soc.*, Vol.10, 103.

109 Bowen Thomas, B. (1945) op. cit., 49–50; Myddleton, W. M. (ed.) *Chirk Accounts 1666–1753*, op. cit., 283, 219.

110 Lewis, E. A. (1933–35) 'The Toll Books of Some North Pembrokeshire Fairs' (1599–1603), *Bulletin of Board of Celtic Studies*, 7, 317; for other purchases, usually of a single cow, by women of unspecified status, see 287, 293, 296, 299.

111 Halliwell, J. O. (ed.) (1860) *A Minute Account of the Social Condition of the People of Anglesea, in the Reign of James the First* (London, privately printed), 32.

112 Roberts, M. 'Women and work in sixteenth-century English towns', in Corfield, P. and Keene, D. (eds.) (1990) *Work in Towns 850–1850* (Leicester, Pinto), 94 and n.67.

113 Myddleton, W. M. (ed.) *Chirk Accounts 1666–1753*, op. cit., 210.

114 Myddleton, W. M. (ed.) *Chirk Accounts 1605–1666*, op. cit., 82. A woman of the same name had been paid £1 in 1651 'for keepinge ye little lame girle Katherine for one whole yeare', ibid., 35.

115 Williams, J. G. (1973–4) op. cit., 2, 32: examination of Susan Addams; Lloyd and Turnor (1794) op. cit., 23.

116 Lewis, W. J. (1967) *Lead Mining in Wales* (Cardiff, University of Wales Press), 274. Substantial numbers of women and girls were also employed in iron works and forges during the Industrial Revolution in south Wales: Boynes, T. and Baber, C. 'The Supply of Labour, 1750–1914', in John, A. H., and Williams, G. (eds.) (1980) *Glamorgan County History, 5 Industrial Glamorgan from 1700 to 1970* (Cardiff, Glamorgan County History Trust Ltd), 330–1.

117 Morgan, W. T. (1961) 'Disputes concerning seats in church before the Consistory courts of St. David's', *Journal of Historical Society of the Church in Wales*, Vol.11, 77.

118 Morgan, W. T. (1962) 'The Persecution of Nonconformists in the Consistory Courts of St. David's, 1661–88', *Journal of Historical Society of the Church in Wales*, Vol.12, 42.

119 Owen, B. (1945) 'Some Details About the Independents in Caernarvonshire', *Transactions of Caernarvonshire Historical Soc.*, 6; Rees, T. (1883) *History of Protestant Nonconformity in Wales* (London, 2nd edn.), 133.

120 Myddleton, W. M. (ed.) *Chirk Accounts 1666–1753*, op. cit., 187–8.

[121] Owen, B. (1945) op. cit.; Rees, T. (1883) *History of Protestant Nonconformity in Wales*, (London 2nd edn.), 133.

[122] Watkin, I. (1907) op. cit., 172–3; cf. Baker-Jones, D. L. (1980) 'The Household Accounts of an 18th Century Mansion', *Carmarthenshire Historian*, Vol.17, 34.

[123] Myddleton, W. M. (ed.) *Chirk Accounts 1605–1666*, op. cit., 123.

[124] Gwynedd Archive Services, [Caernarfon Record Office] XQS/1670/uncatalogued: Justices' Wage Assessment for Caernarvonshire, 1670.

[125] Jones, D. (1902) *Life and Times of Griffith Jones of Llanddowror* (London, SPCK), 118–19.

[126] Ibid. 119.

[127] Ben-Amos, I. K. (1994) op. cit., 138.

[128] Ben-Amos, I. K. (1994) op. cit., 139, 143. This is also borne out by the evidence of numerous poor law schemes for pauper apprenticeship in the eighteenth century.

[129] Davies, W. (1814) op. cit., 291 for instance noted the regional variations in dates at which service contracts commenced in south Wales, in early May in the more pastorally upland east, and in October or November, after the corn harvest, in the west.

[130] Kussmaul, A. (1981) *Servants in Husbandry in Early Modern England* (Cambridge, Cambridge University Press), Chs. 2 and 6; for her analysis of the hierarchy between servants of different ages, Kussmaul draws freely on Jenkins, D. (1971) *The Agricultural Community in south-west Wales at the turn of the Twentieth Century* (Cardiff, University of Wales Press).

[131] Snell, K. D. M. (1985) *Annals of the Labouring Poor: Social Change and Agrarian England 1660–1900* (Cambridge, Cambridge University Press), 94–7.

[132] Howells, B. (ed.) (1973) op. cit., 34–5.

[133] Morris, C. (1988) op. cit., 26, 30.

[134] Myddleton, W. M. (ed.) *Chirk Accounts 1605–1666*, op. cit., 60, 74.

[135] Ibid., 56, 89.

[136] Bowen Thomas, B. (1945) op. cit., 51.

[137] For the anxieties surrounding this transition, see Macdonald, M. (1981) *Mystical Bedlam: Madness, Anxiety and Healing in Seventeenth-Century England* (Cambridge, Cambridge University Press), 85–98.

[138] See for example, Davies, J. C. (1911) op. cit., Ch. 1; Stevens, C. (1993) *Welsh Courting Customs* (Llandysul, Gomer Press).

[139] Axon, W. E. A. (1908) op. cit., 120, for the tragic experience of the five maidservants who were sharing a bedroom at Llangathen, Carmarthenshire around 1620 when they were suffocated by the fumes from a coal fire set to dry out its newly plastered walls.

[140] Opie, I. and Opie, P. (1959) *The Lore and Language of Schoolchildren* (Oxford, Oxford University Press) Ch.6 'Parody and Impropriety'.

[141] Millward, E. G. (1980) 'Delweddau'r Canu Gwerin' (The Images of Folk Song), *Canu Gwerin* 3.

[142] Evans, M. (1981) 'Cefndir a Chynnwys "Hen Hwiangerddi" Ceiriog', *Canu Gwerin* 4, now reprinted in Ffrancon, A. and Jenkins, G. H. (eds.) (1994) *Merêd: Detholiad o Ysgrifau Dr. Meredydd Evans* (Llandysul, Gwasg Gomer). Cf. the account of Rachel Evans of Swyddffynon, Cardiganshire, 'who sometimes sang "Maswedd", or rhymes of doubtful propriety, and used to take the children of the village to see fairy rings', in Davies, J. C. (1911) op. cit., 134.

[143] Huws, D. (1983) 'Dr. J. Lloyd Williams and Traditional Music', *Canu Gwerin* Vol.6, 41.

[144] Williams, M. I. (1959) 'Some Aspects of the Economic and Social Life of the Southern Regions of Glamorgan 1600–1800', *Morgannwg* Vol.3, 23; Davies, E. and Howells, B. (eds.) (1987) *Pembrokeshire County History, 3, Early Modern Pembrokeshire 1536–1815* (Haverfordwest, Pembrokeshire Historical Soc.), 92.

[145] Whyte, I. D. and Whyte, K. A. (1988) 'The Geographical Mobility of Women in Early Modern Scotland', in Leneman, L. (ed.), *Perspectives in Scottish Social History: Essays in Honour of Rosalind Mitchison* (Aberdeen, Aberdeen University Press), p.95.

[146] Owen, T. M. (1974) op. cit., 159–62; *idem* (1991) op. cit., 56–60.

[147] Fleetwood, W. (1705) *The Relative Duties of Parents and Children, Husbands and Wives, Masters and Servants*; Roberts, M. (1989) op. cit., 100.

[148] Myddleton, W. M. (ed.) *Chirk Accounts 1666–1753*, op. cit., 251; see also 50, 190, and Myddleton, W. M. (ed.) *Chirk Accounts 1605–1666*, 59.

[149] Bowen Thomas, B. (1945) op. cit., 39; Myddleton, W. M. (ed.) *Chirk Accounts 1666–1753*, op. cit., 105 for the repair of spinning wheels for 'my younge lady'; cf. Franits, W. E. (1993) *Paragons of Virtue: Women and Domesticity in Seventeenth-Century Dutch Art* (Cambridge, Cambridge University Press) for countless continental examples.

[150] Owen, T. M. (1991) op. cit., 50.

[151] Jones, E. G. (ed.) (1952) *A Description of Caernarvonshire (1809–1811) By Edmund Hyde Hall* (Caernarvon, Caernarvonshire Historical Society Record Series, 2), 323.

[152] In Flintshire, for example, cotton factories which in 1789 were advertising jobs for 'A Great Number of Good Cotton Workers, particularly Young Women, and Boys and Girls' had by the 1840s succumbed to the twin pressures of Lancashire competition and midnight visits from the factory inspectors: Foulkes, E. J. (1964) 'The Cotton-Spinning Factories of Flintshire, 1777–1866', *Flintshire Historical Society*, Vol.21, 93–4.

[153] Cunningham, H. (1990) 'The Employment and Unemployment of Children in England c.1680–1851', *Past and Present*, 126, suggesting that sufficient work was simply not available. This view is contested in Hopkins, E. (1994) *Childhood Transformed: Working-Class Children in Nineteenth-Century England* (Manchester, Manchester University Press), 316–17. In both works some material from Wales is utilized.

[154] Williams, L. J. and Jones, D. (1982) 'Women at Work in Nineteenth Century Wales', *Llafur*, Vol.3 No. 3, 201; cf. Hill, B. (1993) 'Women, Work and the Census: a Problem for Historians of Women', *History Workshop*, 35.

[155] 1851 Census: Ages, Civil Condition, Occupations and Birthplaces, 2. (Irish University Press edn., Population, 9) 837–9, 843–5.

[156] Ibid., 838.

[157] Jenkins, G. H. (1987) *The Foundations of Modern Wales 1642–1780* (Oxford, Oxford University Press), 168–70, 278–9.

[158] Powell, N. M. W. 'Crime and the Community in Denbighshire During the 1590s: The Evidence of the Records of the Court of Great Sessions', in Jones (ed.), (1989) op. cit., 284.

[159] Halliwell, J. O. (ed.) (1860) op. cit., 17.

[160] Teale, A. (1983–4) 'The Battle Against Poverty in North Flintshire c.1660–1714', *Flintshire Historical Society Journal*, Vol.31, 91.

[161] The notion of an 'economy of makeshifts' put together by women on an improvizational basis was first developed in her analysis of eighteenth-century France by Olwen Hufton in (1974) *The Poor of Eighteenth-Century France* (Oxford, Oxford University Press).

[162] Souden, D. ' "Rogues, Whores and Vagabonds"? Indentured servant emigration to North America and the case of mid seventeenth-century Bristol', in Clark, P. and Souden, D. (eds.) (1988) *Migration and Society in Early Modern England* (Totowa, NJ, Barnes and Noble), 158–61.

[163] Houston, R. A. (1992) *The Population History of Britain and Ireland 1500–1750* (London, Macmillan), 59.

[164] Kalm, P. (1892) *Account of His Visit to England on His Way to America in 1748* (Trans. Lucas, J., London), 82–3.

[165] Phillips, Sir Richard (1817) *A Morning Walk from London to Kew* (London), 226–8; Atkins, P. J. (1980) 'The Retail Milk Trade in London c.1790–1914', *Economic History Review*, Vol.33, 523 for an 1811 account of the 'robust Welsh girls' and the presumably rather older 'Irish women' who worked in this trade.

[166] Lipscombe, G. (1802) *Journey Into South Wales in the Year 1799* (London), 101–2. The possibility that evidence from this period was affected by a particularly difficult economic situation needs to be remembered. For a general analysis of female migration, see Hill, B. (1989) *Women, Work and Sexual Politics in Eighteenth-Century England* (Oxford, Blackwell), Ch. 9, and her 'Rural–Urban Migration of Women and their Employment in Towns', *Rural History*, Vol.5 No.2 (1994).

[167] Williams, M. I. (1956–9) 'Seasonal Migrations of Cardiganshire Harvest-Gangs to the Vale of Glamorgan in the Nineteenth Century', *Ceredigion*, 3, 157–8.

[168] Andrews, M. (1989) *The Search for the Picturesque* (London), 145 for tourists' observation of women's work and men's idleness at Aberystwyth.

[169] Clarke, E. D. (1793) *Tour through the South of England, Wales and Part of*

Ireland, Made during the Summer of 1791 (London), 216. For the inversionary donning of male clothes by women as a theme in Welsh popular culture, see Davies, J. H. (1911) *A Bibliography of Welsh Ballads Printed in the Eighteenth Century* (London, Cymmrodorion Society), xii–xiv.

170 The fostering of a national costume for Welsh women by Lady Llanover after 1834 owed much to the desire to promote indigenous industries; but for earlier observers, the fascination with women's dress seems to have been a displaced way of understanding the character of their work, so hard, and yet so evidently done by women. Hence the references to the neatness with which these females were dressed, despite their sleeping under hedges *en route* to London! See Payne, F. G. (1964) 'Welsh Peasant Costume', *Folk Life Studies*, 2; *Bye-Gones* (1913–15), 14, for sleeping under stacks of hay.

171 Thompson, E. P. (1991) *Customs in Common* (London, The Merlin Press), 522–3.

172 Jenkins, D. (1981) 'A Late Seventeenth-Century Llanfyllin Shopkeeper: The Will and Inventory of Cadwalader Jones', *Montgomeryshire Collections*, 69, 53.

173 Mui, H. C. and Mui, L. H. (1989) *Shops and Shopkeeping in Eighteenth-Century England* (London, Routledge/McGill Queen's University Press), 297; for the 'commercialization' of childhood in this period, see Plumb, J. H. (1983) 'The New World of Children', in McKendrick, N. et al. (1983) The *Birth of the Consumer Society: The Commercialization of Eighteenth-Century England* (London, Hutchinson).

174 Mui, H. C. and Mui, L. H. (1989) op. cit., 216–19.

175 Douglas, M. and Isherwood, B. (1981) *The World of Goods* (New York, Basic Books); Appadurai, A. (ed.) (1986) *The Social Life of Things: Commodities in Cultural Perspective* (Cambridge, Cambridge University Press).

176 Smith, K. (1984) *Old Welsh Country Life* (Caernarfon, Melin Productions), 12.

177 Ibid., 22. For another great change, the decline of service, see for instance Pretty, D. A. (1990) 'Women and Trade Unionism in Welsh Rural Society, 1889–1950', *Llafur*, Vol.5 No.3, 6.

178 Woollen, H. and Crawford, A. (1977) *John Thomas 1838–1905: photographer* (Llandysul, Gomer Press) plates 28, 29, 39, 41, 43, 45–6, 47, 49, 53, 56, 59, 62, 63; a similar range of images can be found in *Pobl Wrth Eu Gwaith/People at Work* (Llandysul, Gomer Press 1987). For the role of photographer as observer of work, see Roberts, 'Waiting Upon Chance' (note 78 above).

179 *Pobl Wrth Eu Gwaith*, plates 39, 28.

2

The construction of genteel sensibilities: The socialization of daughters of the gentry in seventeenth- and eighteenth-century Wales

SIMONE CLARKE

I have spent the past three years studying in this country, reading about a great number of individuals, countries and cultures so very different from my own. The differences between cultures are not easily accessible through the eyes of others, but must be experienced at first hand; only by living in a *different* country have I come to understand my *own* country and what it really means to be a part of its culture. Living 'in exile', away from my own people and the way of life to which I had become accustomed has been lonely but has enriched my awareness of beliefs, customs, and manners of others and their relative importance . . .

These sentiments might reflect the experiences of the few daughters of the Welsh gentry who received an education in London in the later seventeenth or eighteenth century. One can imagine their sense of upheaval at leaving Wales and the safe enclave of Welsh gentry society for the bustling and cosmopolitan milieu of the metropolis. Though Welsh gentry society was not averse to English culture and current European fashions, the cultural contrasts must still have seemed quite striking to these girls. In fact the above passage describes my own experiences during the past three years studying at a Welsh university. I have only consciously analysed my own national identity after encountering another culture (namely that of Wales), a culture which is very much formed out of resistance and one that defines itself in relation to another. My awareness of the possible resemblance between aspects of my own experiences and those of the daughters of the Welsh gentry has both awakened my curiosity about these girls, and endowed me with greater empathy towards them. This chapter will examine an aspect of their childhood which is of greatest relevance to my own experiences, namely their education. It will analyse the relationship between the education of these girls and their socialization into accepted gender norms and roles. Historians and sociologists alike recognize this connection. For the sociologist, education both formal and informal is one agent of secondary socialization providing children with a clear insight into the accepted values, beliefs, modes of conduct and, most importantly for our purposes, the gender role models of a given society. Children's education builds upon and generally reinforces primary socialization; a process of learning and imitation by an infant of the actions and expressions of those persons involved in their upbringing, usually in the home. Likewise, the historian Merry Wiesner in her recent and much acclaimed work *Women and Gender in Early Modern Europe* clearly recognizes the close relationship between education and socialization in her discussion of childhood:

> Though society had sharply defined gender roles for adults, children were all dressed alike for the first several years of their lives (there is no early modern equivalent of the pink and blue dichotomy), and comments by parents about their small children show less gender stereotyping than is evident among many contemporary parents. It was when children began their training for adult life, at the age of four or five, that clear distinctions became evident. Girls of all classes were taught skills that they would use in running the household. . . [1]

By way of a prelude to this examination of the education of the daughters of the gentry from Wales[2] I will begin by examining the intellectual context of their experiences, focusing on some of the feminine roles to which they might have been expected to aspire. The remainder of the chapter focuses upon the particular: their lives within the context of the family and educational institutions.

This work is clearly not intended to offer a definitive account of the socialization and education of the daughters of the gentry over two hundred years. The absence of representative material covering the whole period makes generalization difficult. The scarcity, for instance, of anecdotal accounts and personal papers written by women or about women (except for those clustered at the end of the period of study) prevents us from making firm statements about changes in girls' education over this period. Nevertheless, the sources we do have are highly suggestive. By studying them we are offered a window into the Welsh past that has hitherto been largely ignored.

In Welsh historiography the gentry have tended until recently to receive a very bad press. Accused of treacherously neglecting Welsh culture and heritage in favour of English fashions, they have been seen as bringing about the demise of traditional Welsh culture, most notably the bardic tradition, which had, in Prys Morgan's words 'seemed to go back to the dark ages'.[3] These were patriarchs at best and at their worst mere parasites,[4] a group which had, according to Geraint Jenkins, 'avidly pursued the manifold pleasures and temptations of sophisticated London'[5] and 'abandoned their roles as the traditional guardians of Welsh culture'.[6] The juxtaposition here of traditional cultural purity with images of corrupting parasitism, pleasure and sophisticated metropolitan temptations does represent some contemporary attitudes. As Prys Morgan observes, however, 'there was some truth in this attack on the gentry of Wales, but they were a scapegoat for some deeper malaise'.[7] For present purposes the important point is that we seem to be dealing with a historical reconstruction of the gentry in which moral critique may have implications for our interpretation of gender roles. The 'patriarchs' of Wales were gentlemen, and their corruption was achieved through pleasure and temptation. This account reinforces the usual tendency to overlook the experience of girls and women in a particular way. When that experience is examined, its character is found to parallel that of men, but also to offer a kind of forced redemption and transcendence: 'Relieved of domestic chores, blessed with a good education, taste and in abundance of leisure, wives of the gentry often took refuge in intense piety and devotion.'[8] It is for that flight into piety that these women have mostly been remembered.[9] The present chapter re-examines aspects of that experience, on the basis of a limited but unjustifiably neglected body of evidence, in order to recapture the experiences of girls in particular as they grew towards that life of educated leisure. For as recent work has shown, there is scope for a more positive interpretation of what one scholar has termed the 'culture of sensibility' in this period.[10] The suggestion here is that, although in many ways the education of these girls was 'English' in content, we should not view them simply or even primarily as another example of Anglicization, but rather as being culturally bilingual, and European as well as Welsh.[11] The redefinition of Welsh national and cultural identity over the course of this period was paralleled by a redefinition of female roles which made the socialization of girls a process of negotiation between competing models of both Welshness and gentility. There were opportunities for improvization and creativity here which we need not reduce to the single option of piety. The greater exposure to these competing models which the leisure and wealth of the gentry afforded makes their experience a potentially rich field in which to explore the construction of gender and national identities.

Ideals of femininity

One point of departure for this particular journey into the Welsh past is via a brief appraisal of the ideals of femininity current at the time of study, using such sources as prescriptive tracts known to be in possession of the gentry.[12] This literature goes some way to providing an insight into the intellectual fabric into which the experiences of these girls were woven, albeit in a highly stylized way. By the deliberate defining of gender roles, as was one of the purposes of such works, there is a certain rigidity in their portrayal of the models being offered to men and women. That said, they are useful because they suggest at least a degree of plurality in the roles assigned to women that has not received suitable recognition by historians, who have cast them in roles upholding piety, motherhood and wifely obedience. Richard Allestree, a popular theorist among the gentry of Wales, (whose work is to be found in the great libraries of Welsh estates) was a keen advocate of the latter ideal: 'Not let such *wives* think that any fault or provocation of the husband can justify their frowardness [sic].'[13] This is not to imply that there was a strict adherence to the ideals laid down in conduct books. There was probably a dynamic relationship between these theoretical prescriptions and the formation of attitudes concerning gender identities. Baroness Bunsen, in her memoirs, conveys the tensions that could arise between one's own feelings and those beliefs one has been taught. She describes the conflict between notions concerning the importance of outward virtues and her emotional response to these: 'My mother called upon Mrs Darwin, & there I saw the three beautiful daughters, whose appearance is still distinct in my recollection – I always delighted to look upon beauty, but took care not to explain why I stared at the objects of my admiration, because I was always reminded of the solemn untruth "beauty is of no value".'[14]

Similarly, one must consider the possibility of a process of negotiation between ideals of conduct and the reality of female behaviour. Sexual honour among women, for instance, was a highly valued quality and can be seen as the female equivalent of military and later social honour of the Welsh gentleman. Female chastity in marriage had repercussions on family honour and the purity of lineage: a child born within wedlock by a father other than the husband might inherit if the family were not aware of a female's sexual misconduct. Clearly such compelling reasons did not stop some women from committing such 'crimes' when married, such as the sister-in-law of one Eliza Lloyd. In a letter to Mrs Wynne, Eliza Lloyd describes the outrageous behaviour of this unnamed offender and its impact on her husband: 'She has hitherto been remiss in her duty to God and man, I am really concern'd with all my heart for ye disappointment he has met with (for what is more to be valued than a vertuous wife). I am sure I may justly say none of our family's reputation was ever blown upon before, but unspotted and free from aspersions and infamy.'[15]

Many of these images of womanhood were expressed in texts written in English by English writers, and one cannot assume a straightforward assimilation of such ideas into the Welsh intellectual milieu. There was most probably a process of negotiation in the ways in which the gentry of Wales took on board such ideas. Such cases as the presentation of a praise poem in Welsh to the ladies of the Myddelton household at Chirk Castle,[16] for instance, and the use of a harpist and two bards to celebrate an intermarriage between the Wynns of Gwydir,[17] an important rite of passage for the female involved, would seem to show a distinct 'Welsh' way of framing female experience. Rowland Watkyns, though of English origin and writing in English, does seem to have been working within this 'Welsh' framework when he wrote in a genre similar to the praise poetry of bardic fame. In a poem addressed to Mrs Mary Jeffreys, for instance, he offers an ideal of womanhood by proclaiming her many admirable virtues:

> She's rich in beauty, rich in purse, and free
> Her riches most consist in piety.[18]

The desire to convey a sense of distance from one's social inferiors, in ways other than lavish displays by Welsh harpists, cut across cultural and national boundaries by using an array of means that would not have seemed out of place at a European court; such as a delicacy in language,[19] dress[20] and gesture.[21] Elizabeth Baker's account of the gallantry of the sheriff at the ball held after the assizes of August

1784 when she was wearing unsuitable attire, reminds us that dress was seen as an important means of social distinction: 'Observing my dress improper for an Assembly the Sheriff rejoined – "my Address rendered it immaterial", his words too pleasing to scrutinise and I sat by his lady as easy in my old Crape garment as any of the ornamented Belles in the room.'[22] The importance of these qualities is further reflected in the care parents took in the selection of governesses. In a document found in the Peniarth collection, an employer is advised on the qualities most desirable in a governess. In these instructions much emphasis is placed on the aforementioned attributes: 'Her religion, morals, manners and conversation are of the utmost importance . . . as the tutor is now forming the young mind for the woman . . . If the tutor is an accomplished woman, much more may be performed by her.'[23]

Parents and daughters

Though governesses were important role models for those few girls fortunate to have one, parents were of greater importance in the socialization of girls in that they were often enduring figures in their lives. It does not seem unjustified, therefore, to examine the emotional relationship parents might have had with their daughters in so far as the sources permit. A useful starting point for this exercise is to focus upon the nursing of the young baby. Historians in the Stone and Aries school of thought,[24] believe that the use of wet-nurses by the gentry and aristocracy, during the seventeenth and much of the eighteenth century, was symptomatic of a lack of love. By delivering new-born babies into the hands of women outside the family to breast-feed, women from the gentry were released from their nurturing roles. They could then continue with their hectic round of social engagements and could, more importantly, become pregnant again without waiting for their fertility to return after the long period of lactation.[25] This was an advantage for a class so intent on producing as many male heirs as possible, in the hope that one at least would survive to adulthood.[26] For our purposes this custom can be seen as preventing the establishment of a bond, both physical and emotional, between mother and child.

Were the daughters of the Welsh gentry deprived of this important bond? From an appraisal of the personal correspondence and household accounts, in which references to the employment of wet-nurses appears, it seems that this practice was generally confined to the seventeenth century. In 1617, for instance, we find Elizabeth Boswell, in a letter to her father John Wynne, describing the difficulties of finding a suitable wet-nurse.[27] In sources pertaining to the eighteenth century, equivalent examples are hard to find. It is possible that such practices continued, but that the documentation has not survived. This does, however, seem unlikely considering the wealth of sources generated by the gentry in Wales. Perhaps during the eighteenth century the gentry were influenced by the flood of literature, generally written by Protestant writers, which actively criticized this custom on the grounds that it prevented the establishment of an emotional bond between mother and child.[28]

From the brief and sporadic insights derived from the personal papers of the gentry, one can only hazard a guess at the type of emotional relationship the daughters enjoyed with their parents from infancy. It does seem likely, however, that parents played an important role in the emotional lives of these girls. There are repeated references to them buying toys and books for their children, even in the seventeenth century.[29] In letters between husbands and wives written over the course of the period, the children are regularly discussed.[30] If one parent was absent from the home for a period of time, he or she made enquiries about the children. One could even suggest that the depth of emotional attachment parents felt for their daughters was stronger than that for their sons, because girls were more likely to spend most of their childhood at home or in the care of one parent. As evidence later in this chapter will show, girls were less likely to spend a large part of their childhood in educational institutions or in the care of a trained educator.

The relationship between mother and daughter was particularly strong because the mother was viewed as the natural guardian and companion of girls.[31] This is suggested in personal correspondence, in which women make repeated references to the welfare of the daughters in their care. The possibility of a relative degree of emotional distance between fathers and daughters is poignantly introduced by Baroness Bunsen in her memoirs, where she describes a parting from her father during her childhood, sometime in the 1790s: 'He was much affected at parting, & said "it would be hard for him to return to the empty house"– I remember being struck by his emotion & the tears in his eyes – never having reflected on the fact of his being very fond of my Mother & his children.'[32] This particular instance reminds us of the dangers of making rash judgements about the emotional lives of those in the past. Baroness Bunsen was later to learn that her father was very attached to his children, but had difficulty expressing his feelings. Only when a tragedy struck did she realize that her father cared deeply for his daughters. She provides a heart-rending account of his response when her sister, Matilda, died in 1797: 'He came back very shortly, in tears: & when I begged to know the reason, I heard him speak, but only distinguished the words, – "poor Matilda!".'[33]

This example also demonstrates the dichotomy between theory and reality. Parents at the very least bestowed equal care and affection upon their daughters, despite the existence of the commonly held notion that boys were more of a blessing than girls because they represented the continuation of the family line.[34] The birth of a daughter might produce an ambiguous or negative response by the kinship circle, as is evident in a letter from Ellen Godolphin to a new mother, dated 29 November 1740: 'I wish you joy, Dear Mrs Owen, of your daughter, & of your being safe in your bed; had it pleased God, I should rather have congratulated you on the bearth of a son, but God, the giver of all things knows better than we do what is best.'[35] However, if parents initially felt disappointment at the birth of a daughter as opposed to a son, this disappointment soon dissipated. Even if the first born was a girl, parents most probably rejoiced in the survival of mother and daughter, and the reassurance it gave concerning the fertility of their union and the possibility of sons in the future.

The education of girls

Differences in gender undoubtedly underpinned the relationship children might have with their parents. There were subtle differences in the treatment of boys and girls in the family setting even if at present we know little about them. It is in the field of education, however, that there is clear divergence in the experiences of the sons and daughters of the Welsh gentry. Furthermore, this was a sphere of life in which girls could not have failed to realize that they were treated very differently from their brothers. Girls' education differed from that of boys in three basic ways.

Firstly, whilst boys were ostensibly taught by professionally trained educators, girls were taught by a diverse mix of people. Although there are references to the employment of governesses [36] and specialist teachers for such subjects as dance and deportment,[37] it was rare for a girl to be taught by professional educators for a long period of time.[38] Instead, much of their education was carried out by friends of the family and relatives. Miss Mary Myddelton's education, for instance, in the later seventeenth century, was entrusted to the Reverend Thomas Lloyd, a close friend of the Myddelton family of Chirk Castle.[39] Similarly, visits to the houses of acquaintances could provide girls with the opportunity to encounter other educators for the duration of their stay. Thomas Rowlands, of Cayrey, for instance, expressed his gratitude to William Owen for his role in Emma Rowlands's education during her stay at Brogyntyn: 'Yr desire yt Emma shd make a longer stay I shall most readily indulge her with yt satisfaction being fully assur'd that she can no where so much benefit and improve as by the conversation and example of such good company.'[40] Finally, mothers were the most likely persons to educate their daughters. Notable examples include Hester Lynch Thrale who, like her mother before her, played an active role in her daughters' education.[41]

As the daughters of the Welsh gentry were not destined for the public life of politics and business, the resources, both financial and human, bestowed upon their instruction were limited. As this discussion implies, their education was often furthered by chance meetings and friendships or as a result of the closeness a girl experienced with her mother. Not surprisingly, the amount of time a girl could hope to spend in a formal educational setting was also minimal, which introduces the second way in which girls' education differed from that of boys. The sons of the gentry could look forward to attending a grammar school, either locally or in England, and then further education at university or the Inns of Court.[42] Their early education could take place in the home under the instruction of a tutor, but this was generally an introduction to the lessons they were later to receive in educational institutions.

By contrast, a girl received the greater part of her education in the private sphere of the household, within which she was expected to spend her adult life. There are examples of girls going to public school in Wales[43] and London,[44] or lodging with respectable families and taking lessons in the metropolis.[45] In her diary, Elizabeth Baker mentions a visit from Miss Parry of Hendreforion on 17 February 1782 who 'promised to come again before she returns to Chester School which has improv'd her considerably – had she not been sent from Dolgelley there would have been a fine girl totally lost from want of some education; there nothing is to be learnt but what should most carefully be shunned.'[46] The time spent in schools by girls such as Miss Parry was, however, usually severely circumscribed. Instruction in formal educational institutions was seen mainly as a way of finishing a girl's education, not least because the fees levied were often extortionate.[47] Although education in the home is often difficult to document, it seems plausible to suggest that much of the study undertaken by girls was informal and within the context of the household. Mrs Thrale's friend Dr Johnson during his tour of the Hebrides with James Boswell, for instance, suggested that:

> a Chief and his Lady should make their house like a court. They should have a certain number of the gentlemen's daughters to receive their education in the family, to learn pastry and such things from the housekeeper, and manners from my lady. That was the way in the great families of Wales: at Lady Salusbury's, Mrs Thrale's grandmother's and at Lady Philipps' . . . There were always six young ladies at Sir John Philipps'; when one was married, her place was filled up. There was a large school-room where they learnt needlework and other things.[48]

This example is very useful, not least because it provides us with a rare insight into the dynamics of girls' education in certain gentry households. Perhaps what is more interesting, aside from the fact that this is a clear account of instruction within the informal context of the home, is that Johnson goes on to discuss the widely influential sixteenth-century Italian writer Castiglione and the origin of his *Book of the Courtier* at the court of Urbino. Johnson and Boswell during their exchange do not seem to regard Skye or Wales to lie outside this tradition of courtly education.

Wales was certainly not a cultural and social backwater during this period. The gentry had a lively social calendar punctuated by a range of events, some of which older girls could attend. Occasions such as tea-parties, card-playing and dances at the homes of one's contemporaries, for instance, were a regular feature of this social calendar and provided girls with the opportunity to make friends and become part of female networks. During the eighteenth century a number of unnamed females were known to congregate at Bodfan on Saturday nights for card games which quite often ran on into the morning, when they were startled by the ringing of bells at Llandwrog church calling them to Sunday morning service.[49] William Morris of

Anglesey (a renowned antiquarian and letter writer, 1705–63) conveyed the popularity of this pastime among females and his own dissatisfaction at losing to them when he wrote that he was 'tired of playing at cards for some nights past with the ladies with bad success'.[50] One wonders if Morris was not a little piqued by a loss of some male authority to these talented female card masters. In addition, Elizabeth Baker's diary has a number of entries describing her attendance at tea parties. In an entry dated 31 August 1781, she describes a visit to Brynygwyn where 'we were entertained with the Harp all the time of coffee and tea'.[51]

These activities, so popular among the young ladies of the gentry, should not be dismissed as meaningless pastimes undertaken to fill the vacuum created by their shallow and empty lives.[52] Instead, by such activities as tea-drinking, ladies could carve out their own identities as women and as members of the social élite. Tea-drinking provided the opportunity to display social superiority, because tea and the accompanying paraphernalia of china and tea-stands were luxury items beyond the reach of the majority of society. Furthermore, attendance at tea-parties imbued young ladies with the ideals of domestic sociability and social conventions pertaining to the role of hostess, a role they themselves would take on when reaching adulthood.[53] By attending such social events they could also communicate with a large number of their older female counterparts and possibly become conversant in such things as the current literary trends, recent political developments, problems women encountered in the running of households and estates, not to mention the important matters of conception, pregnancy and childbirth. Miss Myddelton and her female entourage, for instance, did not allow the poor communications with polite society to inhibit their knowledge of literary fashions. As the modern historian D. Leslie Davies puts it: 'When the weather was bad and the ways muddied the ladies took to their books, and we know that Miss Myddelton had a good library at Croesnewydd'.[54]

For the daughters of the Welsh gentry, hours of their childhood could be spent in the type of private study at home undertaken by Miss Myddelton and friends.[55] There are numerous examples of girls being supplied with books, of which the most common was the Bible. The daughters of the Philipps family of Picton Castle and the Myddeltons of Chirk, for instance, were all given bibles as a focus for religious study. Sir John Philipps, in a letter dated August 1721, advised his wife to keep their daughter occupied until another governess was found by encouraging her to read her bible.[56] Although books were costly commodities in this period, Elizabeth Baker informs us that difficulties encountered in obtaining a diverse range of books were overcome by the ladies in the Dolgellau area by means of a book sharing arrangement. Rhys Jones's daughters (of Blaenau) were regular lenders to and borrowers from this well-known diarist.[57]

If the array of skills and knowledge girls could hope to acquire from their private study and social encounters were not impressive enough, they could also expect to be taught the traditional female accomplishments of dancing, music, needlework and housewifery,[58] as well as reading, writing, religious catechism and French. A girl from the gentry was casually described in a contemporary lawsuit, for instance, at the beginning of this period, as needing to be brought 'up at her book, needle and other things fitting for her calling and degree'.[59] Possibly the richness of female experience in this respect has been underplayed because the curriculum they encountered was greatly overshadowed by the glittering formal educational opportunities afforded the sons of the Welsh gentry, thus highlighting the third way in which girls' education differed from that of boys. Boys could hope for a more diverse and wide-ranging formal curriculum including such accomplishments as fencing, dancing *and* academic subjects: mathematics, classical languages and natural sciences such as astronomy.[60] It is not surprising to discover, therefore, that the curriculum William Owen had in mind for his daughter was noticeably lacking in academic subjects: 'What you are to doe, you must learn to cypher/and to perfect you hand writing and to learn French dance and if you learnt to singe it would help your voice.'[61]

This range of subject-matter appears to have been staple fare for the daughters of the gentry throughout this period. Despite the aspirations of progressive educational commentators in Western Europe during the later seventeenth and eighteenth centuries,[62] who envisaged a mixture of practical and academic instruction, academic subjects remained the sole reserve of boys. There were, as always, exceptions to this rule. The Welsh gentry nurtured a number of female prodigies who were well-versed in languages (both classical and modern), humanities and sciences. These included such women as Anna Williams,[63] Hester Lynch Thrale, Philip Wharton's daughters [64] and the Waddington sisters. The latter, for instance, 'studied Greek, Latin, Spanish and Italian, Euclid, economics, music, drawing, history, literature and geography, as well as the more feminine employments of embroidery and household management'.[65] The curriculum taught to these girls is, however, well documented by virtue of the fact that *they were* anomalies. One can see them as the eighteenth-century Welsh equivalents of the renowned sixteenth-century female scholars or so-called 'Tudor Paragons', who have been acclaimed as setting the standards to which educators of girls were to aspire during the rest of the early modern period.[66] Although the education girls received was limited in terms of academic subjects, one should not underestimate the importance of instruction in more informal subjects. Their education was no worse than that of their English counterparts, whose instruction also tended towards the traditional female accomplishments. As Mary Astell informs us in 1696:

> And the girls to *Boarding schools*, or other places to learn Needlework, dancing, Singing, Musick, Drawing, Painting and other accomplishments, according to the Humour and Ability of the Parents, or Inclination of the children . . . Here then lies the main Defect, that we are taught only our mother tongue or perhaps *French*, which is now very fashionable, and almost as Familiar amongst women of Quality as Men's whereas the other sex by means of a more extensive Education to the knowledge of the *Roman* and *Greek* languages, have a vaster field for their Imagination to rove in . . .[67]

Just as one should not underestimate the richness of the educational experience of girls as compared to that afforded boys, it would be equally unjustified to view the parallels between the curriculum offered to girls from Wales and England as symptomatic of outright Anglicization. Admittedly, the curriculum and the locations within which the daughters of the gentry of Wales were taught mirrored English fashions. When girls or boys were sent to school, more often than not they were sent to England. The situation, however, is a little more subtle than historians such as G. Dyfnallt Owen would have us believe.[68] Rather than castigating the education of these children as merely English, one could in fact see positive aspects. In effect, by spending part of their time in England, they became educated in the dynamics of another culture. They did not cease to be Welsh. Rather, they became more cosmopolitan in outlook. One can, therefore, argue that there was a particular Welsh dimension to their education by its very diversity in terms of educators, location and the cultural context within which they received instruction, even if the language of instruction was English rather than Welsh.

Furthermore, a taste for such delicacies as tea-drinking which was a fashionable English pastime,[69] (though incidentally not uniquely English in invention but a European phenomenon), did not prevent Welsh girls and boys, when reaching adulthood, from also supporting Welsh culture. Their flirtations with English culture, therefore, merely added a richness and texture to their experiences. The Mary Myddelton mentioned earlier, for instance, who, with her friends, was an avid follower of literary fashions in England and who could not speak Welsh herself, was still an active promoter of the Welsh language and popular culture. She ensured that the Wrexham chapel-of-ease at Minera was provided with sufficient funds to continue services in Welsh.[70] The accounts of Chirk Castle also attest to the fact that the fashionable gentry did not lose interest in everything Welsh. There are entries, for instance, in 1661 for the payment of 1s. 6d. in total 'to the Harper that played at castle xijd. & to the men that sang Welsh carrols vjd.'; and in 1704, 6d. for 'a woman from Scythre for bringing 13 welch bookes (being the lives of the Apostles) from Salop'.[71] Admittedly, the use of such harpers and singers of Welsh carols might be seen as an example of the Welsh gentry patronizing these aspects of Welsh popular culture for their novelty value; entertaining their English guests with examples of 'quaint' Welsh customs. The latter reference to the purchase of Welsh books does, however, display their commitment to the Welsh language. Although we can not be sure whether girls were taught to read these Welsh books, it does seem likely that they learned at least some Welsh. At a time when English-born wives were encouraged to learn Welsh so as not to be cheated by their Welsh-speaking servants, it would be inconceivable to believe that the daughters of the Welsh gentry remained ignorant of their mother tongue.[72] There is room here, too, for an interesting study of the daughters' relationship with servants.

There is perhaps a more tangible way in which the education of these girls can be seen to have had a particularly Welsh dimension, though a way which is probably one of the most difficult to document because it relates to the informal instruction of girls in the home. It would seem likely that by watching and often helping her mother run the household, a daughter would become versed in housewifery and perhaps basic accounting skills.[73] This in itself does not initially seem particularly astounding as the daughters of the English gentry could learn similar skills by observing the 'work' undertaken by their mothers. It does seem likely however, that ladies in Wales had more scope to extend their administrative capacities because their husbands were often away for long periods of time, particularly in the metropolis when they were MPs, entrusting the running of the estate, as well as the household, to their wives.[74] By contrast, in English historiography, this phenomenon has been well documented only during times of crisis; during the Civil War, for instance, whilst husbands were in exile. If there was indeed a greater propensity for women to play a more active and more regular role in the running of the family estate in Wales this may in turn have had repercussions on the socialization of Welsh daughters in that their mothers' actions could imbue them with ideas and aspirations quite out of kilter with such female roles as the obedient wife.

This is not to suggest that in many ways their education did not serve to reinforce ideas about womanhood current at the time, as was indeed the case. As the educational paths of boys and girls diverged in childhood, the daughters of the gentry were probably alerted to a difference in expectation by parents with respect to themselves and their brothers. Their lessons in such subjects as housewifery and needlework emphasized the idea that they were expected to become wives and mothers. In addition, their perceptions of social superiority would have been sharpened whilst being educated at home, because girls could compare their comparatively extensive instruction to that of their lowly female counterparts, not least perhaps their female servants, who only learned such subjects as religious catechism and basic housewifery. Dance and deportment classes most probably reinforced this sense of social distance because they emphasized the cultivation of a delicacy of gesture and manner. William Owen, writing in 1669 to his daughter, emphasized the importance of this aspect of her education: 'think of your Creditt and ours, yt you may improve youself in carradge and learning and breddinge against you Come to ye country [sic]'.[75] The importance placed upon aesthetic qualities possibly prepared these girls for their later experiences when they became beautiful objects in the marriage market; as Baroness Bunsen stated, there was some value in beauty despite attitudes to the contrary.[76]

Conclusion

During this period, women inhabited a world in which they were expected, in theory, to act as good wives, mothers and Christians. The girls from the Welsh gentry were also encouraged to display their social superiority by way of cultivating a delicacy of gesture, manner and language. In many ways their education reinforced these ideas of femininity that were so important in the socialization of these girls into gender roles and the conventions of their class. The roles women were expected to adopt were in keeping with European conventions of the time, rather than being regional or national in form. The lack of a particularly Welsh concept of female gentility may be viewed as yet another example of the Welsh gentry treacherously turning their backs on Welsh culture in favour of English fashions. However, as I have suggested, just because the Welsh gentry read prescriptive texts produced in English, by English authors, one should not be misled into believing that they glibly followed English conventions. We should instead see the Welsh gentry as cultured Europeans, actively involved in the current intellectual debates. Many aspects of the concept of gentility examined by J. Gwynfor Jones owed something to European models developed in the Renaissance.[77] The woman question, for instance, which gained increased currency in the sixteenth and seventeenth centuries, did not escape the attention of Welsh bards, who formed the vanguard of Welsh culture during their time. There are two poems in particular, entitled 'Against Women' (anon)[78] and 'In Defence of Woman' by William Cynwal,[79] which address the woman question. Not only are these poems securely placed in European literary fashions of the time, namely the two concurrent genres of misogynist and defence literature;[80] but also, as the second poem is a direct response to the first, they could be seen as anticipating the Swetnam controversy.[81] In this latter debate, defence literature was written as a reaction against Joseph Swetnam's *Arraignment of Lewd, idle, froward and unconstant women* (1615). It is noteworthy that the Swetnam controversy arose at a time when a Scottish male sovereign, James I, had just succeeded an English female monarch, Queen Elizabeth I. Swetnam's derogation of woman was not merely a misogynist text possibly written to please a new monarch whose disrespect of women is well documented. By attacking women he was in effect supporting the exertion of power by Scotland over England, which resulted from James's succession. Thus in this context nationality and views about gender were inextricably linked.

English stereotypes of Welshness in this period represented the Welsh as a backward and primitive people, overlooking the distinctive way in which inherited notions of decent behaviour were being fused with new ideas spreading across Europe during the Renaissance. Tea-drinking *may* have represented a diminished version of traditional household hospitality, for example, but taken in conjunction with what we know of Welsh gentlewomen's patronage of educational and religious provisions, it might need to be regarded in a more positive light, as part of a Europe-wide re-orientation of genteel sensibilities in response to economic and social change, and taking many different forms across Europe. Not only were the girls of the gentry presented with European images of femininity, they were also educated to the same standard as other European women. This is not to reduce Wales to a mere province of Europe. Such an assertion would be dangerous because the experiences of its daughters were regional as well as continental in form. We noted, for instance, the possibility that mothers of the Welsh gentry sometimes offered a more active role model than those described in theoretical tracts and that there is some evidence to suggest that the Welsh language was not wholly spurned by this class. Furthermore, as Elizabeth Baker was to learn during her stay at Dolgellau, the Welsh gentry continued to treasure their lineage. Baker recalls one occasion when she met a favourable response to her proposition that Mrs Owen displayed a striking resemblance to Mary Queen of Scots, whose mother 'remarked it was probable as she was a near relative of the unfortunate Queen and gave the pedigree up to Owen Tudor Fachan as a proof'.[82]

Encountering other cultures heightens awareness of our own. From the cultural contrasts and diversity of experience to which they were exposed, the daughters of the Welsh gentry received a unique education. As Linda Colley succinctly puts it: 'Men and women decide who they are by reference to who and what they are not.'[83] For these girls, their time in England and their dealings with English culture could have reinforced their own sense of 'Welshness'. The problems of documenting such feelings could account for the propensity of certain historians to naïvely label the experiences of the gentry as 'Anglicized'. We do have a well-documented example that illustrates this stimulus to cultural self-awareness. The founders of such literary clubs as the Honourable Society of Cymmrodorion, that became one of the guardians of traditional Welsh culture, were men also *in exile* in London. Perhaps it is time to begin a re-evaluation of

'Welshness' in this period, as has begun in our own times. Oliver Davies and Fiona Bowie, editors of the recent book, *Discovering Welshness*, rightly note the complexities of this task: 'Welshness, then, is much more than possession of a language. It is a sense of community, identity, a world of culture, poetry, and proximity to the past, all of which draw upon the language, even in those areas in which Welsh is no longer spoken.'[84] I hope that in this chapter I have introduced the reader to another aspect of this Welsh past and culture that has hitherto been neglected.

Notes

1 Wiesner, M. (1993) *Women and Gender in Early Modern Europe* (Cambridge, Cambridge University Press), 43.
2 It should be noted that in this paper I am concerned with the broader category of the gentry from Wales rather than those gentry who were self-consciously 'Welsh' in outlook. Any reference to the 'Welsh gentry' in this article should be viewed in these terms.
3 Morgan, P. (1981) *The Eighteenth Century Renaissance* (Llandybïe, Christopher Davies), 13.
4 This is powerfully conveyed by David Howell (1986) in his choice of these adjectives in the title of his book: *Patriarchs and Parasites: The Gentry of South West Wales in the Eighteenth Century* (Cardiff, University of Wales Press).
5 Jenkins, G. H. (1993) *The Foundations of Modern Wales 1642–1780*, (Oxford, Oxford University Press), 225.
6 Ibid., 245. Jenkins rightly recognizes the pluralistic nature of the gentry whose experiences were by no means homogeneous: 'The lesser gentry of north and west Wales, sheltered against the winds of change in culture and fashion, remained fundamentally Welsh in their speech and outlook' (220).
7 Morgan, P. (1981) op. cit., 25.
8 Jenkins, G. H. (1978) *Literature, Religion and Society in Wales 1660–1730* (Cardiff, University of Wales Press), 274.
9 Deirdre Beddoe has shown how the pious Welsh woman was one of the limited number of images of Welsh women not masked by principally male stereotypes of Welshmen in the nineteenth century. Beddoe, D. 'Images of Welsh Women' in Curtis, T. (ed.) (1986) *Wales: The Imagined Nation. Essays in Cultural and National Identity* (Bridgend, Poetry Wales Press), 227 and 234.
10 Barker-Benfield, G. J. (1992) *The Culture of Sensibility: Sex and Society in Eighteenth Century Britain* (London, University of Chicago Press).
11 Baroness Bunsen, previously Frances Waddington, sister of Lady Llanover who was famed for her role in constructing the stereotypical Welsh female

costume, recalls at the age of seven being sent to play French games in Dr Beddoes' garden in London. M. Fraser, 'The Waddingtons of Llanover 1791–1805: Reminiscences of Baroness Bunsen, née Frances Waddington' in *The National Library of Wales Journal* Vol.II No. 4 (1960), 306. Similarly, it would seem that Lady Wynn Williams's daughters (unnamed) were versed in French, as is evident in a letter from Lady Williams to the estate manager of Wynnstay, dated 6 February 1788, asking him to send a French dictionary from the 'little girls' room' to their London residence (NLW Wynnstay MS 115/13/26). The book catalogues from gentry households also attest to an interest in European literary texts, both classic and 'modern'. For example, refer to footnote 12 below.

[12] The two most popular books of this type were Allestree, R. (1659 edition) *The Whole Duty; Necessary for all Families with Private Devotions for Severall Occasions* (London, Timothy Garthwait) and Locke, J. (1693) *Some Thoughts Concerning Education* (London, A. & J. Churchill). Geraint H. Jenkins (1978 op. cit., p.114) noted that the former was 'enormously popular among the Welsh reading public' and 'it found its way regularly into gentry households.' It reached an even wider audience after its translation into Welsh by John Langford in 1672. This argument is reinforced by a survey of catalogues of books owned by the gentry during this period. Such gentry family estates as Bodewryd (NLW Bodewryd MS 688), Chirk Castle (NLW Chirk, Group A, MSS 29–32) and Picton Castle (NLW Picton Castle MS 1618), for instance, owned at least one copy of both of these books. It should be noted, however, that we rarely encounter references to books actually owned by women. Inventories, for instance, usually listed them collectively as family possessions. We face the problem of not knowing whether women actually read them and, even if they did, what significance they gave to these texts.

[13] Allestree, R., op. cit., 313.

[14] Cited in Fraser, M. (1960) op. cit., 303.

[15] Letter dated 10 January 1713/14 from Eliza Lloyd to Mrs Margaret Wynne of Bodewryd, who was most probably her aunt (NLW Bodewryd Correspondence 147).

[16] See Myddelton, M. (ed.) (1931), *Chirk Castle Accounts AD 1666–1753* (Manchester, Manchester University Press), 3. The date of this entry was 1667.

[17] Entry under the year 1654. Myddelton, M. (ed.) (1908) *Chirk Castle Accounts AD 1605–1666* (St Albans), 46.

[18] Watkyns, R. (1968) *Flamma Sine Fumo* (1662) edited by P. C. Davies (Cardiff, University of Wales Press), 23.

[19] Consider, for instance, Burke, P. (1993) *The Art of Conversation* (London, Polity Press), chapter 4 .

[20] In a poem, for instance, written by an anonymous woman to her daughter, the author suggests that she should wear 'As fine a dress as suits yr fortune.' This reference can be found in a handwritten poem entitled

'Advice to a Daughter going to Bath' in the Llanfair Brynodol collection housed in the National Library of Wales (MS 1, ff. 37–8). Though we have no indication of the identity of the author, we do at least know that the poem was written during the November of 1726, that is at a time of the year when it was not unusual for the gentry to spend at least some time in Bath, where they could take the waters for medicinal purposes and participate in the cultural and social activities of polite society. This poem is interesting in that the author goes to great lengths to stress that her daughter should be moderate in every conceivable circumstance, many of which she discusses.

21 This would be particularly important in this period because of the influence of French culture among the Welsh gentry and also because, at this time, generally throughout Europe, the social and cultural élites were anxious to disassociate themselves from popular culture. Admittedly, this was probably not such a significant movement in Wales because the gentry had never been as active in popular culture as their counterparts elsewhere. Refer to Burke, P. (ed.) (1988) *Popular Culture in Early Modern Europe* (Aldershot, Wildwood) chapter 9. More generally on the importance of gesture and behaviour, see: Keeble, N. H. (1994) *The Cultural Identity of Seventeenth-Century Woman: A Reader* (London, Routledge).

22 Cited in Bowen Thomas, B. (1945) *The Old Order: Based on the Diary of Elizabeth Baker (Dolgelley 1778–1786)* (Cardiff, University of Wales Press), 24.

23 This article entitled 'On the Education of Girls From twelve years and upwards' was, according to the notes at the end of the handwritten transcript, taken from the *Middlesex Journal* of 27 September 1787 (NLW Peniarth MS. 663/514).

24 For a fuller account of these historians and their views, refer to Michael Roberts's article in this volume: note 7.

25 For a discussion of changes in the practice of wet-nursing and its implications: Fildes, V. 'Historical Changes in Patterns of Breast Feeding' in Diggory, P., Potts, M. and Jeper, S. (eds.) (1988), *Natural Human Fertility: Social and Biological Determinants* (London, Macmillan Press).

26 One would have expected that this would have been particularly important from the later seventeenth century when Wales, along with the rest of Britain, experienced a fertility crisis with an accompanying scarcity of male heirs. See Jenkins, J. P. (1982) 'The Demographic Decline of the Landed Gentry in the Eighteenth Century: A South Wales Study' in *The Welsh History Review* Vol.11 No. 1; and Howell, D. (1986) op. cit., Chapter 1.

27 Letter, from Elizabeth to her father at Gwydir, 4 February 1617/18 (NLW 9056E, LIII 82).

28 Crawford, P. 'The Construction and Experience of Maternity in Seventeenth Century England' in Fildes, V. (ed.) (1990), *Women as Mothers in Pre-Industrial England* (London, Routledge), 8–11 *passim*.

[29] In the household accounts of Chirk Castle, for instance, in 1613, there is reference to the purchase of 'ij [2] babies toyes' at the cost of 1s. Myddelton N., *Chirk Castle Accounts AD 1605–1666*, op. cit., 12. In the same volume there are also entries for the purchase of books and primers for the children in 1658 and 1665 on pages 114 and 122 respectively.

[30] For instance in the personal correspondence between Sir John Philipps and his wife covering the year 1713 when Lady Philipps went to Bath with their daughter Kitty, whilst Sir John remained at Picton with their 'young fellows' (NLW Picton Castle MS 1459–61).

[31] Wendy Gibson (1989) also observes this phenomenon in her study of *Women in Seventeenth-Century France* (London, Macmillan), 80: 'Girls seemed much better placed to enjoy maternal solicitude and attention in respect of their education.'

[32] Cited in Fraser, M. (1960) op. cit., 302.

[33] Ibid., 304.

[34] As Astell, M. (1696) noted in her *Essay in Defence of the Female Sex* (London, A. Roper & E. Wilkinson), girls met 'with So many Enemies at their first appearance in the World' (Sig. A2).

[35] Letter from Ell. Godolphin to Mrs Owen, Brogyntyn (NLW Brogyntyn MS 213). Other examples can be found in letters sent to John Myddelton on the birth of his daughter in 1724 and a son in 1726, from Thomas Meredith, Thomas Jones (Llantysilio) and Robert Pigot (Eaton) respectively (NLW Chirk Castle MSS E961, E628 and E3244).

[36] As in a letter from Sir John Philipps, London, to his wife at Picton Castle dated 1 July 1721 (NLW Picton Castle MS 1473) and a letter from Thomas Lewis, Llandeilo to Mrs Elizabeth Johnes, of Dolaucothi, dated 22 September 1816 (NLW Dolaucothi L1202).

[37] See Myddelton, M. (ed.) *Chirk Castle Accounts AD 1605–1666*, 103 and 123, for the years 1662 and 1665 respectively, in which there are entries concerning the payment of Mr Oldam the 'danceinge master' for £2. 16s for '4 daies' teaching in 1662 and £4 in 1665 'for a month worth of dancing lesson for the children'. In many cases of such entries in account books the gender of the children is not specified as the previous examples demonstrate. But, in 1708, we are informed that a Mr Sext[o]n 'the danceing master' was paid £3 'for six days Teach[ing] Madam Myddelton & Master Wm Myddelton to dance': Myddelton, M. (ed.) *Chirk Castle Accounts AD 1666–1753*, op. cit., 380. These short bursts of lessons in this accomplishment were possibly in preparation for a forthcoming ball, which were regular occurrences in the calendar.

[38] There are cases of governesses being employed for a protracted period of time, however. For instance, in a letter from Sir John Philipps to his wife at Picton Castle, during August 1721, we find that they are in search of a replacement governess (NLW Picton Castle MS 359) and Baroness Bunsen's memoirs record that during her girlhood she received regular dancing lessons (Fraser, M. (1960) op. cit., 307).

39 Davies, D. L. (1973) 'Miss Myddelton of Croesnewydd and the Plas Power: A Preliminary Appraisal' in *Denbighshire History Society Transactions* Vol.22, 128.

40 Letter dated 8 September 1746: NLW Brogyntyn MS 1560.

41 Clifford, J. L. (1968) *Hester Lynch Piozzi (Mrs Thrale)* (London, Oxford University Press), 15; and Pollock, L. A. (1983) *Forgotten Children: Parent–Child Relations from 1500 to 1900* (Cambridge, Cambridge University Press), 247. Hester Lynch Piozzi Thrale (1741–1821) was born at Bodfel, near Pwllheli, and was the only daughter of John Salusbury of Bachegraig, Flintshire. She was famous in her day as a minor author and, more importantly, because of her connections with prominent literary figures of her day including Samuel Johnson, with whom she made a tour of north Wales in 1774.

42 For a description see: Jones, E. G. (1954) 'Correspondence of the Owens of Penrhos 1712–42' in *Anglesey Antiquarian Society and Field Club Transactions*, 59–60; Pritchard, T. W. (1982) *The Wynns at Wynnstay* (Caerwys, Old Court Press), 3–5 *passim*; and Howell, D. (1986) op. cit., 172–4.

43 Daughters of the gentry attended schools at Beaumaris, Chester and Oswestry: Bowen Thomas, B. (1945) op. cit., 21.

44 Mrs Elizabeth Gwynn, in a letter to her husband, made a passing reference to a Mrs Middeton who had just arrived home to Wales from London where she had been 'to put her daughter Awbrey to school': Gwynn, E. *The Letters of Mrs Elizabeth Gwynn of Swansea* originally published 1677 (London, Chiswick Press, 1878 edn.), 21. Other references include: NLW Clenennau letters and papers 748 (letter from William Owen at Lladdyn to his daughter Jane at Drury Lane, London; dated 3 July 1669), NLW Brogyntyn Correspondence 1354 (letter from Mary Owen, to her mother at Brogyntyn, dated 21 December 1763); and Roberts, P. R. (1961–4) 'The Social History of the Merioneth Gentry *c.*1660–1840' in *Journal of Merioneth Historical and Record Society* Vol.4, 222.

45 William Owen's daughter, for example, lodged with Mr Robert Busye in Drury Lane, and attended classes in town (NLW Clenennau letter 748).

46 Cited in Bowen Thomas, B. (1945) op. cit., 21–2.

47 Howell, D. (1986) op. cit., 175, notes that Anne Ferrier, the ward of John Colby of Ffynone, Pembrokeshire, received a costly education which amounted to £20. 9*s*. $\frac{1}{2}$*d*. for the six months ending April 1786.

48 Boswell, J. (ed.) (1931) *The Journal of A Tour to the Hebrides with Samuel Johnson* (London, J. M. Dent & Sons), 226–7; entry dated 2 October 1773.

49 Jones, B. D. (1944) 'The Families of Bodvel and Jones of Cefn-y-Coed' in *Transactions of the Caernarvonshire Historical Society* Vol.5, 55.

50 Cited in Nesta Evans, G. (1953) *Religion and Politics in Mid-Eighteenth Century Anglesey* (Cardiff, University of Wales Press), 45.

51 Cited in Bowen Thomas, B. (1945) op. cit., 19.

[52] This is the impression conveyed in Jenkins, G. H. (1993) op. cit., 101.

[53] Amanda Vickery recognizes the importance of tea-drinking in this respect, in her article on 'Women and the world of goods: a Lancashire consumer and her possessions, 1751–81', in John Brewer and Roy Porter (eds.) (1993), *Consumption and the World of Goods* (London, Routledge), 289. In this article she studies the life of Elizabeth Shackleton who lived in an area of northern England that could be seen as comparable to much of Wales in terms of its geographical setting.

[54] Davies, D. L. (1973) op. cit., 143.

[55] For instance in a letter dated 1761, Mrs Owen encourages her daughter, Mary, to use her time fruitfully in private study; 'I hope you spend some of your time in reading and that it will not be long before I be with you' (NLW Brogyntyn Correspondence 1832).

[56] NLW, Picton Castle MS 1473 and Myddelton, M. (ed.) *Chirk Castle Accounts AD 1605–1666*, op. cit. 118 and 148.

[57] Bowen Thomas, B. (1945) op. cit., 18.

[58] Examples to be found in the following letters: NLW Brogyntyn MS 1182 (letter from Ellen Owen at school to her mother Mrs Mary Owen, Brogyntyn, dated 18 May 1754) and NLW Picton Castle MS 359 (day book of the household accounts of the Philipps's London house, 1717–20, in which there is reference to the employment of a dancing instructor).

[59] Cited in Williams, G. (ed.) (1974), *Glamorgan County History (Vol. 4): Early Modern Glamorgan* (Cardiff, Glamorgan County History Trust), 115.

[60] For a discussion of the type of curriculum boys received refer to note 42 above; and for an example of boys being taught these accomplishments; NLW Wynnstay C/164/2 and C/164/3 (letters written by Watt Williams to his father Sir Watkyn Williams at Llanwrda, dated 15 March 1708/9 and 1 April 1709).

[61] Letter sent from William Owen, of Brogyntyn, to his daughter in Drury Lane, London, dated 3 July 1669 (NLW Brogyntyn MS 748).

[62] Notable examples include Makin, B. (1675) in *An Essay to Revive the Ancient Education of Gentlewomen*, and Poulain de la Barre (1673) in his work *De l'Egalité Des Deux Sexes*.

[63] Gooding, K. (1965) 'Anna – Friend of Dr Johnson' in *Country Quest* Vol.63, 51.

[64] Jenkins, P. (1981) 'Mary Wharton and the Rise of the "New Woman"' in *National Library of Wales Journal* Vol.22, 173.

[65] Fraser, M. (1962) 'The Girlhood of Augusta Waddington (Afterward Lady Llanover) – 1802–23' in *The National Library of Wales Journal* Vol.12, No. 4, 312.

[66] The so-called 'Tudor Paragons' were a collection of girls in the sixteenth century whose education was comparable with that of men's. These included such figures as Thomas More's daughters, Princess Mary, Elizabeth Tudor and Lady Jane Grey. See Gardiner, D. (1929) *English*

Girlhood at School: A Study of Women's Education (Oxford, Oxford University Press), 169–76.

67 Astell, M. (1696) op. cit., 37–8.

68 G. D. Owen (1988) *Wales in the Reign of James I* (London, Boydell Press) informs us, with regard to boys' education, that: 'It is likely that many of the young men educated across the border, who came back to Wales, were too influenced by English manners and the constant use of the English language to be re-integrated into the society which had formed their earlier character and dictated their ideas. They were inclined to disregard or, at least, not promote with the enthusiasm of their fathers, that cultural heritage and patronage which had distinguished the Welsh gentry for so many centuries.'(151–2).

69 The importance of tea-drinking in English gentry culture of this period is discussed in Wildeblood, J. (ed.) (1973) *The Polite World: A Guide to English Manners and Deportment* (London, Davis-Poynter), 143–4.

70 Davies, D. L. (1973) op. cit., 146.

71 Myddelton, M. (ed.) *Chirk Castle Accounts AD 1605–1666*, op. cit., 102 and Myddelton, M. (ed.) *Chirk Castle Accounts AD 1666–1753*, op. cit., 355, respectively.

72 Williams, G. (1987) *Recovery, Reorientation and Reformation: Wales c.1415–1642* (Oxford, Oxford University Press), 442 and Williams, *Glamorgan County History*, (op. cit.), 118; noted that wives of the English wives of the gentry in the seventeenth century at least were expected to learn Welsh. B. Bowen Thomas (1945) noted that even Elizabeth Baker during her sojourn in late eighteenth-century Wales 'admitted it was her duty either to learn the language or to accept the inconvenience arising from her incapacity'.

73 This was noted by Gibson, W. (1989) op. cit., 29.

74 We find examples such as Sir John Philipps's wife sending detailed instructions to the estate manager (undated letter, NLW Picton Castle MS 1658) and Mrs Ann Canon, at Hereford, receiving a letter from her tenant Elizabeth Lloyd concerning the renewal of her lease (NLW Picton Castle MS 1598).

75 Taken from the Brogyntyn collection, cited in Roberts, P. R. (1961–4) op. cit., 222.

76 This emphasis on the beautiful and aesthetic was an important feature of gentry culture, evident in the lavish care bestowed on the improvement of their homes and gardens. See Owen, G. D. (1988) op. cit., 147–8.

77 Jones, J. G. (1992) *Concepts of Order and Gentility in Wales 1540–1640* (Llandysul, Gomer Press), xii–xv.

78 Translated in Williams, G. (ed.) (1990), *The Rent Thats Due to Love: A Selection of Welsh poems* (London, Editions Poetry), 56–73.

79 Cynwal, W. (1961) *In Defence of Woman by Wiliam Cynwal* translated and edited by Gwyn Williams (London, The Golden Cockerel Press).

80 Refer to Wiesner, M. (1993) op. cit., chapter 1 *passim* and Purkiss, D.

'Material Girls: The Seventeenth Century Woman Debate' in Brant, C. and Purkiss, D. (eds.) (1992) *Women, Texts and Histories 1575–1760* (London, Routledge).

81 Refer to Shepherd, S. (1985) *The Women's Sharp Revenge: Five Women's Pamphlets from the Renaissance* (London, Fourth Estate), 53–55; Jordan, C. 'Renaissance Women and the Question of Class' in Grantham Turner, J. (ed.) (1993), *Sexuality and Gender in Early Modern Europe: Institutions, Texts, Images* (Cambridge, Cambridge University Press), especially 100–1.

82 The entry in the diary was dated 2 November 1784. Bowen Thomas, B. (1945), op. cit., 17. It should be noted, however, that there was in fact a resurgence of interest in lineage and genealogy during the eighteenth century, this being part of the eighteenth-century Renaissance in Wales examined by Prys Morgan in the book of that name.

83 Colley, L. (1992) *Britons: Forging the Nation 1707–1837* (London, Yale University Press), 6.

84 Davies, O. and Bowie, F. (eds.) (1992), *Discovering Welshness* (Llandysul, Gomer Press), Introduction.

3

The gendering of the elementary and secondary school curriculum in Victorian and early twentieth-century Wales

W. GARETH EVANS

With the re-emergence of the issue of women's rights and the growth of modern feminism during the last thirty years, the relationship between gender and education has attracted considerable interest and has led to wide-ranging research. There has been a growing awareness of the impact of gender on pupils' learning and educational achievements. Educationists are increasingly conscious of the need to avoid discrimination by gender and promote equal opportunity policies in education for both sexes.[1]

As well as empirical research, exploration of the historical background is valuable for understanding the social construction and role of gender in contemporary educational systems. Gender is a social construct shaped by wide-ranging historical forces. Perceptions of femininity and masculinity have been moulded in specific historical periods. Gender roles are the product of historical experience. Masculinity and femininity highlight differences based on historically and culturally determined prejudices and stereotypes. In particular, the study of gender is concerned with power, difference and inequality, and involves a historical awareness of the impact of patriarchy, domination and misconceptions about women.[2]

Historically and culturally moulded roles and attitudes concerning gender have exerted a profound influence in shaping the development of the educational system in England and Wales during the nineteenth and twentieth centuries. The inequitable provision of schooling for girls for much of the nineteenth century, the quest for equal educational opportunities in the late Victorian era, curricular differentiation in the nineteenth and early twentieth centuries, and the inequality and discrimination still evident in twentieth-century schools exemplify the impact of gender as well as social class on educational policy making. The analysis of educational history has benefited considerably in the post-war years from the study of educational developments in their sociological setting and from the writing of social histories of education. It is recognized now that educational developments do not occur in a social and political vacuum. The time is now opportune to broaden the approach of historical study through using the potential of gender analysis:[3] hitherto, little has been attempted in the context of the educational history of Wales.[4] The study of the gendering of the school curriculum in Victorian and early twentieth-century Wales offers new perspectives on the experience of girls in both elementary and intermediate schools.

Images of womanhood

In Victorian Wales, powerful social forces were shaping gender roles. Patriarchal domination of women was well established. The forces of tradition, conservatism and prejudice from many directions, including the churches and chapels, the law and medical professions, projected an image of the woman as the 'weaker sex' both physically and intellectually. Dr Withers Moore's presidential address to the British Medical Association at Brighton in 1886, where he cast doubts on women's suitability to undertake higher education, was widely circulated and exerted much influence on the deliberations concerning intermediate and higher education in Wales. At the National Eisteddfod held at Caernarfon in 1886 he was condemned for arguing that 'it is not for the good of the human race that women should receive an education intended to prepare them for the exercise of brain power in competition with men. This Higher Education will hinder those who would have been the best mothers from being mothers at all.' Regularly in the *Cambrian News*, the influential editor, John Gibson, highlighted the prevalence of tradition and prejudice and the woman's inferior position in Wales. He contended that 'women are still either slaves or are legally, socially and politically non-existent'.[5]

In addition to the irrational views concerning women's mental powers, the impact of social Darwinism also influenced gender attitudes. Its advocacy of separate sex roles tended to consolidate traditional attitudes to the education of females who were regarded as physiologically different and medically weaker than males. But the most powerful determinant of gender identity and role was the prevailing middle-class ideal of womanhood. It was essentially a domestic ideal embodying 'separate spheres' for men and women. The home and family were seen as the female's sphere of interest, while the male's was the workplace. The essential characteristics of the ideal Victorian home were the mother's femininity and indeed 'angelicity'. She was intended to be the perfect wife and mother who infused her home with discipline and moral values. This image of femininity was regularly highlighted in the Welsh press in the Victorian Age. The female was portrayed as a virtuous and divine guide whose duty was the moral elevation of man. For much of the nineteenth century, domestic emancipation and quest for equal educational and professional opportunities were equated with coarsening the female's nature and weakening her moral influence. By the end of the century, however, the feminine ideal was being gradually transformed to accommodate the 'new woman' who sought education, employment and legal and political rights.[6]

Schooling for domesticity

In an age much influenced by the doctrine of 'separate spheres' and girls' eventual domestic roles, it was inevitable that their educational needs were perceived as being different to those of boys. Social class also dictated the need for differentiation in the schooling of middle-class and working-class girls. For much of the Victorian era, 'accomplishments' were deemed appropriate for the former and domestic- oriented elementary education for the latter. The Victorian elementary school embodied gendered forms of domestic ideology.

Prior to the 1870s it was the growing importance of needlework in the education of girls that highlighted its domestic orientation. Competence with the needle became equated with femininity and thrift in a working-class home. The duration of schooling was comparatively brief for both sexes. In 1859, only 38 per cent of the 10,971 boys and 8,882 girls in average attendance in 193 Church of England schools in Wales had been in school for two or more years. With schooling merely a brief interlude in the lives of working-class pupils, teaching focused on the basic skills of literacy and numeracy. There was also recognition of the need to educate the girl for her later role as wife or domestic servant. Her formative influence in the home was clearly perceived by the state.[7]

In the 1840s and 1850s, sewing, needlework and domestic economy were advocated in HMI Reports as important elements in the education of girls who were destined to be 'servants and poor men's wives'. Their sphere was the family, and the role of elementary schooling was perceived in terms of instructing good housewives and mothers: 'Viewed in this way, the education of girls would seem more important than that of boys . . . the welfare of a nation stands or falls with the well being of our homes; the improvement of our girls' schools ought to be considered a national duty and necessity.'[8] In Matthew Arnold's *Report on British and Wesleyan and other Denominational Schools in the Midland District of England and Wales*, 1853–4, attention was drawn to the unsatisfactory state of needlework in elementary schools and the unfortunate tendency to place a higher premium on crochet work and ornamental needlework: 'The importance to a poor family that the daughters should be skilful in plain needlework is obvious to all, yet their ignorance of it is something incredible.'[9] Likewise, Joseph Bowstead, HMI, in his 1853 report, which included reference to schools in south Wales, regretted the neglect of sewing at Aberdare British School and emphasized the general need for greater attention to domestic economy: 'To the wives and mothers of the labouring class a knowledge of domestic economy must be at least as important as an acquaintance with grammar, geography or history and yet in how few girls' schools does the first named subject receive any share of attention, although the others are everywhere taught.'[10] He hoped that the *Manual of Domestic Economy* newly published by the Home and Colonial School Society would prove useful for teachers in this neglected area of the curriculum.

Similarly, in 1854, in his, *Report on schools in Monmouthshire and neighbouring English counties*, H. W. Bellairs HMI called for greater attention by managers and mistresses to industrial work for females: 'There is very little doing in this direction with the exception of needlework. Much more, I am satisfied, might be done if the managers and mistresses would look at the matter in a plain common sense way and consider themselves bound to fit girls for a proper discharge of domestic duties, whether 'in service' or in their own cottages.'[11] In the schools inspected in south Wales, he found that, for reasons of economy, the majority were mixed rather than separate boys' and girls' schools. In such schools, insufficient attention was given to the curricular needs of girls. Needlework was neglected and sometimes only taught by partially qualified teachers. Indeed, overall, 'the female training of the girls which can only be carried out efficiently by a woman is altogether lost sight of. This I conceive to be an evil of no common magnitude, and one which will seriously affect the well-being of the principality in the rising generation.'[12] He believed that teachers over-estimated the importance of book learning, vis-á-vis needlework for girls. There was a serious misconception of the impact of the female on the character of her family and the nation at large, he asserted; the thoughtful, thrifty and skilful housewife and mother was an essential asset for society.

In a detailed survey of education in parts of Merioneth, Neath and Merthyr Tydfil in 1859 for the Newcastle Commission, the Assistant Commissioner, John Jenkins, concluded that insufficient attention was given in the elementary schools to the special requirements of the female. This was seen as a serious defect because the female's potential was thereby not effectively harnessed. 'The girls from these schools enter life without the knowledge proper to woman's sphere of duty, to render a home a sacred refuge from the cares of the world by making it the abode of comfort and of affection.'[13]

Jenkins's report included a comparative analysis of the curriculum of boys and girls in fifty-seven schools in Merioneth and sixty-four in two areas of south Wales. He noted that the data revealed that a higher proportion of boys studied a broader and more advanced range of subjects than did girls. In general, the curriculum was narrow, concentrating on the three R's and religious instruction. Only one pupil in six studied history whilst elements of algebra, mechanics and physical science were taught only to a small number of pupils. Very few of these were girls. But the most significant feature which underlined 'the glaring deficiency in the provision for the special education of females in public schools in Wales' was the fact that only half of the girls in the Neath and Merthyr Tydfil schools and less than 60 per cent in Merioneth were being taught needlework. In particular, where schools were in the charge of male headteachers, and the subject taught by a visiting sewing mistress, an essential element in a woman's education was only given a very peripheral position in the curriculum. Since needlework was essential for women in their domestic life, its neglect 'was a great and most serious defect in the machinery of education in the schools of Wales'. It was recommended that mixed schools should receive financial aid from the state only if a sewing mistress was employed once or twice a week.

The importance of an effective domestic orientation was further underlined by Joseph Bowstead HMI in his *Report on British Schools in South Wales* in 1860. He stressed that needlework, domestic economy and the laws of health ought to be regarded as branches of instruction of paramount importance in every girls' school.[14] The Revised Code of 1862 made needlework compulsory for all girls in elementary schools in receipt of a government grant. Its important status attested to the consolidation of the prevailing domestic ideology which defined the woman's place in terms of the home. It also attested to the dominant position of domestic service amongst the occupations deemed suitable for working-class women. HMI reports in Victorian Wales reflected prevailing social perceptions and contributed to the gender differentiation that was to characterize the curriculum of working-glass girls. The ideology of the sexual division of labour influenced elementary education throughout the Victorian era.

By the end of the century, the education of working-class girls was more sex-specific than in earlier years. From the 1870s, domestic subjects were to assume a more prominent role in the elementary school curriculum for girls. In 1878, domestic economy became a compulsory 'specific' subject whilst cookery and laundry work attracted government grants in 1882 and 1890 respectively. Some middle-class critics voiced their concerns to the Education Department concerning the neglect of essential domestic skills in the curriculum of some Board Schools.

In 1877, in a report on schools in Cardiganshire, Pembrokeshire and part of Carmarthenshire, William Williams HMI emphasized the importance of sewing as 'a subject of primary importance for girls'.[15] Likewise, in 1886, in an address to teachers and managers of Cardiff elementary schools, C. T. Whitmell HMI stressed the importance of instruction in needlework, cookery and domestic economy as a means of raising living standards and promoting moral reform in working-class homes. He contended that 'the wife who can cook well will be a most powerful auxiliary to the cause of temperance'.[16] In 1886 and again in 1889 the importance of cookery was emphasized by the Education Department. Attention was drawn to the grants offered under the Code which were intended to make cookery 'a part of the ordinary course of instruction'. It was maintained that after reading, writing, arithmetic and sewing 'no subject is of such importance for the class of girls who attend public elementary schools'.[17] In 1887 in his Report on the Welsh Division, William Williams HMI noted approvingly that the teaching of needlework was steadily improving and that 'considerable progress had been made of late years'.[18] Curricular developments in elementary schools in late Victorian Wales epitomized the Education Department's policy of curricular differentiation. Emphasis on a domestic-oriented education involved deliberate gendering of the elementary school curriculum. Effective teaching and learning of domestic subjects was intended to improve a girl's competence as wife and mother or as domestic servant. In the introduction to the Education Department's first volume of Special Reports (1896–7) Sir Michael Sadler highlighted the importance of domestic-oriented elementary education for girls. By the turn of the century, a declining birth rate, high infant mortality, military defeats in the Boer War as well as the poor physical condition of young soldiers, raised alarm concerning the degeneration of the race. Attention focused on the relationship between education and the physical condition of the British people. In the 1890s and the early twentieth century, the Education Department and its successor, the Board of Education, were advocating the need for greater attention to domestic subjects in the education of girls in secondary as well as in elementary schools.[19]

Research by Carol Dyhouse and June Purvis has highlighted attempts made in England in this period to orientate girls' education, especially in the elementary schools, towards domestic subjects and mothercraft.[20] The advocates of the inclusion of domestic and technical subjects in post-elementary education called for the utilization of funds raised under the Technical Instruction Act 1889 and Local Taxation Act 1890 to provide instruction in cookery, laundry work, dressmaking, physiology and domestic economy.[21] Likewise in Wales, gender-orientated curricular emphasis in girls' elementary schooling came to be justified in terms of women achieving greater competence in the home as wives and mothers.

Training female teachers: gender considerations

Unsurprisingly, the domestic educational ideology that underpinned the gendered curriculum for girls in elementary schools had also infused the pupil-teacher system and the training of female teachers for the elementary school sector. The pupil-teacher system, introduced in 1846 by Sir James Kay-Shuttleworth to provide the elementary schools with more effective teachers, involved a five-year apprenticeship for promising male and female pupils from thirteen to eighteen years of age. As well as teaching for a stipulated period each day, the pupil-teachers also received instruction from the master or mistress at the school where they were apprenticed. They were examined each year on an official syllabus and duly graded.

Gender stereotyping lay at the heart of the Committee of Council's perception of female pupil-teachers. From 1846, needlework was compulsory for female pupil-teachers. From the 1850s, the importance of cookery and domestic management was regularly emphasized in their course of instruction. Competence in needlework was particularly emphasized in 1866:

> Female pupil-teachers, before admission to apprenticeship, must produce a written attestation from the school-mistresses and managers that they possess reasonable competence as seamstress; and at the annual examinations must bring specimens of plain needlework to the inspector, together with a statement from the schoolmistress specifying whether they have been receiving practical instruction in any other kind of domestic industry.[22]

At eighteen years of age, though they were not obliged to continue as teachers, pupil-teachers could compete for Queen's Scholarships which were tenable at teacher training colleges. The number of female pupil-teachers in Wales increased from forty-three in 1850 to 391 in 1869 and 1,061 in 1877. In the teacher training colleges, attitudes to women students reflected the prevailing gendered perceptions in the elementary schools.

Until the opening of the Swansea Training College in 1872, there was no institution to train schoolmistresses in Wales. The training college opened at Caernarfon in 1856 and the Bangor Normal College, founded in 1858, were exclusively male colleges. Consequently, women students from Wales attended training colleges in England where there were twelve Church of England training colleges exclusively for schoolmistresses, and four training colleges for both men and women, including the well-known non-denominational Borough Road College. Welsh women were enrolled in such colleges as Borough Road, Warrington, Whitelands and Cheltenham from the 1840s. The British Society became increasingly aware of the need to train more women teachers and in 1861 a new women's college was opened at Stockwell.

During their training, the importance of adequate attention to domestic subjects in the schooling of girls was regularly emphasized. It was intended that the prospective women teachers would be acquainted in their training with 'the economics of the poor man's home'. In 1850 a memorandum from the Committee of Council on the training of schoolmistresses in Church of England Training Colleges emphasized their role as 'educators of the mothers of the peasantry, of our domestic servants and to no small extent, of the wives and sisters of the small shopkeepers and tenant farmers'.[23] In the Victorian training colleges, it was official policy to ensure that women teachers were acquainted with the details of housework, sanitary and health matters, and the duties of domestic servants. The importance of needlework and domestic economy were reiterated regularly by HMI. Questions set in the annual domestic economy examination highlighted official perceptions of the social role of female teachers. Typical was this question in 1855: 'What saving may be affected by the use of barley, oatmeal, Indian corn and rice in poor families? State briefly, the nutritious qualities of these articles respectively.'[24] Not only was the teaching of domestic subjects regarded as essential but also the general influence exerted by female teachers on young girls. Teaching was perceived as an appropriate extension of the feminine role because of the link between femininity and domesticity. Women teachers were regarded as key agents in inculcating the daughters of their own working class with those fundamental principles and skills of femininity and domesticity deemed appropriate for their station in life as wives and mothers or as domestic servants in middle-class households.

The Swansea Training College of the 1870s saw its role as a provider of 'careful training not only in the usual elementary subjects but also in habits of order, industry and economy and in the principles of religion and morality'.[25] As well as being orientated by gender considerations concerning domesticity, the training of female teachers was also influenced by prevailing concerns about their health. Victorian women, in contrast to men, were regarded as particularly vulnerable to the stress and strain of study and examinations. At Swansea, concern about the possible dangers to the health of women students was regularly voiced in the college reports.

In the 1880s and 1890s, students at Swansea Training College and other training colleges in England where there were women from Wales were, as ever, subject to the dictates of the regulations and policies of the Education Department and HMI and their perceptions of femininity and the role of elementary education. The improvement of what was perceived as a largely thriftless working-class society was emphasized. In evidence to the Cross Commission in 1886, T. E. Ellis MP referred to the interrelationship of educational and social reform. In advocating the provision of more places for the training of schoolmistresses in Wales, he was conscious of the misery of many homes caused by 'ignorance of domestic economy and lack of habits of thrift'. Schoolmistresses, he thought, could exert a profound influence on girls and sharpen an awareness of the implications of femininity.[26]

The establishment of three Day Training Departments attached to the University Colleges – Cardiff 1890, Aberystwyth 1892, Bangor 1894 – was a most significant development for teacher training in Wales. By 1897 there were 131 female and 126 male students enrolled. But, significantly, teacher training in the University Colleges was perceived within well-established social conventions. Domestic economy and needlework were to be compulsory elements in the course of studies for prospective female elementary school teachers. The establishment of the South Wales and Monmouthshire Training School of Cookery and Domestic Arts in Cardiff in 1891, in conjunction with the University College and the local School Board, also exemplified an awareness of the role of women teachers in improving the quality of life in working-class homes.[27]

In Victorian Wales, domestic ideology influenced the training of women teachers and the curriculum for girls in the elementary schools. With the growing feminization of the teaching profession by the 1890s, the relationship between femininity, schooling and domesticity was strengthened. The formation of gender identity was consolidated. Until well into the twentieth century, gender differentiation and stereotyping were to exert a profound influence on the development of the curriculum and schools in Wales.

Accomplishments education

Unsurprisingly, gender considerations also influenced attitudes towards the significant developments in secondary education which occurred in Victorian Wales.

By the mid-nineteenth century, the daughters of middle-class families in Wales attended private schools of varying quality. The curricular emphasis was primarily on accomplishments which usually included music, art, modern languages, grammar, literature, composition and elocution. Needlework and dancing or callisthenics were also given some attention. At 'The Ladies' Seminary', Well Street, Rhuthun, there were resident French and German governesses in 1859. A similar ethos percolated the numerous other 'Young Ladies' Establishments' and 'Ladies' Boarding and Day Schools' throughout Wales. Schools at Chester, Bristol, London and elsewhere also advertised in newspapers circulating in Wales. In 1860 the well-endowed Howell schools at Denbigh and Llandaff were opened. Their role also was to educate cultivated middle-class wives, mothers and governesses. The Taunton Report (1868) concluded that the accomplishments – French, music, drawing – were being carefully taught at both schools.[28]

The domination of the schools' curriculum by accomplishments epitomized the prevailing conception of middle-class culture and womanhood. Only subjects regarded as 'ladylike' – music, art, French, German, fancy needlework – were taught. The role of the schools was to inculcate femininity. In a patriarchal society, the home was deemed the proper sphere of the middle-class woman and accomplishment education the most appropriate. This was in sharp contrast to the classics-dominated boys' grammar schools.

Not everyone approved of this type of education, and criticism was voiced of the over-emphasis on accomplishments. In 1859, Thomas Gee condemned the attention given 'to the study of inessentials',[29] whilst a decade later assistant commissioner H. M. Bompas reported to the Taunton Commission that 'in the case of girls, the necessity of mental training seems to be to a great extent overlooked . . . subjects which would exercise the reasoning powers and other mental faculties such as maths, classics or science in any but its elementary forms are seldom taught'.[30] It was accurately suggested that this reflected Victorian society's differing roles for the male and female. For the middle-class girl the prospect of marriage and home-making, rather than a career in business or in a profession, provided no incentive to pursue a rigorous academic education.

Academic emulation

During the 1870s and 1880s there was growing demand for greater provision of secondary education for girls in Wales. This attested to the emergence of 'the woman question' and the beginning of the quest for female emancipation.[31] It was concerned with the long tradition of female subjugation and masculine domination in every sphere of society – employment, politics, marriage, the law and education. Rejection of the assumed intellectual inferiority of girls led to criticisms of the domination of the accomplishments curriculum in the existing private schools. There was some response by a few schools, through modification of their curricula, to accommodate more academically challenging subjects and provide preparation for recognized examinations.

Typical was Kingston House, Wrexham, which in 1878 was preparing girls for the Oxford and Cambridge Local Examinations and for College of Preceptors examinations. It claimed to provide thorough grounding in all subjects. The Ladies' College at Holt claimed in 1889 to be not only a finishing school, but also an institution providing thorough preparation for the University Colleges in Wales, and for the Oxford and Cambridge local examinations as well as the music examinations of the Royal Academy of Music and Trinity College. In 1889, Elwy Hall School, Rhyl, pronounced that its aim was 'thoroughness', and referred to its excellent results in the Oxford and Cambridge Local Examinations and College of Preceptors examinations. The balance of accomplishments and an academic education varied from one establishment to another. At the Howell schools at Llandaff and Denbigh, accomplishments remained prominent though more academic oriented courses became evident in the 1880s. At Llandaff, the appointment of Miss Maria Kendall as headmistress in 1880 led to the provision of a chemistry laboratory, the appointment of specialist subject teachers and preparation for the Oxford and Cambridge Board examinations. Likewise, at Denbigh, the school gave regular attention to the demands of external examinations. In 1885, Principal Reichel of UCNW Bangor was giving fortnightly lectures to senior pupils. In 1890, the first Drapers' Company scholarships tenable at UCNW Bangor were awarded.[32]

The provision of schooling for middle-class girls in Wales was extended through the establishment of the endowed Dr Williams' School at Dolgellau in 1878, the opening of a Diocesan High School for Girls at Carmarthen in 1880 and a Girls' Public Day High School at Swansea in 1888. Their curricula reflected the growing debate concerning the relationship of academic subjects and domestic subjects and the tradition of an accomplishments-oriented education for middle-class girls. In the 1880s and 1890s the women's movement in England and Wales gained increasing support in the quest for wide-ranging emancipation and equal opportunities for both sexes. The adoption of an academic curriculum and preparation of girls for the same external exams as boys came to be regarded by the headteachers of girls' high schools as the essential way to achieve equality of recognition. Girls would be shown to be of the same intellectual calibre as boys and entitled to break free from the bonds of domesticity and enter the professions. This was a challenge to the domestic ideology which had earlier in the century enthroned an accomplishments-orientated curriculum for middle-class girls.

Also influential had been the preconceived notions that women had less mental capacity than men and were not suited for an academic education. At the Caernarfon National Eisteddfod 1886, Miss Dilys Davies, a teacher at the influential North London Collegiate School founded by Miss Buss, and one of the leading protagonists of the female education cause in late Victorian Wales, condemned the pronouncements of Dr Withers Moore, president of the British Medical Association, concerning women's unsuitability to undertake higher education. She contended that there was no place for mere concentration on accomplishments that characterized so many girls' schools – 'that smattering of a foreign language or two and facility on the piano'. There was a 'fatal gap' in the Welsh system of education – the lack of intermediate schools for girls.[33] Later, in January 1888 at the important Shrewsbury Conference organized by the Honourable Society of Cymmrodorion, she called for the establishment in Wales of girls' schools modelled on the academic-oriented Girls' Public Day Schools in England. Again she firmly rejected the commonest objection to the provision of academic schooling for girls – the danger to their health: 'the health of girls and women engaged in mental work would be found on due examination to compare most favourably with that of women who spent their lives in the pursuit of pleasure.'[34]

By the end of the Victorian era, the Dr Williams' School at Dolgellau and the Howell schools at Llandaff and Denbigh were regarded as the most successful girls' schools in Wales. Their increasingly academic and examination-oriented courses of instruction epitomized the prevailing quest for equality of recognition and the bridging of the gender gap. Serious study was replacing accomplishments, and girls' studies were becoming assimilated to those of boys. But new pressures from the Board of Education on behalf of domestic subjects reminded girls' high schools that a degree of gendering should continue to characterize their curriculum.[35] At Dr Williams' School in 1895, the Charity Commissioner noted that all the girls were learning cookery. The school authorities were well aware of the prevailing debate concerning a balanced liberal education and the need to accommodate an element of curricular differentiation based on considerations of gender.

Intermediate education: curricular debate in the 1890s

By this time a network of publicly funded intermediate schools was being established throughout Wales. The Welsh Intermediate and Technical Education Act (1889) was one of the supreme achievements of Victorian Wales.[36] It was the product of a long and often acrimonious struggle for legislation that was intended to ensure that the aspirations of the Welsh people for greater educational opportunity would be met. Treasury funding – a novel principle at the time – was now made available for a network of ninety-three intermediate-secondary schools established throughout Wales in the 1890s. Not until after the Balfour Education Act of 1902 were similar arrangements established for England.[37] The need for better provision of intermediate or secondary education had been highlighted in the Aberdare Report (1881),[38] but only after many years of political pressure involving influential Welshmen and women was the essential legislation enacted in 1889. Vigorous campaigning, particularly by the Honourable Society of Cymmrodorion and the Association for Promoting the Education of Girls in Wales, ensured that the principle of equal opportunities for both sexes was embodied in the terms of the legislation. It was intended that boys and girls would have the opportunity to study academic-based intermediate education encompassing classics, modern languages, mathematics and sciences as well as to acquire a practical and commercially oriented technical education.

The establishment of intermediate schools attested to the great fervour for extending educational opportunities in late Victorian Wales. Throughout Wales, the essential fund-raising to erect school buildings and the location of the new schools on a county basis was achieved comparatively quickly and ratified by the Charity Commission and Education Department. By 1900, there were 3,513 girls and 3,877 boys enrolled in ninety-three intermediate schools. Unsurprisingly, their curriculum was overwhelmingly academic in nature with only a minimum of concession to technical education and gender differentiation.

The intermediate schools were established at a time when the academic tradition of boys' grammar schools was being assimilated into the more ambitious English girls' high schools. The quest for equal educational provision for girls as well as boys in Wales had endeavoured to explode the myth of the female's inferior intellectual calibre. The Education Department were also conscious of the new professional and job opportunities available for the suitably educated woman freed from the chains of domesticity. The provision of an academic-based liberal education in the girls' schools, and their goal of examination results comparable with those of boys' schools, was intended not only to fulfil the main objective of the 1889 Act but also to show that girls possessed the same intellectual calibre as boys. Subjects such as Latin, German and mathematics were regarded as essential for sharpening the intellectual faculties of both sexes. Miss Holme, headmistress of Carmarthen Intermediate School for Girls spoke for many of her colleagues in 1897 in emphasizing that the prime objective of intermediate education was to inculcate culture and cultivate 'manhood or womanhood in contact with the best thought of the world'.[39]

They were also well aware of the obligation to deliver an effective practical-oriented technical education equated with domestic economy, needlework and the laws of health, and of the prevailing debate in English girls' high schools in the 1890s concerning the place of domestic subjects in a primarily academic curriculum. Whilst the majority of the headteachers favoured the same academic-oriented curriculum for girls as well as boys, there was some support for Sara Burstall, headmistress of Manchester High School and the leading advocate of the inclusion of domestic subjects.[40] However, the Girls' Public Day Schools Trust was critical of the Education Department's advocacy of greater attention to domestic subjects in girls' secondary as well as elementary education.

In Wales in the 1890s the curricular debate was well represented in the deliberations and publications of the Association for Promoting the Education of Girls in Wales.[41] The inclusion of domestic subjects in all the county schemes for intermediate education was welcomed by the Association in 1892. Publications such as *Manual Training for*

Girls in Wales (1894) and *Technical Education for Women* (1894) highlighted the case for curricular differentiation in girls' schools. Effective instruction in cookery, nursing, dressmaking and hygiene was advocated as essential 'technical education' for girls. It was contended that 'a just compromise between the useful and the mere humanistic' was essential not only to implement the spirit of the 1889 Act but also to address society's gender expectations. The intermediate schools were expected to educate women to be not only learned but also equipped with skills useful in the home and in society at large where there were increasing job opportunities for the female. But at the turn of the century in both boys' and girls' intermediate schools, technical subjects remained on the periphery of the curriculum. The uniformity of academic subjects predominated in the emerging system of intermediate education in Wales. Any significant degree of differentiation to accommodate the gender stereotyping associated with domestic subjects would have been regarded as incompatible with the redefined objectives of girls' secondary education. Miss Annie Dobell, headmistress of Ffestiniog Intermediate School, summed up the feelings of many when she said that domestic economy was 'a little more than nothing whilst cookery could only be justified if taught scientifically. Girls should not be taught differently to boys because their mental capacities [are] similar.'[42]

Curricular differentiation

The dawn of a new century saw intensification of the curricular debate concerning intermediate and secondary education in both England and Wales. In the Edwardian and pre-war years much interest was shown by the newly established Board of Education and its Welsh Department after 1907, as well as the Central Welsh Board which had examining and inspecting duties in intermediate schools since 1897. Gender considerations figured prominently in debates concerning alleged curricular uniformity and rigidity and the possibility of differentiation.

It was a period that saw growing concern about the alleged physical deterioration of the nation. The role of domestic subjects in girls' education was viewed within the context of wider issues relating to femininity and the role of women in British Society. Through general circulars, regulations in 1904, 1908 and 1909, annual reports, inspection of schools and through a Consultative Committee in 1923, the Board of Education underlined the importance of domestic subjects in girls' education in the Edwardian and pre-war years.[43] In England and in Wales, bifurcation and differentiation, involving a more central role for domestic subjects in particular, characterized the debate concerning girls' secondary education.

There was regular criticism of the academic orientation of the curriculum of girls' schools in both HMI and Central Welsh Board (CWB) Reports.[44] The slavish emulation of the curriculum of boys' schools, overemphasis on academic work geared for external examinations and university entrance and the neglect of domestic subjects were highlighted. In the Board of Education (Welsh Department) General Report on secondary schools in Cardiganshire in 1913 'the one determining goal seems to have been University Matriculation or its equivalent'.[45] Unsurprisingly, effective teaching of domestic subjects was not a priority. Likewise, at Holyhead, a CWB inspector reported in 1910 that 'a day spent in this school leaves the impression that the girls' side wants a new start and fresh life – their subjects a more important place on the time table'.[46] There was concern that the overemphasis on academic and examination-oriented work was causing overpressure and was detrimental to the health of many pupils. The Board of Education (Welsh Department), and particularly its inspiring chief inspector, O. M. Edwards, was well aware that the examination system was the most dominating feature of the intermediate schools of Wales. External exams also retarded the development of curricular differentiation. In 1915 it was acknowledged that 'the problem of secondary education today is to make the pupils' education a preparation for the duties of life without ceasing to be a liberal education'.[47]

A gendered education for girls expressed in terms of curricular bifurcation and differentiation was regularly advocated by the Board of Education and the Central Welsh Board. As well as giving more attention to domestic subjects, the provision of an effective programme of domestic studies was regarded as a valid alternative to foreign languages, mathematics or science in the education of girls. Science teaching in many girls' schools was regarded as too academic in nature and divorced from the study of domestic subjects. In 1912 the CWB welcomed the arrangements at Hawarden Intermediate School where 'in Form IV, physics will be taught to boys only, and girls will learn instead needlework, domestic economy and more literature'.[48] Likewise, at Aberystwyth it was recommended in 1910 that, for girls, chemistry should be replaced by household management in Form IV. At Tredegar, where the boys studied chemistry and physics and the girls botany, further differentiation was recommended with the provision of a higher domestic course as an alternative to mathematics and foreign languages. By 1914, a limited degree of curricular differentiation based on domestic subjects to accommodate the perceived needs of girls as future wives and mothers was evident in Welsh intermediate and secondary schools. But, overall, the schools' curricula remained insufficiently gendered for both the Board of Education (Welsh Department) and the CWB. Their criticisms of curricular uniformity and their advocacy of more differentiation based on domestic subjects were reiterated during the First World War and the inter-war years. But little was achieved. Secondary education for girls had been transformed in the late nineteenth century. A core of 'accomplishments' and the accompanying overtones of domesticity and the implied inferiority of the weaker sex had been discarded. Equality of opportunity for the female sex was based on emulating the academic curriculum and examination successes of boys' grammar schools. Confirmation of intellectual equality had demanded curricular similarity and assimilation. Only a minimum of differentiation based on gendered perceptions could be accommodated. Academic study was a sign of intellectual superiority and a criterion of the educability of girls, and, in many schools, housecraft was equated with unskilled drudgery. In 1917, O. M. Edwards attributed the neglect of domestic subjects to 'the inadequate idea of the purpose and scope of the Secondary School which is still widely prevalent'. Domestic subjects would be regarded as an essential element of the curriculum for girls only when 'the schools and public opinion, acting and reacting on one another, rise to a fuller conception of the aim of secondary education'.[49]

Conclusion

During the Victorian and Edwardian years, there had been significant educational achievements. A network of elementary and intermediate schools had been established in Wales. Gender considerations had been of major importance in the changing pattern of both working-class elementary and middle-class secondary schooling. They continued to influence policy-making during the First World War and the inter-war years. But a focus on socio-economic bias and injustices in access to secondary education rather than on gender-based curricular differentiation was the main priority for education reformers and politicians. Thereafter, almost half a century elapsed before the re-emergence of significant interest in the curricular implications of gender and sex-role stereotyping in the schools of Wales.

The prime objective of schooling had been to provide a general or liberal education for boys and girls to the age of sixteen years. The 1944 Education Act addressed inequality of educational opportunity through providing 'secondary education for all'.[50] But in the wide-ranging wartime deliberations, the nature of the curriculum for boys and girls was not examined from the standpoint of gender requirements or differences.

For over four decades neither the Board of Education nor the LEAs gave gender issues a high profile. Nevertheless, there was a gender ideology which held that there were necessary differences between boys and girls and that a degree of curricular differentiation was necessary in elementary and secondary schools to cater for girls' domestic role in the home and society as future wives and mothers. With boys' education regarded as the norm, gender differentiation in the years pre-1944 was equated with a domestic bias in the curriculum for girls. This was embodied in the Board of Education's regulations for elementary and secondary schools.[51] With secondary education equated with the delivery of a traditional arts and science based liberal education, domestic subjects were not given equal curricular status. The view of many headmistresses was that girls should not be denied identical opportunities with boys of preparing themselves for academic careers.

In 1949 the Ministry of Education in *The Future of Secondary Education in Wales* saw a need to reconsider the question of curricular differentiation for girls.[52] It recommended the integration of domestic studies within the basic curriculum for all girls. In secondary modern and technical high schools, home-making should be given especial emphasis in the curriculum for older girls. The need for all girls to study domestic subjects had been emphasized in the Norwood Report (1943) – *Curriculum and Examinations in Secondary Schools*[53] – and by John Newsom: *The Education of Girls* (1948) which was highly critical of the failure to relate the curriculum of girls to their 'biological and social function'.[54] No real attempt had been made to synthesize the education and social function of women. It was considered that marriage, motherhood and home-making for which the majority of women were destined, needed to be addressed effectively in schools.

The post-war emphasis on the virtues of domesticity and the educational implications was re-affirmed in the Crowther Report (1959) – *15 to 18*[55] – and in the Newsom Report (1963) – *Half Our Future* – which underlined the differential interests of girls and boys, and influenced the growth of attention to domestic subjects in secondary modern schools in the 1950s and 1960s.[56] In her presidential address to the Welsh Secondary Schools Association in 1961, Miss Margaret Copland, headmistress of Grove Park Grammar School for Girls, Wrexham, emphasized the importance of 'home-making' as the essential core of the curriculum for girls leaving at sixteen years. Indeed, she held that all girls would benefit from the combination of a very practical domestic science course with traditional GCE subjects.[57]

The growing criticism in the 1950s and 1960s of the post-war tripartite system of secondary education focused primarily on unequal opportunities and social class divisions.[58] Considerations of gender equality and its curricular implications awaited the growth of modern feminism in the 1960s and 1970s and the accompanying gender scrutiny of the educational system. The Sex Discrimination Act 1975,[59] the curriculum reform movement of the 1970s and 1980s and the introduction of a National Curriculum in 1988,[60] which included a commitment to equal entitlement for both girls and boys to all curricular areas, highlighted the growing awareness of gender inequality. Arguably, the growth of gender awareness was influenced by efforts made by feminists in particular to make gender a key dimension of educational politics and policy-making. The gendering of the school curriculum in Victorian and early twentieth-century Wales established a tradition that remains of significance in the current deliberations and quest for a de-gendered education in the 1990s.

Notes

[1] Blair, M. and Holland, J. (eds.) (1995) *Identity and Diversity: Gender and the Experience of Education* (Clevedon, Open University Press); Dawtrey, L., Holland, J. and Hammer, M. (eds.)(1995) *Equality and Inequality in Education Policy* (Clevedon, Open University Press); Holland, J., and Blair, M. (eds.) (1995) *Debates and Issues in Feminist Research and Pedagogy* (Clevedon, Open University Press); Measor, L. and Sikes, P. J. (1990) *Gender and Schools* (London, Cassell); Weiner, G. (1994)

Feminisms in Education: An Introduction (Buckingham, Open University Press).

2 Linsey, L. (1994) *Gender Roles: A Sociological Perspective* (New Jersey, Prentice Hall).

3 Scott, J. W. (1988) *Gender and the Politics of History* (New York, Columbia University Press).

4 Evans, W. G. (1992) 'Gender stereotyping and the training of female elementary school teachers: the experience of Victorian Wales' in *History of Education* Vol.21, No.2, 189–204.

5 Gibson, John (Sir) (1992) *The Emancipation of Women*. Introduction by W. Gareth Evans (Llandysul, Gwasg Gomer).

6 Evans, W. G. (1990) *Education and Female Emancipation: The Welsh Experience 1847–1914* (Cardiff, University of Wales Press).

7 Dyhouse, C. (1977) 'Good wives and little mothers: social anxieties and the schoolgirls' curriculum' in *Oxford Review of Education* 3(1), 21–35.

8 Minutes of the Committee of Council on Education 1852–3, 806–7.

9 Ibid., 1853–4, 1050.

10 Ibid., 1853–4, 1092–93.

11 Ibid., 1854–5, 405.

12 Ibid., 1854–5, 407–8.

13 *Newcastle Report* Vol.II, 544–6: Vol.IV, 544–6.

14 Minutes of Committee of Council of Education 1860–1, 360.

15 Ibid., 1876–7, 651.

16 C. T. Whitmell HMI 'Education in the Cardiff District' (1886), 4.

17 Minutes of Committee of Council on Education, 1889–90, xxii–xxiii.

18 Ibid., 1886–7, 359.

19 Purvis, J. (1981) 'Separate spheres and inequality in the education of working class women 1850–1900' in *History of Education* 10(4), 227–43.

20 Dyhouse, C. (1981) *Girls Growing Up in Late Victorian and Edwardian England* (London, Routledge & Kegal Paul). Purvis, J. (1991) *A History of Women's Education in England* (Milton Keynes, Open University Press).

21 Technical Instruction Act 1889 (52 & 53 Vict. c.41). Local Taxation (Customs and Excise) Act 1890 (53 & 54 Vict.c.60).

22 Minutes of Committee of Council on Education 1865–6, xxvi–xxvii.

23 Ibid., 1850–1, 80.

24 Ibid., 1854–5, 70.

25 Swansea Training College Report 1878, 6. Significantly, Swansea Training College Testimonial Form 1872 included the question: 'Is she a good needlewoman?'

26 *South Wales Daily News*, 2 October 1886.

27 Davies, H. (1894) 'Technical Education for Women'; School of Cookery Minutes 1890–5.

28 Schools' Inquiry Commission [or Taunton Commission] Report, Vol. VIII and Vol. XX, 152–3.

29 *Baner ac Amserau Cymru*, 6 December 1859.

[30] Taunton Report Vol.1, 547–8.

[31] Evans, W. G. (1990) op. cit.

[32] Howell's School Denbigh, Governors' Minute Book, 7 October 1890.

[33] *Sixth Annual Report, National Eisteddfod Association*, 1886, 62–9.

[34] Ibid., 67.

[35] Dyhouse, C. (1976) 'Social Darwinistic ideas and the development of women's education in England 1880–1920', *History of Education* Vol.V, No.1, 44–58.

[36] Evans, W. G. (1990) 'The Welsh Intermediate and Technical Education Act, 1889: a centenary appreciation', *History of Education* Vol.19, No.3, 195–210.

[37] Education Act 1902 (2 Ed.VII, C.42).

[38] Aberdare Report: *Report of the Committee Appointed to Inquire into the Condition of Intermediate and Higher Education in Wales* (London 1881).

[39] *The Welshman*, 24 December 1897.

[40] Education Department, Special Reports 1896–7, 166–72.

[41] Annual Reports and Pamphlets 1887–1901.

[42] *The Cambrian News*, 15 April 1898.

[43] *Code of Regulations for Public Elementary Schools 1904*, and subsequent years to 1925. *Report of the Consultative Committee on Differentiation of the Curriculum for Boys and Girls Respectively, in Secondary Schools*, 1923 (HMSO). Hunt, F. (1991) *Gender and Policy in English Education 1902–1944* (Hemel Hempstead, Harvester Wheatsheaf).

[44] Board of Education (Welsh Department): Annual Reports 1907–25; Central Welsh Board, Reports of Inspection and Examination 1897–1920.

[45] Report: County of Cardigan 1913, 37.

[46] CWB: Reports of Inspection and Examination 1910.

[47] Board of Education Report (Welsh Department) 1915, 6.

[48] CWB: Reports of Inspection and Examination 1912.

[49] Board of Education (Welsh Department), Memo 14 May 1917.

[50] Education Act 1944 (HMSO). Dent, H. C. (1968) *The Education Act 1944* (University of London Press) 12th edn.

[51] Hunt, F. (1991) op. cit.

[52] Ministry of Education (1949): *The Future of Secondary Education in Wales* (London, HMSO).

[53] *Report of the Secondary Schools Examinations Council (Norwood) Curriculum and Examinations in Secondary Schools* (1943) (London, HMSO).

[54] Newsom, Sir John (1948) *The Education of Girls*. (London, Faber and Faber).

[55] Report of the Central Advisory Council for Education (England): *15–18* (Crowther) 1959 (HMSO).

[56] Report of the Central Advisory Council for Education (England): *Half Our Future* (Newsom) (1963) (HMSO).

[57] WSS Review Vol.48, December 1961, No.1, p.26.

58 Floud, J. and Halsey, A. H. (1957) 'Social class, intelligence, tests and selection for secondary schools', *British Journal of Sociology*, Vol.V111, No.1, 339. Banks, O. (1955) *Parity and Prestige in English Secondary Education* (London, Routledge and Kegan Paul).

59 The Sex Discrimination Act 1975 (London, HMSO).

60 Education Reform Act 1988 (London, HMSO).

4

Opportunity denied: The voices of the lost grammar school girls of the inter-war years

GRAHAM GOODE AND SARA DELAMONT

Introduction

This chapter is based on material collected from interviews with twenty-four people who had 'passed the scholarship' but had been unable to take up their places in the years between 1918 and 1944.[1] Eleven of the informants were women. The chapter presents extracts from the interviews – predominantly from the women respondents – to give a voice to a generation of Welsh people whose education suffered because of the economic situation of Wales between the wars, and, additionally in the case of girls, because of prevalent gender stereotypes. The respondents were interviewed by Graham Goode in the late 1970s, but their reminiscences bring the Great Depression vividly to life. The injustice – being denied a secondary schooling – still rankled, and the gendered bias of that injustice is illustrated.

The historical context

Selection for secondary education during the inter-war period was a competitive scramble for places on a narrow educational ladder. Despite their limitations, and the questionable premises on which the selection examinations were based, they were intended to identify children capable of profiting from a secondary education. By passing the selection examinations, each of the respondents was set apart from those candidates who sat the examination but failed to achieve the qualifying standard. The offer of a secondary school place indicated that the respondents had passed with sufficient merit to satisfy whatever criteria their LEA used. All of them were deemed capable of profiting from a secondary education and were pointed in the direction of secondary schooling by the offer of a place. In the case of the respondents below, the offer was not taken up so they were categorized as 'refusers' of secondary education. If the passing of the secondary education selection examination is taken as an indicator of a particular kind of educational achievement, refusal of the secondary education to which it gave access may be seen as a symptom of the contemporary inequalities of educational opportunity based on the types of schooling available.

The term 'Scholarship' was used frequently by the respondents in a colloquial sense which encapsulated the variety of selection procedures, whether with or without financial awards or maintenance provision, whereby pupils from elementary, non-provided, or private schools were chosen for entry to the secondary schools. The phrase 'eleven plus', more commonly associated with the post-1944 era, is used by some respondents but is to be taken as synonymous with 'Scholarship'. 'Secondary schools' developed in various ways but generally conformed to a curricular pattern in preparation for higher education and entry into the professions. The terms 'high school' and 'grammar school' are synonymous with 'secondary school' wherever they appear in the transcripts.

The work of Floud demonstrated that the chances of obtaining a free place favoured the pupils drawn from the top of the occupational scale.[2] In 1929 there were sixty-six free secondary schools in England and Wales. Twenty-one were in Wales (of which Glamorgan had ten and Cardiff four), all in industrial areas.[3] This seemed to indicate that the greatest demand for free places and increased educational opportunities came from what Culshaw[4] described as 'the artisan classes'. By the time the special-place system was introduced and thrown open to all comers, lower income groups were in competition for the free-place system. The Board of Education's policy to make the schools accessible to all was, in Banks's view,[5] a reaction to class bias but foundered on the rocks of meagre scholarship provision whilst prosperous middle-class parentage remained the best hope of obtaining secondary education.[6] Bernbaum[7] saw widening opportunities for the lower middle class; and the work of Campbell[8] indicated that in London the scholarship schemes in operation favoured the children of skilled workers, clerks, shopkeepers and the like, hardly touching the children of the unskilled labouring class. In relation to an evident trend of opinion it can be said of the majority of the respondents in this study that the rules of the game did not favour them. But in contrast to the evidence of the larger geographical scale there was undoubtedly a high proportion of the population in south Wales classified as working class. There is little support, however, from a Welsh perspective, for the argument of one witness cited in the 1920 Departmental Committee of Scholarships and Free Places that 'there is no social difficulty in education and no middle class'.[9]

The competition for secondary places may have been more within a single class than between social classes in the smaller region. Thus a more precise analysis of the working class, against whom social bias evidently operated, would have enabled a truer judgement to be obtained. Within a social class the circumstances of individuals may have ameliorated or exacerbated the demonstrable bias of the prevailing educational system. It was possible to delve into the experiences of the group of respondents investigated in a bid to identify those factors which they saw as having interacted to limit their educational opportunity.

For the respondents as a whole, the occupations of their fathers and/or mothers were of importance mainly in terms of the way that the regularity or irregularity of the pay packet or lack of it controlled their family's standard of living. The majority of respondents had a strong recollected awareness of poverty at the time they sat the Scholarship.

The voices of the past

Central to the respondents' memories of their childhood were poverty, unemployment and insecurity. Father's irregular employment with long periods on the dole was a repeated recollection within the sample. Skilled manual workers were as likely to be hit by the recession as the unskilled who were traditionally victims in the labour market competition:

> They would report for work and if they worked three days in a week they
> received no dole.   (Mrs A)

'Three days on the dole, often laid off and long periods on the sick' was a description given by Mrs D of her father's plight as a wheelwright. Being on the dole varied in duration, with periods of up to three years in the 1930s being recalled by Mrs E whose father was a printer, although he was in employment when she passed the Scholarship. Periods of sickness and 'escape' through alcohol were mentioned in passing, along with generalizations which indicate a felt condition of poverty:

> Most of the fathers in my area were nearly all unemployed.   (Mrs K)

> *Your father was in full-time employment. Would you have known at that age what kind of income he had?*
> About £3. My mother always said, 'Your father earned £3. I kept nine children on £3.'   (Mrs V)

Mrs V was adamant that in the early 1930s her father's dole money was 23*s*. a week. It was during this time that the working class, with a virtual breakdown of the economic system under which they lived, had a profound sense of uncertainty, according to Branson and Heinemann.[10] Just under three million were unemployed, of which nearly one in five were continuously out of work for more than six months. Long-term unemployment was a feature of depressed areas like south Wales and indeed of some of the respondents' parents.

> I'm going back now to 1932, 1933 er, 1931, 1932, but my father who had prior to that been employed drawing a horse and cart for a haulage contractor in Swansea – one of the biggest then, about three horses, three horsemen drawers, you know – and he decided to sell the three horses and buy a lorry; which meant that the three men would have an opportunity to work one week in three. And the week my father worked he could earn £2.10*s*. and the following week because he'd worked a week he drew 30*s*. 3*d*. dole to keep seven of us and out of that we paid 12*s*. 5*d*. rent.   (Mrs P)

Poverty was not just a function of net wages but involved the amount of housekeeping given to the wife. In the context of her mother's differentiation between sons and daughters, Mrs E gave a glimpse of how ends were made to meet:

> My father had a lot of ill health and he was on the sick for many years and I can remember every Saturday my mother being in tears. She used to have little piles of money saying, 'This is for the baker and this is for the butcher.' She'd be robbing Peter to pay Paul as she put it, and I think she just thought she looked on me getting a job with security not getting in the position she'd been in.   (Mrs E)

The survey findings of Orr,[11] supported by Rowntree,[12] indicated that the wage of even a skilled man was insufficient for a healthy diet if there were at least three children under working age; the typical unskilled wage meant that the diet would be inadequate if there were any dependent children at all. Virtually all families living on unemployment benefit or assistance were too poor to afford what the BMA in 1933 optimistically declared to be a minimum diet to sustain physical health.[13]

The respondents were asked how they would describe their family home:

We were poor but I never remember going home not to a cooked meal.
(Mrs D)

We were fed and clothed but we never had very much and we didn't go very far and if we did we always had to walk.   (Mrs L)

Poor. My most vivid memory is of my mother worrying constantly because there wasn't enough money. Um, it was bare. We had enough food – never hungry or anything like that. I can remember her crying once because she didn't have any money for coal. They came to turn off the water, we were that poor. It was a very bad time the thirties, I think.
What was your dad doing?
Well he had been in business but that had collapsed at the beginning of the Depression. I remember him walking down the docks getting work unloading fish off the Neale and West boats and finally he got a job driving a lorry. Then he used to do a bit of firewatching in the war and things like that, and then they got a bit better off as everybody did after the war I suppose.   (Mrs H)

Specific evidence of the kind which allows quantifiable gradations of poverty in terms of, for instance, minimum nutritional standards or a subsistence datum claim were not expected nor catered for in the interview sessions, but sufficient account was presented to show that the early lives of the respondents were extensively influenced, moulded and coloured by poverty. Only two of the respondents recorded that they '. . . didn't go short of anything' – Mrs O and Mr M.

And how would you describe your home?
Poor, but I never thought so, mind. Like everybody else's around here . . . I think we had people in rooms at the time. The back bedroom wouldn't have been furnished.

And it's now when you look back that you say you were poor?
Oh yes, I wasn't aware. Well I didn't happen to have the classy things. Like the one particular girl that er, went to high school. When we joined the Urdd she looked extremely smart; a really first class blazer whereas mine was second grade. (Mrs Y)

The nineteenth-century tradition of the private investor supplying the working class with houses to rent continued into the inter-war period. Although the 1930s may have set the stage for the slow eclipse of the private landlord nationally, renting and leasehold tenure is still a prominent feature of south Wales housing conditions and in the thirties council tenancy was in its early stages. Owner-occupation was a minority feature reflected in only two cases in our sample. For these two respondents, whose families lived on slender means, owner-occupancy may have been a practical liability. Mrs V's mother had to manage on her husband's wage of £3 a week to keep nine children:

You were staying in a rented house?
No we bought it. My grandmother had left my father £50 and he put it on the house. You put £50 down and the railway advanced the rest. (Mrs V)

You said that you were ratepayers so were your mother and father buying the house you were in?
They owned the house. It was where he was running his business from originally, you see. He had a fish and chip shop. Well actually they had a lot of fish and chip shops but they are, or were, a wealthy family. Quite well to do now, the family. Quite prosperous. My father being the eldest . . . don't know what happened but something went wrong you know. He was the one whose business went first.
Was he paying a mortgage at the time do you know?
No I don't think he was paying a mortgage but I remember we had to go up the City Hall to pay rates. And then they used to get summoned because they couldn't pay the rates and my mother used to send me in to a big fat policeman sitting behind the desk to pay 5s. off the rates. (Mrs H)

Resourcefulness may have hidden the extent to which some lived in need. The wearing of hand-me-downs was often quoted as a feature of childhood. Thrift was seen as a practical necessity rather than a virtue.

My father had an allotment and he used to grow all his own vegetables. My mother used to pickle, and we also used to be taken out in the summer holidays and various times picking blackberries and things like that. And she used to make a lot of jam. She was very thrifty. (Mrs L)

Social historians like Branson and Heinemann[14] maintain that there was a prejudice against married women working which was common to all social classes and reflected in the employment of women in the public sector, namely the teachers and civil servants compelled to retire on marriage. The majority of the respondents' mothers did not work at the time they sat the Scholarship.

How about your mother? Did she work?
Oh no, no, my mother didn't work; neither did hardly anybody else's. Didn't see many women working in those days. (Mrs K)

Did your mother work at all?
Oh gosh no, she had enough to keep five of us going. (Mrs Q)

The prejudice may have existed but for some families the need to supplement their incomes resulted in mothers taking on extra domestic burdens distinct from full-time paid occupations.

Did your mother work?
No, not work to go out to do a job, but I knew she used to take in washing. (Mrs L)

Taking in washing supplemented the family income in the case of three other informants (Mrs G, Mrs J, Mr T); two mothers were part-time cleaners (Mrs D, Mr N) and one joined the Territorial Army and as a result served full-time when war broke out. Mrs Y's mother let out rooms in their family home.

Such strategies point to the ubiquity of poverty in the experiences of the respondents and their attempts to cope with their circumstances without resorting to the meagre public provisions for subsistence. The official viewpoint on unemployment benefit was that of a 'ceiling' not a 'floor'. In 1931 unemployment insurance benefit was 17s. for a man, 9s. for a dependent wife and 2s. for each child. In the same year the National Government economy measures reduced benefits for adults to 15s. 3d. and 8s. respectively but maintained child benefit at 2s. whilst for those at work weekly unemployment insurance contributions were increased. A limit of twenty-six weeks was imposed on the drawing of unemployment benefit and then an unpopular and degrading Means Test was applied by the Poor Law Authority – the Public Assistance Committee – to assess amounts of benefit (not exceeding the above scale) to be paid to those unemployed for longer than six months. The indignities of the Means Test rankled, particularly amongst men who had paid insurance contributions for many years. Disclosure of the entire resources of a household, under threat of prosecution, was necessary and deducted from the recommended payment so that some Public Assistance Committees became notorious for their low scales and strict use of the Means Test. Glamorgan County, Merthyr Tydfil and Swansea Public Assistance Committees were, however, admonished for awarding nearly every claimant the maximum permitted allowances regardless of family circumstances.[15] As a result of Government disciplinary action, recalcitrant Public Assistance Committees were forced to toe the line and the small improvements in benefit (back to the pre-1931 payments in 1934; child allowances raised to 3s. in 1935 and increases up to 17s. for a man and 10s. for his wife in 1939) reflected an opinion given by Ramsay MacDonald in his broadcast to the nation on 25 August 1931: 'Unemployment benefit is not a living wage; it was never meant to be that.' The relationship between benefit and wages seemed to be an obsession in Whitehall where the fear was that a man might feel as well off out of work as in work.[16] Where wages were low there was little disparity between them and benefit rates – indeed those working intermittently during a week could sometimes be better off on the dole.

The demeaning process involved in obtaining benefit seemed to have been a last resort for many and an indication of dire financial circumstances. The plight of the working-class widow poignantly illustrates the difficulties encountered through poverty and the kind of strategies adopted to survive.

How did your mother earn her living? She obviously did not work while your father was alive did she?
Oh no! She was only married ten years and she had five children during that time. So it was Parish Relief or whatever they called it in those days, public assistance I think it was. One time she said, thinking back very carefully, she didn't have any money at all and they used to give her food vouchers, food coupons, you know – you could take it to the shop and if the manager of the shop knew you and liked you he might pop you, er, the odd shilling or two as well as the groceries or instead of.

Was the Parish Relief a very demeaning affair?

Very demeaning. I remember my mother locking doors and picking up a little bit of carpet they had or a little bit of what they thought might be considered valuable because they could take it you see, sell it and live on it for a week.

Did she have anything particular that she did not want sold?

Well this one coffer that she had given her from the proprietor of the hotel as a wedding present. It was a beautiful coffer, beautiful polished doors and a set of cupboards at the top, and two long drawers, very thick wood. They would have taken it without doubt if they had known about it. She used to keep that in the front room and shut the door.

And how did she supplement the Parish Relief?

Well, what they would call moonlighting today, really, you know. She used to go papering. She used to take in sewing particularly mourning sewing: black dresses, black hats. She used to darn socks, anything, she would do anything – money to support us you see, to support us.   (Miss F)

To put generalized impressions of wages, supplemented incomes and benefit rates into perspective is difficult. Branson and Heinemann[17] have attempted to assess real earnings and a number of their points of comparison may prove useful in tempering the oral accounts of the respondents.

Real wages in the thirties were very low by comparison with recent standards and the impact of recession on different industries and sections of the population was uneven. In the old industrial areas, where there was heavy unemployment, the earnings of employed workers were particularly low. In addition, as a result of the Means Test, many employed workers were forced to maintain unemployed members of their household and even the few shillings earned by juvenile labour (often in demand even where there was no work for skilled adults) was taken into account by the Means Test calculations of allowances for parents and younger brothers and sisters. Some of the oral evidence indicates that prices were low and Branson and Heinemann[18] estimate that they were low in comparison with those of the mid-sixties; but for those on unemployment benefit, 30s. a week, on which a man, wife and two children had to manage, was in real terms about half the amount considered necessary for minimum subsistence by the National Assistance Board in the mid-sixties. Rowntree's[19] minimum standard below which no worker should be forced to live, i.e. about 53s. a week in 1936 and about 56s. in 1939 for a family consisting of man, wife and three children, seems not to have been met by a large proportion of the families of the respondents interviewed. Both unemployed and employed seemed to be barely subsisting, and poverty was woven into the fabric of the lives of the majority.

The thirties saw increased agitation to feed children at risk of malnutrition. LEAs were entitled to supply free school meals to particularly needy children – those who 'were unable by reason of lack of food, to take full advantage of the education provided for them'. There were also local arrangements of long standing for the provision of subsidized meals for necessitous children.[20] By 1938/9, only about 4 per cent nationally got free school meals, with much local variation explained in part by the attitude and prosperity of the LEA in relation to the recipient's degree of poverty. But the Poor Law stigma attached to attendance at a dinner-centre meant that such meals were taken only as a last resort.

> There were no dinners served in the school. They had to walk down to the dinner place so everyone knew who they were. I could understand my mother not having me join them. (Mrs D)

> Well, there was this, um, it's not done now, but there was this stigma of having free dinners and free milk. I mean it was done, looking back, it was done in a very crude way because the children whose parents were unemployed, they were issued with a dinner ticket, five for a week, and they had to take their ticket. There was a house on Splott Road, rather a big house on the corner and I assume the lady who either used to own or rent the house she would be employed by the Council and the children would go up there for their free dinners. So we would see them all in crowds standing outside. (Mrs L)

The unacceptability of parading your poverty might also have been a factor in refusing to take school milk for which children paid $2\frac{1}{2}d.$ a day for one-third of a pint of milk under the first subsidized scheme for cheap milk introduced in 1934.

> *Would you have been eligible for the 'Soup Queue'?*
> I don't think so. I wasn't the poorest by a long way. I remember somebody coming to school once and asking us to put our arms up. I was so incredibly thin, and then they asked me what my father did and I said he was a lorry driver and they said 'You would qualify for free milk', and I wouldn't accept it. I still took my $2\frac{1}{2}d.$ and paid for the milk because I wouldn't accept it.

Because this would have done what?
I don't know. It would have put me in with the poor ones I suppose, and I wasn't quite the poorest.

(Mrs H)

Cost was a significant factor as can be seen by the fact that the proportion of schoolchildren taking school milk rose dramatically from about 45 per cent in 1936 to more than 90 per cent when it was issued free during the war. Prior to this, even at $2\frac{1}{2}d$. a bottle many families did not feel able to budget for it.

How poor was poor? Constantly the respondents qualified their impoverished condition, seeking a gradation by comparison with friends or acquaintances. This can be seen in their responses to questions about those of their peers who passed the Scholarship and did go on to a secondary school.

And of the people who went on, were their family backgrounds any different from yours?

Yes they were a little better off.

(Mrs J)

Yes, a lot different, yes a lot better off obviously.

(Mrs S)

Her father was a railway worker and they had better money.

(Mrs Y)

Oh yes, his family circumstances were better off financially. Yes, I don't know quite what his father did but um, he was um, you know, he was um, a white collar worker and my father was a railway guard.

(Mr M)

Well this one girl – Joan – her father owned a shop and um, she was an only child, so I don't think they had any financial difficulties.

(Mrs L)

Such comparisons together with an awareness of what Roberts called an 'undermass'[21] proved to be reference points for a kind of self-assessment of relative deprivation. The majority of the respondents did not perceive themselves as being at the bottom of their neighbourhood social order.

And were you aware of families poorer than yourselves?
Well, not in this street. But in another road just down there. She was one of about ten. Well, she was always lousy.

(Mrs Y)

Although times were hard for you were you aware that there were people in your district worse off than yourselves?
Oh absolutely. Very much worse off and very proud too – they would never

admit it but one of my best friends used to have to queue up just around the corner from where the shop was for soup in a big white jug and they used to have boots with eyelets – I remember that very vividly.
And what were the boots with the eyelets in?
They were the sort of parish allowance for big families[22] that had no money to buy shoes.

As I was saying although I thought we were poor there were a lot more far poorer than we were. And of course um, we never played with the children over in Thomas Street – that was a big Catholic community where they had so many children they didn't know what to do. We just didn't talk to those people down there.   (Mrs H)

There were lots of children in Splott perhaps their parents weren't um, employed, and of course there was a lot of people used to spend their money in the Wimbourne Hotel and the children were neglected. I can remember in my school the teacher used to have a cupboard with old clothes, you know, supposing I'd grown out of something you'd take it along and um, then the teachers would perhaps rig out some of the more unfortunate children.   (Mrs L)

The special handicaps of gender

Many of Goode's respondents were convinced that a combination of insecurity, poverty and gender made parental refusal of a secondary school place particularly likely for a bright girl. While the male respondents told poignant enough stories, those of the women were mostly grounded in an explicit claim that parents could not, or would not, make the same sacrifices for a girl that they might have stretched to for her brother.

It wasn't important for a girl, it was important for my two brothers but it wasn't important for me, and I was going to commercial school and no questions asked.   (Mrs E)

The school gave out letters notifying the candidates of their results and Mrs E described herself as being highly excited about passing.

What was your mother's reaction?
Delighted but she sort of convinced me it wasn't for me. It was much more important for the boys to go because books, uniform had to be bought. She certainly had it cut and dried.   (Mrs E)

Mrs A sat the first of two parts of the Scholarship in Cardiff but through 'illness' was prevented from sitting the second part of the examination. Mrs A recollected that the real reason for her not taking the examination was that her mother needed her at home to help out in the days immediately following the birth of the youngest son of the family. Mrs J felt that a contributory factor in her parents' decision not to let her go to High School was to free her from schooling at the earliest opportunity to look after her brother who was ten years younger than Mrs J.

> If I hadn't been free to mind the baby er, my mother couldn't have taken a job.
> *Do you think she had that in mind at the time?*
> I think so, yes, because I was already involved very much with the baby anyway. (Mrs J)

> My mother was very close, but I always – I felt it was a dirty trick. It wasn't fair because she was not allowing me to show what I was capable of doing. I wasn't having the same chance my brothers were having. (Mrs E)

> He had the money. I think perhaps I would not have been so defiant or pushing if I'd known my parents could not afford for me to go – by my parents I mean my father – but I knew he could afford it. (Mrs C)

The nearest that the oral evidence came towards an impression of parental hostility to the kind of education provided by the secondary schools was the record of Mrs E and, to some extent, that of Mrs L. Speaking of a friend who also passed the Scholarship:

> There again she didn't go to the High School either. We were in the minority possibly because our parents couldn't afford to send us really and the fact that my mother had it planned out for me. It wasn't important for a girl. It was important for my brothers but it wasn't important for me and I was going to commercial school and no questions asked. (Mrs E)

> Oh yes, I can hear my mother saying 'Girls only grow up and get married, what's the point of keeping them in school till they're sixteen', and that was it. (Mrs L)

Here apparently, was an antagonism born of sex bias – a devaluing of the educational needs of a girl and, in the case of Mrs E whose destiny was secretarial work, a somewhat stereotyped perception of female vocation.

Not all the parents were hostile to secondary education for girls. Mrs B recalled that her father 'was always very keen on education' and tried to borrow money to finance her schooling in 1919. Miss F's widowed mother tried to move heaven and earth to let her go to the Ferndale Secondary School in 1926. Describing her mother's feelings about the insurmountable barrier of finance, Miss F recalled:

> Well, she was terribly upset at the time. I don't know. I don't think she ever got over it, in a way, you know, but, she tried to get grants for it, she collected for the British Legion. She was a big woman in the British Legion at the time. She was treasurer of the Women's British Legion in Tylorstown and she did get grants for ex-servicemen's widows and wives and children to help start up a little business or maybe help them in any extreme poverty or put the children in school. She thought of my father having served in the Boer War would have qualified for some sort of grant, but apparently not. He had had to have spent one day in the Army or the Air Force or whatever it may be, for him to have even qualified for sixpence . . . and he went to the Forest of Dean to enlist but he had a bad heart; they wouldn't take him on. He came home. That was it. He died in 1918.
> *So there were no other sorts of bodies who –*
> There were no Social whatsoever. She did go over to the Director of Education in Pentre or Treorch y . . . she had to go over Penrhys Mountain. It was an awfully long walk and there were no charabancs or buses, you had to walk. You had to walk up the one side and down the other, Penrhys Mountain. And er, he tried I think – Mr Berry the man's name was – very concerned that I couldn't go because he said it was a shame. He told her he understood that I was being deprived of an education that should have been mine but there was nothing at all, there was no Socials at all available in those days. None whatsoever. If you had not the money in the home then that was it. (Miss F)

This particular parent may have fallen between two stools in the matter of grants in 1926. The respondent did not qualify for the minor county scholarships nor was she able to benefit from the limited generosity of the school governors; expansion of awards was most rapid in the wake of the 1933 special-place provision. The local education official's response indicates the tragic shortfall between principles and practices in secondary education provision.

Sometimes there were disputes over the issue, with the child wanting to take the place and the parent refusing to accept it; sometimes the child did not want to go and was able to get parental support for the refusal.

But in two cases at least, the child was an active and catalytic influence in the parents' deliberations at the time her entrance for the Scholarship was first drawn to their attention.

> Well . . . it's the first time I've ever admitted this. I initially heard my Mam and Dad talking – should they allow me to pass. And I eavesdropped and I remember quite distinctly it was the first time in my life I ever eavesdropped on their conversation. I stood on the stairs and I overheard them talking: What would happen if I passed? Would they be able to afford to send me? A great sacrifice for them. So the following day I just asked them if I sat the Scholarship, if I passed, would they promise not to send me. So they promised. I'd have a present for passing. (Mrs Y)

In the case of Mrs G, her eldest sister was withdrawn early from secondary school partly as a result of her family's financial hardships. She laid great store, however, in remaining with her friends:

> Our parents seemed to let us please ourselves about education. They didn't push us at all because the day I said I didn't think I wanted to go because my friends were not going, except Jean who I told you about, they didn't mind. 'Cos I cried they signed the form so I didn't go.
> *So the decision really was yours?*
> Yes it was my decision but it was . . . I had no opposition. (Mrs G)

It is tempting to assume that the end of the quotation reveals the more decisive factor in this instance. The obdurate child might almost clinch the matter, but determination to force the issue could result in a suspense prolonged by parental prevarication, as Mrs C discovered. At first, her father signed the form accepting the offer of a place at Howard Gardens School in the face of her relentless pressure, but her mother was not convinced they could afford to meet all the expenses involved.

> So although my father had signed I remember a few weeks before I was due to start school I think my father phoned up or we had some contact with the Education to say then that I wasn't going. My father did sign but then it was cancelled. (Mrs C)

Sitting the entrance examination as a forlorn hope in the face of parental inertia permeates the collective evidence of the respondents. Domestic dynamics are pointed to as important determining factors in the rejection of a secondary school place.

The overwhelming impression is given of families approximating to what Bernstein[23] called 'position', with distinct separation of roles and with the right to command based on formal status such as age or sex. As a type, parental expectations of the role of children seemed to lean towards the adage 'children should be seen but not heard' – a phrase used in some interviews to embrace the kinds of relationships existing between children and their parents. To see the child as a party to the business of education was exceptional in the context of secondary school place refusal within the small sample. The obdurate child could almost steer the decision her way, as Mrs C recalled, but the hierarchical 'position' family makes little leeway for those at its base:

> Were we gutless?
> *Compared to your children today?*
> We accepted things without question.   (Mrs E)

Clothes, books, hockey sticks and lost earnings

Many of the respondents recalled that their parents were deterred by the costs of secondary education. The *lessons* might be free, but the schools demanded uniforms, textbooks, equipment, and attendance until sixteen.

> Well I didn't go because of purely financial reasons, purely financial reasons, my mother couldn't afford it. She was getting about – well 7s. 6d. must have been the most – and she just could not afford the sporting equipment which was necessary, or the uniform. Because the uniform in those days, it was a round hat with a badge on the front, the gymslip and a coloured belt and a purse on a strap and black shoes and stockings; I should imagine, you know, special blouses. Well, she made all my clothes. She bought the material in Pontypridd market and she used to make all my school clothes but she couldn't make those you see. Couldn't make the uniform, it was out of the question. That and the transport. Although I could have walked. But everything combined it was out of the question. She couldn't do it, so that was it.   (Miss F)

> My mother had already decided that even if I passed she wasn't going to send me.
> *Why was that?*
> Well I think there were two reasons. First of all, er, as I explained, my mother was a country woman. She wasn't very well educated herself and I

don't think she thought that a girl needed to be educated. That was one aspect. But the other one was that she had er, quite a job to manage, from what I can make out, you know looking back. I have seen her taking in washing, and doing all this cooking and tending this allotment and one thing and another, mending, patching. She would cut my sister's clothes down for me and mine down for my younger sister and I don't think that she could afford it. I didn't realize it at the time but when I came home and told her that I was in this Scholarship class she said, 'Oh, you're not going.' Just like that.

That was before you ever sat?

Yes. I don't think she had any doubt in her mind that I would fail the exam or she wouldn't have said that to me, and she did tend to brag to her neighbours and my relatives that I was 'brainy' as she called it. I can remember that.

(Mrs L)

Books, unlike clothing, were not always part of the daily family requirements and could have been an unknown quantity which would have to be taken into account. Mrs L provided an interesting estimate of costs which adds substance to the above extract.

Well, you had to buy all the books and, as far as I can remember, when you were a first-year entrant second-year pupils used to sort of find out who was going and they would come around and sell their books to you second-hand. Some of them were rather tatty because they wouldn't be second-hand, they would, perhaps, be third, fourth and fifth-hand.

Yes.

Of course those books in those days I suppose they would have been about half a crown each, which was a lot of money. It sounds a very small sum now but in those days when people were only earning £2 per week you know, I suppose it was a lot of money. Then of course, you had to buy school uniform. I can remember you had to have a special gymslip. In the summer it was a white blouse and in the winter it was a certain colour jumper which you wore under this gymslip. And you had to wear navy blue knickers, I can remember that, and black stockings and shoes. And you had to have a navy um, kind of a school hat, a velour hat, you don't see them now, with a school band. They were rather expensive; I think they were about 7s. 6d. each. And in the summer you had to wear a Panama hat, and again with the school colours on the band of the hat.

Yes.

Then you had to have a tennis racquet and a hockey stick. And boys would have to have cricket gear and so on. So it was rather a lot for people to lay out you see.

(Mrs L)

Such expenses were frequently quoted as a factor in the rejection of a Scholarship place, although schools in Cardiff and Glamorgan had shown an awareness of the burdens imposed on some of their pupils by setting up internal trading and barter arrangements in second-hand school clothing and books.

Furthermore, to keep a child at school beyond the age of fourteen was viewed as a loss of earnings – a view consistent with the stratagems employed by families to reduce the effects of their poverty. None of the respondents recalled specific and explicit reference made to them on this issue by their parents, but just over one-third of them were convinced it was implicit in the decision made about the offer of a place at secondary school.

> *What were the reasons why you did not take up your Scholarship place?*
> Well firstly, my father would not pay. I don't think it was so much paying because what I can remember about this pass I had when I filled in the form – if you passed high enough you could go to the school of your choice – and of course I put the school of my choice down which was Howard Gardens, and I also think I won a scholarship high enough to pay for my books and also give me a grant for the clothes. So really my father would not have had to have paid anything out, but I think the main thing was that he knew I could leave school at fourteen and go to work, whereas if I went on to High School I would have to stay in school until sixteen and I would be able to come out at fifteen if he paid money to let me come out and there was no chance to leave at fourteen. They didn't want me to go because of these two years. (Mrs C)

> She realized if I went on to school beyond fourteen no money would be coming in – my mother was not one for education. (Mrs D)

Other respondents continued the same line of thought in a slightly different context.

> *Why do you think your parents didn't show the same kind of interest in education as you do?*
> I don't know. Whether my parents were more apathetic towards education or whether they knew in their minds that they couldn't send me up, you know. At the back of their minds they were waiting for us to go to work, you know what I mean. (Mrs G)

> *How about your mother and father's attitude towards education?*
> They weren't like the modern parents today, interested in their children's education. All they wanted was to see you leave school and earn money,

which was the general attitude, I would have thought, at the time. All they were interested in was to see us get out and earn.

(Mr K)

Life after denial

Graham Goode asked his respondents to recall how their elementary school responded to the parental refusal, what effect that refusal had on their subsequent education and careers and on their attitudes to the education of their own children. These data are not reported here but in this final section a few of the most poignant comments made by women about 'what might have been' have been extracted from the thesis, to serve as a conclusion.

Time and again, respondents indicated that they considered their Scholarship success, on reflection, as a feather in their caps, a kind of touchstone in their self-assessment – an endorsement of their potential in meeting a challenge on what they saw as equal terms with their peers. The result could bolster self-esteem, as half the sample testified.

I've always considered myself a bit brainy. You know you're not a fool.

(Mrs B)

I think although I didn't go to High School I am as bright as the people who went . . . just to think that I passed . . . I got there really. (Mrs C)

It makes me feel I'm not that dull, you know what I mean? (Mrs G)

I think it gave you a certain confidence, you know, you were a little bit better than the ones who didn't pass. (Mrs H)

I knew I'd passed the Scholarship so I ought to have something upstairs.

(Mrs O)

I think it made me feel I'm not too stupid, that's about all. (Mrs Y)

This kind of pride of achievement was a private satisfaction for the majority. It was usually noted on school leaving cards but only two respondents used it to make a public claim at job interviews. The overwhelming belief was that in terms of passing through promotion barriers, or even in securing a job, the fact that they had achieved success in the Scholarship was totally irrelevant. It could even be an embarrassment.

Did you ever mention your Scholarship success when you went for a job?
Yes. I did used to say I passed the Scholarship but didn't go, and felt rather ashamed at having to admit it . . . I felt it was a lame excuse.   (Mrs E)

During the interviews it was not always possible to separate the initial reaction of the interviewees from their current feelings about the refusal. In some cases it was evident that strength of feeling was continuous from the time of the event and often in direct proportion to the degree of satisfaction or excitement at actually having passed the examination.

It destroyed me that I couldn't go but it didn't do anything for me to think that I passed. I just felt very bitter that I didn't – I couldn't go.   (Mrs J)

Almost two-thirds of the informants registered much stronger emotions. Bitterness and resentment featured in most cases. This was directed at parents where it was felt by the respondents that there was an element of reneging. For some it was generalized in chafing at the injustice of the system prevailing during their schooldays. Two examples illustrate these emotions:

I felt cheated; that I had been let down. It was settled I would go; my parents had agreed. They later changed their minds. It's quite possible, as my husband says, I have a chip on my shoulder because I feel cheated. I should have been going where the others went. The reason given to me was they couldn't afford it and as a child I had to learn to accept it. I had to accept it.
(Mrs D)

What were and are your feelings about being unable to take up your place?
Resentment! Resentment always, all my life, that I wasn't allowed to do what I wanted to do. I wanted to go to College to be a teacher. Resentment even now. I resent the fact that children get such wonderful chances these days and so many waste their opportunities . . . you had to fight every inch of the way. Resentment at being poor. I have been very bitter – I love schooling. Possibly I might have made something of myself, maybe not.
(Mrs B)

The underlying cause of regret and disappointment was not easy to articulate, but it can be summed up in terms of lost opportunity.

As well as the possible effects on job prospects, Mrs A and Mrs J (the only respondents who, through marriage, moved down a rung on the social classification ladder) ventured opinions about the effect their lost opportunity had on their social life.

> *So you feel if you had gone on, what?*
> Yes I feel I could have made something better of my life. I would probably not have married, well, quite as young, I know that. I married to get away from the home, and had I had a good job, a nice job, you see I didn't have a job, right up until . . . well, I think I did a small job for six months before I was married, but my main idea of getting married was to get away from the home, to get away from this, this . . .
> *Domestic?*
> Domestic situation [laughter]. (Mrs J)

> The biggest difference I feel it has made, and it was not financial or anything like that or perhaps not so much opportunity; I think that a high level of education enables you to mix with different people and that's the main thing. If I was educated I would never have married at eighteen, my circle would have been wider. (Mrs A)

Mrs A was to describe one of the tenets of investigations of social mobility:

> My social circulation was not limited by my own capabilities but um, by my husband's capabilities. (Mrs A)

For a few female respondents in particular, recollection of their peers who received secondary education suggested that the majority left school at sixteen and took the same kinds of office jobs obtainable by those who had left school earlier.

> What I did notice though was that lots of girls who went to High School when they came out, unless they went on to University, they really came out with more depth of knowledge. Yet if they wanted a job they still had to learn shorthand and typing or learn something else, so they were no further up the scale than me. (Mrs E)

Despite this, a sense of social distancing was experienced.

> Once these people had passed the Scholarship and went, the line was drawn straight away. We were looked down upon as the sort of underdogs. Some girls actually stopped speaking to me. (Mrs E)

The childhood experiences of many of these women may be summed up in the final heartfelt words of Mrs D:

> Having been cheated myself, I was determined that my sons would get what they could. (Mrs D)

Notes

1 Sara Delamont produced this paper from Graham Goode's M.Ed. thesis.
2 Floud, J. *et al.* (1954) *Social Class and Educational Opportunity* (London, William Heinemann).
3 Board of Education Pamphlet No.63 on Examination for Free Places in Secondary Schools 1928 (HMSO).
4 Culshaw, J. E. (1929) 'The Development of the Free Place System and its Effects on the Secondary School System' (Unpublished MA, University of London) 31.
5 Banks, O. (1955) *Parity and Prestige in English Secondary Education* (London, Routledge and Kegan Paul) 64.
6 Evans, K. (1975) *The Development and Structure of the English Educational System* (London, University of London Press) 80.
7 Bernbaum, G. (1967) *Social Change and the Schools 1918–1944* (London, Routledge and Kegan Paul) 50.
8 Campbell, F. C. (1956) *Eleven Plus and All That* (London, Watts).
9 Board of Education (1920) *Report of the Departmental Committee on Scholarships and Free Places* (HMSO) 44.
10 Branson, N. and Heinemann, M. (1971) *Britain in the Nineteen Thirties* (London, Weidenfeld and Nicholson) 5.
11 Orr, J. B. (1936) 'Food Health and Income' in Branson, N. and Heinemann, M. (1971) op. cit.
12 Rowntree, B. S. (1941) 'Poverty and Progress: Second Social Survey of York' in Branson, N. and Heinemann, M. (1971) op. cit.
13 Branson, N. and Heinemann, M. (1971) op. cit.
14 Ibid., 157.
15 Ibid., 27.
16 Ibid., 32.
17 Ibid., 133–47.
18 Ibid., 20.
19 Rowntree, B. S. (1936) 'Human Needs of Labour' in Branson, N. and Heinemann, M. (1971) op. cit.
20 School Canteen Committee Minutes, CEC, Vols. 18, 19, 20.
21 Roberts, R. (1971) *The Classic Slum* (Manchester, Manchester University Press).
22 Reference to this provision is found in numerous reports in the Education Committee minutes, e.g. Medical Inspection Sub-Committee Report No.98, Glamorgan County Minutes October 8 1936.
23 Bernstein (1971) *Class, Codes and Control* Vol. 1 (London, Routledge and Kegan Paul) 151–2.

PART TWO

Gendering and Education in Contemporary Wales

5

The culture and aspirations of Welsh secondary school pupils: A comparison between the sexes

RICHARD STARTUP AND BENJAMIN M. DRESSEL

Introduction

The purpose of the research described in this chapter (which formed part of a larger transatlantic comparative study)[1] was to investigate and to compare and contrast the attitudes and aspirations of male and female secondary school students in Wales regarding education and occupations. The intention was also to increase understanding of those aspirations and expectations by placing them within the context of peer group culture. It is believed that insight may thereby be gained into the links between the schooling of boys and girls and wider cultural values. In this connection it is important to enquire whether, in the changing economic conditions of the 1990s, there is any evidence of differential educational motivation between the sexes, and to establish to what extent career choices continue to be made in conventionally gendered ways.

The research has taken place against a background of rapid educational and economic change. The 1980s was a period of intense flux and reform in education[2] alongside rapidly changing labour markets. As far as sixteen-plus education is concerned, there has been steady progress in recent decades from a situation where school subjects tended to be sex typed, and with overall male performance outstripping that of females, to one in which the relative performance of girls across the curriculum has so improved that their overall achieved standard on some measures clearly exceeds that of boys. For instance, of pupils aged fifteen in Wales in 1992/3, 42 per cent of girls but only 32 per cent of boys achieved five or more grade C or better GCSE passes.[3] Indeed, worries are now being expressed in several quarters regarding apparent male underperformance. Changes in the acquisition of educational qualifications have proceeded alongside changes in patterns of employment which are almost all relatively favourable to women. In recent years, male employment has fallen while female employment, particularly on a part-time basis, has increased. Indeed a recent review notes that over the period 1981 to 1993, 'the number of female part-time workers has increased by 44 per cent in Wales and by 25 per cent nationally'.[4] A comparative study of the aspirations of girl and boy secondary students is surely therefore timely, and Wales is a particularly interesting place in which to conduct it, given its experience of economic change in unusually acute form, for example the shift from the heavy industries of coal and steel towards lighter engineering industries.[5]

The familiar traditional picture was of the Welsh regarding themselves as having an unusually high respect for education,[6] but the pattern described by Rees and Rees, reviewing evidence of the late 1970s, was of Welsh schools producing both high proportions of well-qualified school-leavers and very high proportions with no formal qualifications at all.[7] However, in a recent review any note of optimism has given way to the dismal conclusion that, compared with the rest of the UK, 'there is now lower attainment in Wales across the board'.[8] Disturbing as they are, the data presented in support of this assertion provide further evidence of a 'gender gap' favourable to females, which appears to be even greater in Wales than England (e.g. in respect of GCE Advanced Level results). Particularly relevant for present purposes are the figures quoted that there were in Wales, in 1993, 25 per cent of females but 35 per cent of males who did not remain in education at minimum school-leaving age.[9] An objective of this study is to increase understanding of factors contributing to this differential. As regards the educational context, Istance and Rees draw attention to the more complete comprehensivization of public-sector secondary education in Wales compared to England and the lower proportion of secondary schools which have so far 'opted out' and acquired grant-maintained status.

Among the earlier sociological studies which can inform an investigation of pupil aspirations and expectations are those of Turner[10] and Hopper.[11] These authors examine various national systems of education and analyse their differences in respect of the tendency to 'warm up' or 'cool out' student aspirations at various stages. In exploring further sources of pupil motivation and inequality, influential American studies highlighted achievement ideology, social status and the social organization of the school.[12]

More recently, insight has been gained into the formation of pupil attitudes and responses through the idea that education may be understood as a response to the economic needs of industrial capitalism.[13] Although early British work focused, for instance, on social class inequalities in educational performance, it tended to throw rather little light on links between motivation and the schooling process. However, more latterly there has been something of a move towards cultural explanations, the claim being made, for instance, that working-class pupils have their own distinctive outlook and ambitions.[14] Arguably, the position has been reached where much work can be said to link systematically to the concept of cultural reproduction a notion that directs attention *inter alia* to the means whereby schools reinforce variations in cultural values.[15]

Of even more immediate relevance for present purposes is the empirical study of Welsh pupils conducted by Brown.[16] This study decisively rejects the bi-polar, pro- and anti-school, culturally oriented model of student behaviour evident in some earlier work[17] and is concerned to explore the outlook of the ordinary 'invisible majority' of students who neither excel in nor rebel against school. Brown indicates three main culturally defined categories, or student 'types', which differ in their 'frame of reference', a classification implying variations in pupil attitudes and aspirations in relation to education and work. He is also critical of the new vocational emphasis in British education and raises the possibility of fundamental changes in attitude in conditions of high unemployment. The intention here is to evaluate these ideas further, by examining the links between educational and occupational aspirations in the 1990s.

Method

Following the work of Brown, the research interest was in 'ordinary' or 'average' types of students,[18] so it was decided to select schools which were good representative examples of average (English-language) comprehensives, each with an intake which represented a cross-section of the local community. To keep fieldwork manageable it was decided that one rural and one urban school from Wales should be selected. To further the research objectives, an initial idea had been to include the urban school in south Wales studied by Brown, but access was denied and a further school of a similar nature, although not quite as 'working class', was located.

Access to the schools being assured, a key decision concerned the age cohort to sample. It was judged that the fifth form, the fifteen to sixteen age group, was the most desirable, as these students were at a stage when they needed to form ideas about future plans for education and work. Equally important, however, was the point that this would be the oldest group from whom it would be possible to sample students across the whole of the ability range. Altogether, 136 students were taken into the sample from the appropriate school classes. Importantly, it also transpired that the socio-economic background of the sample was very similar to that of the region of Wales within which the schools were located: for instance, (allowing for non-respondents) of fathers or stepfathers of the sample 46 per cent were in non-manual employment, 10 per cent in personal services, 39 per cent in manual employment, 4 per cent were unemployed and 2 per cent homemakers. On the other hand, the occupational profile of the mothers or stepmothers of the sample was: 41 per cent in non-manual employment, 35 per cent in personal services, 6 per cent in manual employment, 1 per cent unemployed and 17 per cent homemakers.

It had been decided that a combination of quantitatively and qualitatively oriented methods of data collection would be most thorough: the use of a questionnaire survey followed up by intensive interviewing of a representative sub-sample in which issues could be explored in greater depth. The questionnaire itself comprised four sections, the first of which dealt with biographical and related matters. The second concerned attitudes to school and educational aspirations, while the third probed the approach to employment. A final section was concerned with wider interests and activities. Given the background and purpose of the investigation, some use was made of questions formulated by Brown which is here gratefully acknowledged.[19] Data collection was conducted during 1990–91.

Informal pupil culture

An examination will first be made of the informal pupil culture evident in the Welsh schools, and there follows a more quantitatively detailed exploration of the data regarding aspirations. As Brown affirms, informal culture is important, 'because it represents the social and cultural context in which school is experienced on a daily basis, and the sociological context needed to bring the study of pupil orientations to life'.[20]

Students were initially asked to identify the main types of pupils in their schools and also to state how each category might be referred to in everyday terms. It transpired that classification was relatively straightforward, probably implying a fair measure of agreement on criteria. There was a strong tendency to identify peers in terms of three predominantly academically based categories, which were the same as those described by Brown.[21] Altogether each of these three identities was cited by more than 65 per cent of the respondents while no other single identity was referred to by more than 12 per cent.

As many as 87 per cent identified the 'swot', a term with a somewhat negative connotation, and the implication is of a pupil who conforms or over-conforms to the academic ideals of teachers through study and other scholarly patterns. In addition, a substantial 78 per cent identified students who were relatively unsuccessful academically and who also tended to reject the school ethos: 'rems', 'trouble makers' and 'wasters' were the most common terms for this category (with clearly negative overtones). The third type of pupil, identified by 66 per cent, was the 'ordinary' student: this partly functioned as a residual category with respect to the other two and the main behavioural criteria would seem to be a mixture of both work and play, and of conformity and dissent. The only other student type to emerge was the 'sporty' individual but this was identified as a distinct category by only 11 per cent of respondents.

Altogether the largest number of students identified themselves as belonging to the 'ordinary' category. Gina, a highly motivated student aspiring to be an electrical engineer, characterized the groups in this way:

> Well, there are people who are just working all the time and don't enjoy themselves and others who do work but enjoy themselves and then others who don't do any work but just spend all the time enjoying themselves.

From the point of view of a 'rem' Gina would be considered a 'swot', yet she placed herself firmly in the middle group of those who 'do a bit of work and a bit of play'. As long as one is seen to enjoy oneself some of the time, it is possible to avoid the 'swot' label, but one must be seen to do enough work to avoid the 'waster' label.

It would be fair comment that the majority of those interviewed appeared to be making some use of their ability to make academic progress while maintaining a certain amount of personal distance from the staff-centred academic ethos of the school. Overall the impression was that even among the 'swots', students wished to play down their academic achievements in order to be thought of as more average or at least so as not to stand out from the rest. The most common outlook is suggested by the participation in GCSE work: whereas 80 per cent of respondents were attempting seven or more GCSE subjects, only 32 per cent expressed an unequivocally positive orientation toward school.

The clear inference regarding the informal categories employed is their reliance on an academic framework with respect to which students are judged. Few responses varied from the pattern outlined but even when they did there were still references back to the academic. For instance, some students spoke of 'in' groups and 'out' groups (e.g. when commenting on friendship patterns) but qualified their comments in terms of individuals' compliance with the school's academic ethos.

As indicated above, no attempt was made to classify individual respondents by reference to the judgements of their peers, but clear patterned differences could be noted in the tendency to identify boys and girls as belonging to the various types. In particular, girls were more often identified as 'swots', while boys were over-represented within the 'rem/waster' and 'sporty' categories. Allied to this, it seems from interview comments that boys were more reluctant or even afraid to be labelled a 'swot'[22] and more of them were felt to have a negative orientation towards the school. On the other hand, a sporting identification had a mildly positive overall flavour but those to whom it applied effectively disqualified themselves from being seen as swots.

Aspirations and orientation to school

As well as analysing relevant cultural differences, the intention was to explore pupils' educational and occupational aspirations with a view to clarifying any broad sex differences in respect of the orientation to schooling and the acquisition of qualifications. To this end questions were asked about the amount of higher education respondents hoped to receive and the type of occupation they wished to enter. The answers were then used to classify individuals into a typology consisting of: (a) 'high aspirers' i.e. those hoping for more than two years of higher education together with professional or semi-professional employment; (b) 'low aspirers', i.e. those not hoping to enter higher education and seeking skilled, semi-skilled or unskilled work; (c) 'moderate aspirers' i.e. those with other patterns of response but most often hoping for two years or less of higher education together with either an associated intermediate occupation or, as in some cases, without firm occupational aspirations. It transpired that the average level of aspirations was significantly higher among girls than boys (Table 5.1). Some of the details of these aspirations are 'unpacked' later but, at this point, as well as noting the tendency for female aspirations to be higher, one is struck by the large proportions of young people of each sex aspiring to a higher education/professional or semi-professional route together with the small proportion without interest in higher education and hoping for, at most, skilled work. Striking too, was the lack of any statistically significant association between extent of aspirations and father's or stepfather's occupation. Indeed, of those from working-class backgrounds, 37 per cent were high aspirers, 49 per cent moderate aspirers and 14 per cent low aspirers, so these students were virtually as sanguine as the others. This is striking evidence and differs from Brown's picture of 'ordinary kids' tending to want to 'get on' *within* the working class.[23]

Table 5.1: Student types by percentage

	Girls	Boys	All
High aspirers	55.7	30.3	43.4
Moderate aspirers	38.6	54.5	46.3
Low aspirers	5.7	15.2	10.3
Total 90	100.0	100.0	100.0
Number	70	66	136

Note: There was a statistically significant difference between the sexes ($p < 0.01$).

A further question probed the extent to which the respondents felt they liked school and, again, there were patterned differences for the two sexes. Of the female sample, 20 per cent said they liked school a lot, 69 per cent said they liked it a bit, while 7 per cent disliked it a bit, and 4 per cent disliked it a lot. The corresponding figures for males were 9 per cent, 65 per cent, 20 per cent and 6 per cent respectively, so the main differences were that relatively more girls liked school a lot while more boys disliked it a bit. It is also noticeable that the proportion of boys disliking school to any extent was more than double the corresponding female figure.

An examination was made of the relation between the responses to this last question and the aspiration typology described earlier. It transpired that among high aspirers 97 per cent liked school (at least to some extent) while only 3 per cent disliked it, and among moderate aspirers 81 per cent liked school and 19 per cent disliked it, but of low aspirers only 21 per cent liked school and 79 per cent disliked it. So, overall, there was a clear positive correlation between a higher level of aspiration and a liking for school, and it was also discernible that there was a relatively small (8–9%) disaffected category, consisting predominantly of males, with low aspirations.

A further question sought in a summary way to identify the aspect of school life which students enjoyed the most. Twenty-seven per cent of girls as compared with 16 per cent of boys responded that they enjoyed school because 'they liked to learn', while 70 per cent and 79 per cent respectively indicated that they enjoyed school 'for social reasons'. The numbers indicating that neither of these aspects was a source of enjoyment to them were small (3% of girls; 5% of boys). Nevertheless it seems that rather more females than males responded positively to the intrinsic nature of the academic experience. A further slight difference emerged when the respondents were asked to assess the importance of education to their futures. Whereas 90 per cent of girls indicated that it was very important, the figure for boys was somewhat lower, at 76 per cent. In response to further probing, both females and males divided approximately in the ratio of eight to one in favour of the statement that education was 'important for obtaining a good job' rather than it being 'important for its own sake'. Hence the predominant stance of both girls and boys was utilitarian.

Educational plans and occupational aspirations

Given their frequently high aspirations and their tendency towards instrumentalism, how precisely did these students see their own futures shaping up? It must be stressed that one is concerned with ideas expressed before GCSE courses were completed or subject results known. Against that background when asked to state their educational or vocational plans for the next year, fully 55 per cent of girls said they aimed to stay on at school and study for GCE Advanced Level. A further 6 per cent of girls aimed to stay on but to study a sixth-form vocational course. An additional 26 per cent said they planned to proceed to a further education or technical college, while only 12 per cent planned to enter work; the remaining one per cent indicated other routes. The corresponding figures for boys were: 46 per cent aiming at GCE Advanced Level; 3 per cent, a sixth-form vocational course; 23 per cent, a further education or technical college; 20 per cent, planning to enter work; 8 per cent indicating other routes. Therefore rather more females were inclined towards GCE Advanced Level, while relatively more males wished directly to enter the labour market. Even though these various plans might be modified in the light of subsequent GCSE results, the students were clearly oriented to further study beyond the minimum school leaving age and to the acquisition of additional qualifications.

The extent of these students' ambitions becomes even more apparent when one considers responses to a question concerning progression to a university. In this case the sex difference was even more marked. A startlingly high figure of 51 per cent of girls (boys, 33%) did indeed say they had at any rate tentative plans in that direction, while 20 per cent of girls (boys, 33%) had no such plans and 29 per cent (boys, 33%) were not sure. In the light of projected numbers in UK higher education it seems likely that a significant proportion of these respondents will be unable to execute their admittedly provisional plans. In this connection there is no intention to imply that the students exhibited undue rigidity in defining educational goals. No doubt they made judgements in respect of future possibilities with limited and variable knowledge, but interview discussion with them revealed that most understood the necessarily tentative and conditional nature of the exercise. There was a growing awareness that much of importance might depend upon good GCSE results and beyond that the performance at GCE Advanced Level (or BTEC). Nevertheless, there is no avoiding the inference that aspirations tended to be high with a correspondingly enhanced risk of disappointment.

The reasons why females were, in their future plans, even more positively disposed than males towards education may be complex, but one factor would appear to be parental expectations or influence. This was revealed when respondents were asked what their parents wanted them to do in the forthcoming year. Of each sex approximately 10 per cent responded by saying that the parents wanted whatever they wanted, but the pattern of responses was different for the two other popular answers. It transpired that rather more girls indicated that their parents wanted them to stay at school (74% compared with 64%), while rather more boys believed that their parents wanted them to find a job (18% compared with 6%). Although this difference must not be exaggerated, there is perhaps a hint, particularly on the latter point, that in some cases it is not so much the expectations of pupils themselves which are conventional, but rather those of their parents.

Table 5.2: Occupational aspirations (%)

	Girls	Boys	All
Higher professional	7.4	3.0	5.2
Lower professional	27.9	15.2	21.6
Intermediate	4.4	18.2	11.2
Armed Forces officer	2.9	4.5	3.7
Professional or semi-professional – sub-total:	42.6	40.9	41.7
Skilled non-manual	13.2	3.0	8.2
Police/Fire	0.0	10.6	5.2
Entertainment	5.9	9.1	7.5
Medical, not doctor	17.6	0.0	9.0
Armed Forces, other	2.9	3.0	3.0
Services, etc. sub-total:	39.6	25.7	32.9
Skilled manual	1.5	12.1	6.7
Semi-skilled manual	5.9	0.0	3.0
Unskilled manual	0.0	0.0	0.0
Manual sub-total:	7.4	12.1	9.7
Other	0	4.5	2.2
Undecided	10.3	16.7	13.4
Total %:	99.9	99.9	99.9
Total number:	68.0	66.0	134.0
Missing:	2.0	0.0	2.0

Note: There was a statistically significant difference in the occupational distributions for the two sexes ($p < 0.01$).

The students were also asked to indicate their career or occupational aspirations and a high proportion proved able to do so, at least in outline. As Table 5.2 reveals, the proportion as yet undecided was 10 per cent of girls and 17 per cent of boys. Overall, the difference between the two distributions is statistically significant, but it is nevertheless interesting how similar they are. Of each sex more than two-fifths had professional or semi-professional employment in mind, while the expressed interest in manual work was slight (despite the fact that approximately two-fifths of the overall sample had fathers or stepfathers in manual employment). There were some rather more 'traditional' patterns in occupational preferences, for example rather more girls were inclined towards nursing or ancillary medical occupations; relatively more boys went for the police and fire services. Again, more boys chose computing and information technology, an area which Holland claims is increasingly gendered.[24] However, choices of a discernibly gendered type were very much in a minority and the most marked tendency for both sexes was to aspire upwards in conventional socio-economic status terms.

At this stage one may be inclined to infer at least that educational and occupational aspirations were in a broad sense appropriately related. Earlier it was noted how widespread was the interest in extended education and, in particular, in higher education, and it now becomes apparent that the tendency was towards careers which required a substantial amount of formal education. In order to increase understanding further on this point, an attempt was made to explore the relation between the educational and occupational aspirations of individuals. These did indeed prove to be in general meaningfully related, but, as expected, there were discrepancies. For instance, not all those aspiring to the higher professions anticipated a formal education beyond GCE Advanced Level. The inference may be tentatively drawn from this analysis that the level of 'realism' was in this respect reasonably high while being clearly less than perfect.

There is also evidence bearing on the issue as to whether the occupational aspirations were themselves 'realistic'. In human life, hopes not infrequently outstrip expectations, but did the students in fact anticipate achievement of their stated occupational aspirations? The difference between the patterns of responses of the two sexes to this question was noticeable without being statistically significant. Fully 50 per cent of girls replied in the affirmative with 4 per cent saying no and a further 46 per cent indicating that they were not sure; the corresponding figures for boys were 39 per cent, 5 per cent and 56 per cent respectively. So the girls proved to be more often confident about the realization of their hopes. An extended analysis was made to see whether the patterns of expectations of the sexes varied with the level of occupational aspirations, and it transpired that the variation was slight. Although the inference must necessarily be tentative, there is little evidence here of girls anticipating any gender barrier to their upward mobility.

What does, however, strongly suggest itself both from these data and from observation within the schools is the relative openness of the GCSE system of examinations. Students are not banded in such a sharp way as under the previous, bifurcated GCE Ordinary Level and CSE arrangements, hence a different signal is being sent by the school. The change represents a further move towards a 'contest' and away from a 'sponsored' system of mobility.[25] The newer system appears to be particularly effective in 'warming up' pupil aspirations, which no doubt are then in some cases modified or 'cooled out' by subsequent examinations.

Concepts of success

It was felt that the respondents' aspirations could be more readily understood and interpreted if taken in conjunction with their criteria of success and ideas about what it takes to be successful in life. For example, there is recognized to be a variety of ways of 'doing well' and these may lead in different occupational directions. During the interviews this topic was explored and an attempt made to identify each student's main criterion of success in life. It transpired that the resultant distributions of responses for the two sexes were broadly similar. The yardstick of 'financial rewards and material wealth' was tied in first place in terms of its frequency of mention. However, what was striking was the relatively small proportion of respondents, 26 per cent, who identified that aspect as their main criterion. Also in joint first place was 'achieving a stated goal or career'. When taken in conjunction with the fact that the next most prominent responses, following the two already noted, were 'having a good education', 'trying one's best' and 'having enough to get by', the relatively non-materialistic tendency among the students becomes even clearer. Interestingly though, the criteria of 'status and respect within the community' and 'getting on well with others' had no takers of either sex; hence success tended to be defined in individualistic as opposed to social or relational terms.

Both survey and interview data point to girl respondents being disinclined to cite their gender as a disadvantage in achieving success. In the survey, in relation to sources of occupational achievement, fully 92 per cent of girls indicated agreement with the statement that 'anyone can be successful as long as they are willing to work hard', while only 4 per cent felt that 'it's not what you know but who you know that gets you ahead' and 2 per cent that 'there is no point in trying because I'll never be successful'. Again in the interviews, after exploring their concepts of success, the students were asked whether or not they felt everyone had the same opportunity of becoming successful. The patterns of responses were similar for the two sexes with 39 per cent of girls replying 'yes, regardless', 44 per cent responding 'some better than others' and 17 per cent saying 'no, not always'. Those giving the first response were broadly adamant concerning the ability of individuals to achieve what they wanted through hard work and application. The second category tended to develop the point that opportunities were widely available but some individuals were better placed to take advantage of them, for example because of greater scholastic aptitude. The third category in fact tended to gravitate towards a similar point, for instance by drawing attention to individual 'handicaps' like not being intelligent enough to do well at school. Conventional sex-typing of occupations was not cited as a problem. On the other hand, three girls expressed the view that gender could even be turned to their advantage in present circumstances should they seek to enter what had previously been largely male areas of employment such as carpentry and the building trades.

Also taken up in interviews was the issue of what it takes to be successful. A classification of the main emphases of students' responses yielded the same rank order of items for the two sexes. 'Hard work' was cited by the largest proportion of respondents, 60 per cent, while 'a good education' came second with 24 per cent. This last was the main point of any real difference between the sexes for it was cited by 31 per cent of girls but only 19 per cent of boys. There were also less frequent references by both sexes to 'doing something you enjoy', 'being ambitious' and 'being encouraged'. However, the importance of 'having connections' was stressed by only one respondent. The overall tendency in discussion was thus again towards individualism this time combined with the culturally familiar theme of the efficacy of hard work.

The significance of social and extra-curricular activities

In this exploration of culture and aspirations, it is important to review briefly the sphere of students' extra-curricular involvements. A key reason why the latter is significant is that it provides a major context where pupils exercise choice and is therefore highly relevant to their outlook on, and motivation towards, their schooling.

Those pupils interviewed were asked about the number of activities of a school-based extra-curricular type in which they engaged. Overall, 31 per cent said they had two such activities, 10 per cent said one, but the clear majority, 59 per cent, indicated none. Involvement in sports teams was most often referred to but various other clubs (mainly of a non-academic kind) were also mentioned. In the survey the respondents were asked about their primary participation in clubs and societies in general (i.e. not just in school) and sports again proved to be the most prominent item but with a clear sex difference. Of the girls, 32 per cent were involved in sports, 15 per cent in social clubs, 15 per cent in various other types of associations and 4 per cent in academic or school-related clubs; as many as 34 per cent indicated no participation. The corresponding figures for the boys were 62 per cent sports, 5 per cent social clubs, 15 per cent other associations and 5 per cent academic or school related, with 14 per cent indicating no participation (a statistically different pattern at the 1% level). On a thematically related point the respondents were then asked to indicate their main (free time) interest and, as expected, there was again a clear sex difference, with 32 per cent of girls and 16 per cent of boys referring to socializing with friends, while 27 per cent of girls and 53 per cent of boys indicated an interest in a sport.

A number of tentative inferences may be drawn. The whole emphasis of these activities is on sports (both within and outside school) with the ratio of male to female involvement being about 2:1. (Boys almost invariably participated in sports teams; the girls were sometimes involved in other ways.) Evidently the provision of sports facilities and sporting opportunities was great. On the other hand, the low level of involvement in academic or school-related clubs may seem to suggest that few opportunities were available within the schools themselves. (A further possibility is that to participate in that way tends to attract the 'swot' label and is therefore avoided.) For whatever reason, there appeared to be rather few school-based initiatives to link from academic concerns to students' free-time interests. In addition, it seems fair comment that, although the interest in sport among girls is far from being negligible, the overall pattern of extra-curricular opportunities and facilities tends to reflect male rather than female interests.[26]

These data can usefully be considered in conjunction with the replies to a final question. The respondents were asked how they would like to be remembered after they had left school and the pattern of their replies revealed a striking sex difference. Fully 69 per cent of girls responded by saying that they wished to be remembered as good students, while a further 27 per cent said they wanted to be remembered as popular, and only 3 per cent as good athletes or sportswomen; 2 per cent gave other replies. On the other hand, among boys there were 36 per cent who wished to be remembered as popular, 31 per cent as athletes or sportsmen and only 23 per cent as good students; 11 per cent gave other replies (a significantly different pattern at the 1% level). The main tendency among girls was thus to respond in a way which was in harmony with the academic emphasis within school life. In contrast, on this evidence, rather more males were being drawn towards the auxiliary sporting side as against the mainline academic. That substantial numbers of students (but rather more males) put their emphasis on popularity may not be unexpected, but it is a further reminder of the importance of peer pressure which probably serves in this age group to accentuate rather than diminish the differing orientations of the two sexes towards school life. Hence these data provide additional support for the notion that it is more acceptable or approved for girls as opposed to boys to be 'swotty' or to be seen to be making a real effort to succeed academically. Allied to this, the academic side may be pursued more wholeheartedly by girls as a means of achievement because they lack an outlet equivalent in importance to that which sport represents for boys.

Conclusion

Initially an attempt was made to identify the way in which Welsh pupils conceptualized the peer groups within their schools. It emerged that students seemed to have rather limited freedom of movement within their broad groupings, which were based predominantly on the degree of commitment to the externally prescribed academic ethos of the school. This seemed to be the case for the three prominent categories of swots, rems and ordinary kids, while the only other significant dimension of involvement was that indicated by the 'sporty' identification. As regards sex differences it transpired that there were rather more girl 'swots' and relatively more boys found within the 'rem/waster' and 'sporty' categories. The implications of peer pressure for *differential* performance appeared to be in the direction of promoting female academic careers and male sporting involvement.

With the assistance of an analysis in terms of student types it was shown that girls tended to be higher overall aspirers in educational and occupational terms than boys. In addition there is evidence that females more often liked school a lot than did their male counterparts and more often positively embraced the central learning experience. Also striking, for both sexes, was the marked positive correlation between higher aspirations and a liking for school. In fact the predominant approach to education of both sexes can be fairly characterized as utilitarian, but, if anything, rather more girls than boys saw education as very important to their future. It was also noticeable that although there was a small, predominantly male, disaffected category with relatively low aspirations, hardly any students rejected school outright or in a way which would lead one to speak of an associated counter-school subculture.

In respect of future educational or vocational plans, even more girls than boys indicated an intention in the following year to embark upon GCE Advanced Level and beyond that to pursue a university education. Parental encouragement generally pointed in this same direction but, perhaps significantly, there were relatively more boys among the minority whose parents favoured their offspring finding a job in the near future. Nevertheless, the main interest was in the pursuance of careers requiring a substantial amount of formal education. That this was so often the case for girls contrasts with the earlier findings of McRobbie[27] and Holland[28] who describe females as often being straitjacketed by 'stereotypical' expectations. There is little evidence here of girls feeling conscious of formal barriers; indeed, in some cases there was even believed to be an advantage in terms of informal 'positive discrimination'.

Brown points to the possibility that in conditions of high

unemployment, education may be delegitimated for 'ordinary kids' given its failure to assist them to 'get on' in working-class terms.[29] In some respects the opposite appears to be happening in that, far from rejecting school, the majority – including relatively more girls – are embracing the notion of their own need for qualifications more strongly. This in turn, of course, generates its own set of problems. Given the likely availability of places in higher education, some of the young aspirants stand to be disappointed. Even more so does it seem probable that, if and when educationally qualified, large numbers will have their hopes for professional or semi-professional employment frustrated. Indeed, a majority of this sample expressed serious doubt about the achievement of their occupational aspirations. Nevertheless, on this evidence, the integration of GCE Ordinary Level and CSE into the GCSE system of examinations seems to have prolonged the 'warming up' process for a majority of pupils and it must therefore be the failure to achieve sufficiently high grades in GCSE or subsequently in GCE Advanced Level which performs for many the necessary 'cooling out' function.[30]

Although students differed in the extent of their aspirations, it seems that criteria of success were diffuse in nature and widely shared. Respondents of both sexes appeared to be at least as concerned with 'job satisfaction' and other qualitative considerations as they were with straightforward material advancement. This finding may help to counteract a materialistic stereotype. What was also striking, however, was the way in which success, and also the means of achieving it, were identified in individualistic terms, rather than incorporating the social or relational.

Evaluating this evidence in structuralist terms, there would seem to be forces in operation which resemble the 'correspondence principle' favoured by Bowles and Gintis.[31] That is not to suggest that the role of schools is to be seen as passive provider of a submissive and obedient workforce. Rather it is the strongly individualist and achievement-oriented element of capitalism, highlighted politically by the Thatcher/Major years, which seems to have found its way into the British school system through educational policy.[32] The individualist outlook would seem to have been adopted even by the working-class students of this sample and is manifested in the generally high level of their aspirations, which did not differ greatly from those of the middle class. Even more dramatic is the way in which female aspirations have risen to the level where they even begin to exceed those of males. There is no denying the point that since Turner provided his influential comparative analysis,[33] public sector education in this country has come to express some 'contest' principles in a way which resembles their operation in the USA and this substantially arises from a convergence on educational policies geared to the promotion of capitalistic action. This would seem to be an instance, therefore, where, far from the operation of capitalistic principles acting in a biased way against females, on the contrary, the persistent application, and working through, of those principles has been a powerful underlying factor promoting formal and ultimately substantive sexual equality.

A further intriguing suggestion arises from the evidence which has been presented. Sex differences were apparent in respect of the pursuance of extra-curricular activities; most notably, boys were more often involved in sport. No doubt too the choice of both timetabled and extra-curricular sports was heavily gendered. We have seen in addition that boys were more often classified by their peers as 'sporty' and more frequently wished to be remembered as good athletes or sportsmen. (The reader will hardly need reminding that prowess at rugby is in south Wales exemplary in relation to a prevalent conception of masculinity; in a wider UK context soccer and cricket, as well as rugby, are all significant in this respect.) This evidence regarding the place of sport may then appropriately be considered in conjunction with the recent phenomenon whereby female academic performance has overtaken male (at least up to the compulsory school-leaving age). The notion which inevitably suggests itself is that in conditions of equality of opportunity in respect of the academic curriculum, boys are under-performing academically partly because of the place of sport in prevailing conceptions of masculinity. By contrast, contest principles and contemporary conceptions of femininity seem to be serving schoolgirls well.

Notes

1 Dressel, B. M. and Startup, R. (1994) 'Peer group culture and pupil aspirations: a USA/UK and rural/urban comparison', *International Journal of Sociology and Social Policy*, Vol.14, 6/7, 51–69.
2 David, M. (1991) 'Comparisons of "educational reform" in Britain and the USA: a new era', *International Studies in Sociology of Education*, Vol.1, 87–109.

3 Welsh Office (1994) *Statistics of Education and Training in Wales: Schools, No. 2 1994*, Table 8.04 (Cardiff, Welsh Office).

4 Blackaby, D., Murphy, P. and Thomas, D. E. L. (1994) 'Wales: an economic survey', *Contemporary Wales*, Vol.7, 193.

5 Ibid., 181.

6 Central Advisory Council on Education (Wales) (1967) *Primary Education in Wales* (The Gittins Report) (London, HMSO).

7 Rees, G. and Rees, T. L. (1980) 'Educational inequality in Wales: some problems and paradoxes', in Rees, G. and Rees, T. L. (eds.) *Poverty and Social Inequality in Wales* (London, Croom Helm).

8 Istance, D. and Rees, G. (1994) 'Education and training in Wales: problems and paradoxes revisited', *Contemporary Wales*, Vol.7, 13.

9 Ibid., 16.

10 Turner, R. H. (1960) 'Sponsored and contest mobility and the school system', *American Sociological Review*, Vol.25, 855–67.

11 Hopper, E. (1971a) 'A typology for the classification of educational systems', in Hopper, E. (ed.) *Readings in the Theory of Educational Systems* (London, Hutchinson).

12 Coleman, J. S. (1961) *The Adolescent Society* (New York, Free Press); Cicourel, A. V. and Kitsuse, J. I. (1963) *The Educational Decision-Makers* (New York, Bobbs-Merrill).

13 Bowles, S. and Gintis, H. (1976) *Schooling in Capitalist America* (London, Routledge & Kegan Paul).

14 Willis, P. (1977) *Learning to Labour: How Working Class Kids Get Working Class Jobs*, (Farnborough, Saxon House).

15 See Bourdieu, P. and Passeron, J. C. (1977) *Reproduction: In Education, Society and Culture* (London, Sage); Bourdieu, P. (1986) *Distinction: A Social Critique of Judgements of Taste* (London, Routledge & Kegan Paul); Bourdieu, P. (1988) *Language and Symbolic Power* (Cambridge, Polity)

16 Brown, P. (1987) *Schooling Ordinary Kids: Inequality, Unemployment and the New Vocationalism* (London, Tavistock).

17 Willis, P. (1977) op. cit.

18 Brown, P. (1987) op. cit.

19 Brown, P. (1985) 'Schooling and the School/Post-School Transition in Urban South Wales', (University of Wales, Ph.D. thesis) Appendix.

20 Brown, P. (1987) op. cit., 69.

21 Ibid., Ch.4.

22 Cf. Brown, ibid., 87.

23 Ibid., 106.

24 Holland, J. (1988) 'Girls and occupational choice: in search of meaning', in Pollard, A., Purvis, J. and Walford, G. (eds.) *Education, Training and the New Vocationalism: Experience and Policy* (Milton Keynes, Open University Press).

25 See Turner, R. (1960) op. cit.

26 See Sutton, Hutson and Thomas in this volume.
27 McRobbie, A. (1978) `Working class girls and the culture of femininity', in Women's Studies Group, Centre for Contemporary Cultural Studies, *Women Take Issue: Aspects of Women's Subordination* (London, Hutchinson).
28 Holland, J. (1988) op. cit.
29 Brown, P. (1987) op. cit., 185.
30 Hopper, E. (1971b) `Appendix II: Educational systems and selected consequences of patterns of mobility and non-mobility in industrial societies: a theoretical discussion', in E. Hopper (ed.) *Readings in the Theory of Educational Systems* (London, Hutchinson).
31 Bowles, S. and Gintis, H. (1976) op. cit., 131.
32 David, M. (1991) op. cit., 109; Ball, S. J. (1993) 'Education markets, choice and social class', *British Journal of Sociology of Education*, Vol.14, 3–19.
33 Turner, R. (1960) op. cit.

6

Sex, lies and the PSE curriculum

LESLEY PUGSLEY

Growing up in south Wales in the 1950s as the child of working-class parents, in common with many of my contemporaries I lacked any formal sex education. It was considered neither 'necessary' nor 'nice' to talk about such matters and, in consequence, any sex education we received was gained during conversations with friends. Initially I recall sitting in a group outside the park keeper's hut on the local recreation ground, listening avidly, if somewhat disbelievingly, to various tales from older children about the mysteries of sex. Over time the location may have altered – the youth club, the patch of waste ground near the river, behind the tennis courts at the grammar school – however, the format and content was much the same, the stories were often wildly exaggerated and frequently highly inaccurate. It was not until some way into the 'swinging sixties' that I felt competent and confident enough to be able to dissociate the fantasies from the 'facts of life'.

Now in the mid-1990s, what do our daughters know about sex? What do they want to know? And who do they look to for their information? Are parents comfortable discussing issues such as contraception, masturbation and sexually transmitted diseases, with their daughters or with their sons for that matter? Do schools deal adequately with sex education? Are teenagers satisfied with the ways in which information and advice about sex and sexuality is transmitted to them? This chapter sets out to address some of these issues and does so with reference to a survey which was conducted with Year 12, lower-sixth pupils, in three comprehensive schools in south Wales.[1] The study was undertaken in order to determine the attitudes and opinions of young people, of both gender groups, in respect of the sex education which they had received to date. It also offers an analysis of the attitude of the Conservative government to the teaching of sex education in schools, as reflected by the education policy which has been installed over the past decade.

The moral crusade

'Surely school is not just text books, homework and exams? It must prepare us to live in the real world too.' This quote comes from a female pupil in the sixth form of a south Wales comprehensive school. Despite what conservative ideologies would have us believe, schools allow pupils to witness and experience at first hand the ways in which sex and sexuality influence and shape behaviour, conversation, attitudes, identities and relationships. Kelly suggests that such reality exists alongside 'the cautious inclusion or the deliberate exclusion of sexuality in the formal taught curriculum'.[2] So who is it that decides what our daughters should know about sex?

Issues of sexuality are guaranteed to attract media attention and stimulate public interest, indeed, Weeks states that 'few topics evoke so much anxiety and pleasure as the erotic possibilities of our bodies'.[3] Similarly, over the past two or three decades there has been both a political and social discourse surrounding education which has been and, continues to be, both vociferous and turbulent. Therefore any attempt to combine topics on sex with education ensures not only widescale debate, but banner headlines, which bring about outbreaks of rhetoric and moral panic as an automatic consequence.

During the 1980s, the high levels of teenage and schoolgirl pregnancy in England and Wales together with the HIV/AIDS pandemic, resulted in a dichotomy of political opinion. There was a recognition and acceptance by health professionals, educators and some politicians, of the vital need to provide an effective programme of sex and health education in schools as a means of protecting the young. However, in some areas a 'blame the victim' model emerged, which suggested that the perceived increase in levels of promiscuity among the young were directly attributable to progressive teaching methods and liberal ideologies.[4] The political emphasis of the 'New Right' began to dominate, and located the problem firmly within issues of self control, morality and family values.

The government began to put sex education within a legal framework in the 1986 Education Act[5] since this clearly stated that the responsibility for the formulation of a policy for sex education in schools lay with the individual governing bodies. Lay school governors were given discretionary powers to determine whether or not sex education should be taught and, where applicable, they could specify the inclusion or the exclusion of any topic areas. However, the Act provided a moral framework stating that any sex education which was provided should be given in a manner such as to have 'due regard to moral consideration and family life'. The Act further instructed governors to provide a written policy for sex education, if it were provided, but the research evidence indicates that many governing bodies, aware of the sensitivity of the subject area, preferred to avoid controversy and, in consequence, where statements did exist, they were very bland.[6]

The non-statutory guidelines on sex education issued by the DES in 1987 underlined the emphasis which was to be placed on morality, stressing that pupils should be helped to appreciate the benefits of a stable married family life. While it concluded that schools could not avoid tackling controversial issues such as contraception and abortion, it particularly stressed that in no circumstances should schools teach anything which might be seen to be presenting homosexuality as a 'norm'. Such caveats proved limiting for the provision of a comprehensive curriculum and served to create feelings of paranoia in all those associated with the provision and promotion of sex education. In consequence, many schools chose to shy away from 'difficult' areas of sex education and many topics were avoided or evaded in the classrooms. Such a climate served to undermine the attempts to provide a holistic approach to teaching the subject-matter in schools.

While the 1988 Education Reform Act[7] restated the role of the school governors in formulating sex-education policies, it attempted to curtail their discretionary powers somewhat by indicating that all pupils were to be taught topics necessary to comply with the Science syllabus. However, the National Curriculum which was installed by the Act provided for a core syllabus which resulted in the creation of a subject hierarchy. In consequence the personal and social education syllabus which contains sex-education programmes as an integral component has become marginalized. The low priority which schools now afford to the implementation of cross-curricula themes, has further ensured that sex education has become a very low-status subject.

Correspondingly, the increasing emphasis on a more academic

orientation to the school curriculum has ensured that those areas which would have included topics on sex and health education, such as 'Child Care' and 'Human Biology' no longer constitute 'approved courses of study'. However, statistics indicate that most of the unplanned or unwanted pregnancies are to be found within the lower socio-economic groups[8] and it is mainly children from within these groups who opt for the less academic subject choices in schools. Furthermore, studies have shown that working-class parents are less likely than those in the middle class to discuss sexual issues with their children.[9] For many pupils in these socio-economic groups the only opportunity which they have to receive a formalized sex education is through the school curriculum. Thus, for these pupils, the implications which are associated with the removal of such subjects from the syllabus are self-evident.

The Conservative government under the leadership of John Major has continued with considerable zeal the 'moral crusade' begun during the Thatcher era. The policies of the 'New Right' reflect an underlying fundamentalist Christian influence and demonstrate a commitment to a cultural restoration which can be seen to be reflected in the construct and content of the school curriculum. Ball suggests that within such an approach there is an identifiable 'regression to Victorianism'.[10]

Therefore, given the political climate which pervaded in the early part of the 1990s and the low status afforded to the topic of sex education as a consequence of the pressures on teaching staff to 'deliver' the National Curriculum, it was decided to implement an evaluative study of the sex education which had been offered to pupils in south Wales up until 1993.

The study

There have been a number of studies which have set out to determine the attitudes, experiences and behaviour patterns of teenagers in respect of issues associated with sex and sexuality. However, most of the data generated has come from studies conducted in England. Allen undertook a major survey for the Policy Studies Institute into the attitudes of parents and teenagers in three English cities[11] and Wyness looked at the ways in which parents and children accommodate 'the normalization of sex talk within the home'.[12] There has also been considerable research into unplanned and unwanted teenage pregnancies and teenage and schoolgirl mothers.[13] While Ford carried out a study of the socio-sexual lifestyles of young people in the south-west of England.[14]

Although Alison George specifically researched the social and cultural aspects of menstruation using Welsh women as her study group,[15] in the main the attitudes and experiences of teenagers in connection with issues of sexuality and sex education has been, and remains, a much-neglected and under-researched area in Wales. The research project described here sought to provide a small-scale study of young people in one, mainly English-speaking, area of south Wales in an attempt to rectify this omission. Nevertheless, there is still a desperate shortage of any data on teenage sexuality which looks specifically at both rural areas and the Welsh-speaking communities of Wales.

Three comprehensive schools in south Wales were selected for the study. A total of 120 pupils, forty from each of the three schools, were involved. All of the pupils were in Year 12, lower sixth forms of their schools. This cohort was selected because this year group is not entered for public examination so the research could slot into the lesson timetabled for Personal and Social Education without being disruptive to studies. A further consideration was that all the pupils involved in the study were over the age of sixteen and this avoided the need to obtain parental consent for their participation in the survey. Self-administered questionnaires (see Appendix 1) were completed by the pupils during lessons timetabled for PSE. Each of the pupils received an assurance as to the confidentiality of the study and participation in the survey was entirely voluntary.

An initial aim of the research had been to investigate the link between the religious identity of schools and the approach towards the teaching of the PSE curriculum. Accordingly, the schools selected represented varying religious affiliations.

Redstones School is a large co-educational local-authority-controlled comprehensive school situated in a city suburb of south Wales. Pupils attending the school come from a variety of homes since the catchment area serves a number of small, middle-class, private housing estates and also a medium-sized council-owned estate.

St Asaph is a medium-sized Church in Wales co-educational comprehensive located in a select middle-class suburb of the same city. As a voluntary-aided Church school, it too takes pupils from a wide catchment, however this area is delineated such that the majority of pupils come from the more prosperous middle-class areas of the city and its suburbs. The Cardinal Hume Tertiary College, also a co-educational school, serves as a Roman Catholic sixth form, receiving pupils from a number of Catholic comprehensive schools in and around the city. It has a number of pupils from non-Catholic backgrounds and is also located in a middle-class suburb. However, since it is the main Catholic tertiary college in the area, this school has the widest socio-economic mix of pupils because of the variety of feeder schools which it serves.

In the event, the religious identity of the school proved not to be significant. Neither the religious affiliation of the school, nor that of individual pupils, had any significant impact on the attitudes and opinions of young people with respect to sex and sexuality. As will be shown later in this chapter, it was gender which emerged as the important factor. Girls had very different opinions from boys about the quality of the sex education they had received in school, its relevance to their needs and life-styles and the topic areas which they would like covered within the PSE curriculum.

Whilst the major concern of the research was to investigate the attitudes and opinions of pupils, a secondary concern was to investigate parental attitudes to sex education and provision and to determine the extent of knowledge which parents had of the form and content of sex education programmes offered to their children in school. The relationship between home and school is an important dimension in understanding young peoples attitudes to sex education.

Passing the buck

The evidence from the study of parents (see Appendix 2) supported that of other researchers regarding the extent of parental support for the teaching of sex education in schools.[16] All of the parents in the survey (N = 40), thought that sex education should be taught in schools, although many were vague as to the actual individual practices in the schools which their own children attended. While the 1986 Act made it a legal requirement that all schools in which sex education was taught should have a written statement of policy, 71 per cent of parents surveyed were unaware of this and could not say if such a policy statement existed in their child's school. Only 58 per cent of parents were able to confirm that their child/children did receive some sex education in school. However, they were all unsure as to the nature and extent of the instruction provided or who actually taught the course.

Many parents admitted to feeling either embarrassed or inadequate when attempting to discuss issues related to sex with their children. These findings replicate those of earlier studies.[17] Other parents felt they 'were not qualified' to talk to their children about such topics. Although all the parents surveyed supported the idea of sex education as a school subject, half of them felt that a 'specialist' teacher was the best person to deal with the subject while the remainder expressed concerns about the possibility of individual teacher bias being translated into the presentation of certain topics thus allowing value judgements to interfere with the presentation of factual material. Twenty-three per cent of parents were concerned that sex education might be presented to children at either too early an age or stage in their development. These findings suggest a rather negative analysis of the professionalism of teachers on the part of the parents.

Particularly significant was that parental interest and involvement appeared to be so limited in what is a crucial area of education and one which has a tremendous impact on the physical and emotional well-being of both our daughters and our sons. In total, 55 per cent of parents who were surveyed failed to identify any specific topics which they felt should be covered in a sex education programme and 89 per cent did not signify any areas or issues which they felt should be specifically omitted from such courses. In the main, those parents who did respond to the question of areas of importance which they felt should be taught indicated that teenagers should learn about contraception and the transmission of HIV and AIDS.

Only one parent identified female assertiveness training as a useful and valid option for inclusion in a personal and social health education programme. It can be argued that an emphasis on the inclusion of teaching policies within the curriculum which are aimed at improving the self-confidence of young people and promoting a positive self-image among both gender groups would provide a significant contribution towards resolving many of the problems associated with the uncertainties and insecurities which teenagers constantly experience. Furthermore, a programme of assertiveness training for girls, provided as part of the formal curriculum within schools, could do much to address many of the gender stereotypical attitudes, assumptions and behaviour patterns which are a 'taken for granted' part of the socialization experiences of the young.

Whilst parents appeared in principle to support the idea of sex education in schools, many of their responses indicated a high degree of indifference, unconcern, embarrassment or ignorance with respect to the subject-matter covered during such lessons. This may be interpreted as an abrogation of responsibility for informing their children about sex onto teachers and schools. Alternatively it may reflect a lack of communication between home and school.

At the chalk face

Given the extent of the political rhetoric, the school practices and parental attitudes to sex education, what of the young people themselves? How did the pupils evaluate the sex education they received and what needs did they identify?

The overwhelming majority of pupils (96 per cent) were in complete agreement that information about sex and sexuality was an important part of their overall education. However, 78 per cent of girls compared to only 31 per cent of boys rated it as essential. No girls, but a minority of boys (15 per cent) considered sex education in school to be a 'waste of time'.

Gendered differences were also evident when pupils were asked specifically about the relevance of the subject-matter which was covered in their sex education lessons. Only 8 per cent of boys and 2 per cent of girls indicated that they had found the information *very* relevant to their needs or life-styles. Overall, 38 per cent of the pupils had found the lessons *quite* relevant, but this figure was lower for boys (34 per cent) than girls (42 per cent). Twenty-seven per cent of boys and 33 per cent of the girls indicated that the lessons were *not at all* relevant to their needs.

Girls were evidently more able to recognize in principle the importance of a fully comprehensive programme of sex education than were their male counterparts. They were also more discriminatory than boys since they were able to acknowledge that the existing approaches and formats were often not particularly relevant or appropriate and in consequence frequently failed to address their needs.

Pupils were also asked where, ideally, they felt it would be best to receive sex education. Fifty-one per cent felt that it was best to receive sex education from a combination of sources, including the home and school. Again attitudes were gendered, since when asked to indicate a preference, nearly 60 per cent of the girls indicated a preference for receiving information from the home and in particular from the mother. This was particularly the case in respect of information and advice about menstruation and reproduction. Fewer than half the girls surveyed (40 per cent) felt that schools should be totally responsible for sex education as compared with 60 per cent of the boys who felt that schools were the best place to learn about sex and sexuality. When asked where they had actually obtained their information the students indicated all the major sources which they felt had been instrumental in providing them with some sex education. These sources included the home, school, friends and the media. Again there were gender differences. Thirty-six per cent of girls and 27 per cent of boys cited the home as a source of information while 45 per cent of girls compared with only 26 per cent of boys cited the school.

Most significant was the use of friends as a source of information. The figures revealed that the informal transmission of knowledge, via peer relationships, played an almost equally significant role in providing sex education as did the more formal curriculum transmitted within the school and the home. In total, 42 per cent of the female pupils and 26 per cent of males indicated that they had received information from their peer group. In contrast, almost equal numbers of girls and boys, 23 per cent and 21 per cent respectively, indicated that they had received information about sex from the media. Whilst the media in general was a source of information for both girls and boys, magazines were clearly more important to girls. Although there are magazines aimed specifically at the young male market, none of the boys who responded to the survey indicated that they saw magazines as a source of information concerning sex.

Teen magazines influenced girls in shaping their approach to personal relationships and premarital sex. A number of the girls indicated that they felt magazines promoted the idea that it was 'OK' to have sex with a boy if you 'loved him'. However, only one girl reported that magazine articles had influenced her to feel that there was no need to 'give in' to a boy and engage in premarital activity if that was not what she wanted. A brief survey of some of the more popular magazines aimed specifically at the young female adolescent market revealed that some of the content was focused towards issues associated with sexual attitudes and behaviours among young people.

The style and presentation of such literature varied enormously, sometimes presenting an over romanticised approach to the subject.

A very small percentage of the magazines presented a somewhat aggressive approach to certain aspects of sexuality with an inference that the most important consideration in sexual activity should be self-gratification. In the main, however, they adopted a responsible approach to the subject-matter and presented information on a wide range of topics covering practical issues such as contraception, sexuality, sexually transmitted diseases, and providing the addresses of clinics, counselling centres and help lines. Increasingly it would seem that the popular press are aware of the trend for young people to look to sources other than the home and school for information and advice and they are responding to this need. In fact, the Family Planning Association booklet of sexuality includes a section by the author of a popular teenage magazine advice column.

Overall, girls seem to be more methodical in their quest for sex education. They seek out information from a wider variety of sources. Boys on the other hand appear to adopt a much more 'casual' approach to the acquisition of the 'facts of life'. Over a quarter of those boys who were surveyed (27 per cent) indicated that they 'had just picked up' their knowledge. This may suggest a lack of any systematic effort on their part to ensure that what information they had received was either comprehensive or accurate.

The students were also asked what sources they would use if they needed advice or help with any sexual or personal issues. Peer influence was clearly evident since the majority of pupils said they would choose to ask their friends for help. However, this figure was much higher for girls than boys. Almost 80 per cent of girls said they would use friends as a source of advice compared with 51 per cent of boys. For both girls and boys, parents were seen as a second option and just over a quarter of the pupils said they would go to them. Of the teenagers who expressed a preference to speak to one or other parent, 60 per cent indicated that it would be the mother they would speak to while 37 per cent specifically noted that they could not talk to their fathers about sex-related issues.

Less than 3 per cent of pupils said that they would choose to talk to a schoolteacher about personal problems and 70 per cent of students specifically indicated that they would *not* want to talk to teachers. Interestingly it was the girls who were far more reluctant to speak to teachers about personal matters than boys. Eighty-three per cent of girls compared with 56 per cent of boys said that they would be unwilling to use any members of staff as a source of advice. It may be significant to note that in all three schools the gender balance of teachers was very heavily male orientated and in two of the schools the responsibility for teaching sex education rested with the class tutors, only two of whom were female, one being a middle-aged spinster. The third school, which taught sex education through the religious and moral studies department, also had a predominantly male staff. Both the head of department and the deputy were men and the only female teacher was again a middle-aged 'Miss'. This may well be a consideration when pupils, particularly girls, are looking for someone to confide in.

Pupils were also asked to identify 'gaps' in the programmes of sex education which they had received in school and to make suggestions concerning possible improvements. Previous studies have found that for most young heterosexuals the major focus of concern is the risk of unwanted pregnancy.[18] Therefore, it was interesting to note that in this study while contraception was a commonly identified topic area about which pupils suggested they wanted more information, they were also anxious to receive information about sexually transmitted diseases. Again these concerns and needs were gender differentiated: 77 per cent of girls compared with 55 per cent of boys wanted more information about sexually transmitted diseases and HIV and AIDS. Forty-three per cent of girls compared with only 23 per cent of boys indicated the need for further contraceptive advice.

Do we conclude from these figures that our daughters are concerned with these issues to a greater extent than our sons because the implications associated with unprotected sex are greater for them? Or is it that young women have begun to recognize and acknowledge that it is they who will ultimately need to accept the responsibility for the protection of both partners and the prevention of unwanted pregnancies in any heterosexual encounters?

Girls were also more concerned than boys to receive information on emotional issues with the figures being 49 per cent and 28 per cent respectively. However, slightly more boys (26 per cent) than girls (21 per cent) expressed a need for advice about physical concerns with topics ranging from acne to the size of genitalia.

All pupils expressed a preference for sex education to be taught in mixed rather than single-sex groups and all indicated that they were concerned to have information presented to them in a more interesting and up-to-date manner. Twenty-seven per cent suggested that lessons should include more informal discussion with group and forum debates to allow a more relaxed exchange of ideas and information. Over a third of all students said that they would welcome the opportunity to hear guest speakers who had specific expertise in areas related to sex. All the respondents expressed considerable dissatisfaction with the way in which they had been taught to date and many of the young people expressed the sentiment that the instruction which they received was 'far too little, far too late'. This survey thus supports the findings of other research in this area in suggesting that schools seemed to avoid or evade many of the more contentious issues and subject areas which often include topics which are of the greatest concern to the young.[19] It can be suggested that the approach to the teaching of sex education and the consequent disaffection can be directly attributed to the low status afforded to a personal and social curriculum by schools.

From the evidence of this study it would appear that girls are becoming increasingly aware of the importance of sex education. They are appreciative of the necessity to take full control of their own lives and accept that they may need to be the dominant partner in so far as safe sexual practices are concerned. Their quest for information and their identification of perceived need bears witness to this. But girls must seek to achieve these goals within a still prevailing structure of traditional sexual attitudes and codes of behaviour. Delamont refers to 'folk models and myths' transmitted through youth culture[20] and it is widely acknowledged that a sexual code exists within schools which pupils adopt in order to identify, via a series of covert messages, 'who likes who'!

To be accepted into their peer group, pupils need to successfully negotiate this code, but they must also be aware of and conform to the double standard frequently associated with sexual conduct. A majority of pupils apply moral judgements to sexual attitudes and activities which allow them to make distinctions between 'nice girls' and 'slags'.[21] These, male-owned distinctions are well known to the female pupils in the schools who accept them and seem prepared to go to extremes to avoid 'having a reputation'. Such avoidance behaviour involves the girls in self-imposed sanctions in their styles of dress, their make-up, their use of 'bad' language and their sexual conduct.

One of the strategies commonly used by boys to identify 'slags' is the degree of familiarity which girls admit to in respect of issues concerning contraception and contraceptive use. If a girl appears to have a wide knowledge of contraceptive devices and their use, boys may consider this tantamount to an admission of sexual experience. Such 'evidence' of promiscuity would immediately result in the girl being labelled a 'slag' or a 'tart'. For a girl to carry a supply of condoms or to instigate any suggestion that they should be used during sexual intercourse would be considered to be the actions of an 'easy lay'; many girls seemingly run the risks associated with unwanted pregnancy or sexually transmitted disease, rather than chance being labelled as a 'slut'.[22]

The ready acceptance by both gender groups of the double standards which are associated with sexual activity must be addressed and countered through social education. Labelling as 'promiscuous' any girl who chooses to adopt the same approach to sexual encounters as her male 'stud' counterpart must be shown to be not only unjust, but unrealistic. Girls need to be allowed the freedom to challenge such traditional sexual stereotyping since the evidence from this study indicates quite clearly that it is they who are the more concerned and the more enquiring about sex education. Their responses suggest that they are aware of the dangers and anxious to take more of the 'responsibility' within relationships, but they are constrained by the imposition of a double standard of sexual conduct.

Both gender groups need to accept that carrying a condom does not mean that a girl is automatically going to say 'yes' to any boy who asks. Rather what such a practice does is to provide her with a choice, and should she decide to say 'yes' then she will not run the risk of either an unwanted pregnancy or a sexually transmitted disease. Such a radical change of attitude can only be encouraged and developed if there are opportunities for open debates of topics related to sex and sexuality set within the context of a comprehensive programme of sex education within schools.

Conclusion

From the evidence of this and a number of other studies,[23] it is apparent that both parents and pupils are aware of the importance of sex education. However, there appears to be a barrier to the extent to which 'formal' sex education is being provided within the context of the home. While parents feel that they should be involved in telling their children about reproduction and sex, they are often 'intimidated' by the thought of engaging in any formal discussion with them and would prefer to abrogate the responsibility to the school. Similarly, while 60 per cent of the girls surveyed would ideally like to get advice and information from the home, and especially the mother, there are obvious barriers to communication since the majority indicated that they were often more comfortable approaching their peers when they wanted advice. Many parents are unclear as to the exact content of the sex education curriculum provided for their children. This study further indicates that parents and pupils place differing degrees of emphasis on the content of sex education programmes. Parents seem to be almost completely in agreement that the curriculum should cover the 'mechanics' of sex. They want their children to be taught 'the facts': reproduction, contraception, AIDS and HIV and other sexually transmitted diseases. However, in contrast, many of the teenagers surveyed, whilst admitting the need for such factual information, were also anxious to receive advice and guidance about emotional and physical issues.

The role of the school in promoting sex education to facilitate the healthy and well-informed development of the young is vital and inevitably the burden of this responsibility will lie within the pastoral care programme. The present government has adopted an increasingly moralizing stance with regard to the teaching of sex education in schools. Right-wing influences have resulted in the formulation and installation of legislation which has had serious implications for the transmission of knowledge through the personal and social education curriculum in schools. Such determination by government to pontificate and prescribe the formulation of sex education programmes for schools serves merely to present the young with a censored account of the 'real world'.

There is a need to improve both the quality and range of sex education offered in schools. The findings of this study indicate high levels of pupil dissatisfaction with current teaching programmes which are clearly failing to address their needs. This may continue to be the case unless the subject area is afforded much higher status within the curriculum hierarchy. It is evident that gender is a powerful and significant factor in determining the needs, attitudes and beliefs of the young in respect of issues of sexuality. Therefore, efforts must be made to devise a 'gender conscious' curriculum aimed at addressing those powerful 'folk models' which do much to prohibit the successful dissemination of information among young people. Delamont has suggested that the use of TV 'soaps' could be one possible way forward in attempting to address the problems of stereotypical gender roles.[24] Such a model could perhaps be applied to the teaching of personal and social education in schools since it is apparent that there is a definite need for a more modern 'youth friendly' approach if its messages are to have the desired impact on teenagers.

The study indicates that a much higher profile needs to be afforded to the whole area of sex education and personal relationships provided within the school curriculum. Teaching needs to incorporate a variety of styles and to utilize a range of resources to allow for a comprehensive dissemination of information about issues such as contraception, physical and emotional development and sexuality and matters related to HIV and AIDS. The crucial role of the school in preventing the spread of HIV and AIDS has been noted by Rogers who argues that 'education is the only means of preventing infection'.[25] To this end the personal and social education curriculum in schools is vital in the transmission of factual information in a format which is readily understood by pupils.

Sexuality raises a whole host of contentious issues for the young. To allow that our children should receive either a false or a censored account of the 'facts of life' is an abuse of their trust. Our daughters and sons neither want, nor deserve that they should receive their sex education 'behind the bike sheds'. They should and must be allowed access to a well prepared and presented programme of sex education throughout their school careers. This study has demonstrated the ways in which girls are seeking to develop new attitudes and behaviours but they are currently struggling to do so within a context of constraints. Girls are attempting to assimilate knowledge about sex and confront the issues associated with sexuality and sex education in a mature way. Yet they are having to contend with the traditional sexual stereotypes, the reluctance on the part of parents to provide a home-based context of sex education, and the inadequacies of formal educational provision

The 'real world' which one female pupil identified, presents both our daughters and our sons with myriad options and dilemmas in respect of their sexuality and sexual behaviour. Surely then, there is also an obligation to ensure that all aspects of sex education are clearly and comprehensively presented such that both gender groups are allowed the opportunity to make rational, informed decisions in this, as in all other aspects of their lives. Sex education must be seen as a vital and integral part of the school curriculum for all children.

The present policy which dictates the shape of the PSE programme is firmly rooted in Victorian values and this has ensured that sex education is taught within a prescriptive, moralistic and moralizing framework. Such an approach is counterproductive and will ensure that as a consequence our daughters and our sons will be denied access to vital areas of information both about sex and their own sexuality. Furthermore, their moral, physical, and emotional development will be confined and constrained within a narrow framework of gendered stereotype and expectation.

Our daughters have indicated quite firmly that they are willing and indeed anxious to take control of their own lives in respect of their sexual behaviour and physical well-being. They recognize that sex education is the key which will allow them to do this and they want up-to-date information presented in a clear and easily accessible format in order that they can make rational, educated choices. We cannot allow their requests to continue to go unanswered. We need to adopt a comprehensive approach to the transmission of sexual knowledge in order that a critique of 'far too little – far too late' can no longer be applied to sex education in Wales.

Notes

1 Pugsley, L. A. (1993) 'Sex, Lies and the PSE Curriculum' (University of Wales Cardiff, unpublished undergraduate dissertation).
2 Kelly, L. (1992) 'Not in front of the children' in Arnot, M. and Barton, L. (eds.) *Voicing Concerns. Sociological Perspectives on Contemporary Education Reforms* (Oxford, Triangle).
3 Weeks, J. (1985) *Sexuality and its Discontent* (London, Routledge and Kegan Paul).
4 Gillick *v.* West Norfolk and Wesbech AHA & the DHSS (1986).
5 Department of Education and Science/Welsh Office (1986) *Education Act* (No 2), 1986c (London, HMSO).
6 Allen, I. (1987) *Education in Sex and Personal Relationships*, PSI Report No.665. (Dorset, Blackmore); and Peckham, S. (1992) *Unplanned Pregnancy and Teenage Pregnancy* (Southampton, Institute for Health Policy Studies, Southampton University Press).
7 Department of Education and Science/Welsh Office (1988) *Education Reform Act* (London, HMSO).
8 OPCS (1991b) *Statistics on Unplanned and Unwanted Pregnancy* (London, HMSO).

[9] Farrell, C. (1978) *My Mother Said* (London, Routledge and Kegan Paul) cites studies by the Newsons (1968), Douglas (1964) and Gill Reid and Smith (1974).

[10] Ball, S. (1993) *Education Reform. A Critical and Post-structural Approach* (Buckinghamshire, Open University Press).

[11] Allen, I. (1987) op. cit.

[12] Wyness, M. G. (1992) 'Schooling and the normalisation of sex talk within the home' in the *British Journal of Sociology of Education* Vol.13, No. 1, pp. 89–103.

[13] Dawson, N. (1987) 'In a Class of Their Own: A Study of School Girl Pregnancy and Motherhood' (University of Bristol, unpublished M.Ed. thesis); and Dawson, N. (1993) 'The Decision-Making Processes and personal Constructs of Pregnant Schoolgirls and Schoolgirl Mothers' (University of Bristol, unpublished Ph.D. thesis); and Miles, M. (1979) *Pregnant at School* (London, National Council for One-Parent Families).

[14] Ford, N. (1991) *The Socio-sexual Lifestyles of Young People in the South West of England* (Exeter University, Institute of Population Studies).

[15] George, A. (1989) 'Social and Cultural Aspects of Menstruation: an Ethnographic Analysis.' (University of Wales, Cardiff, unpublished Ph.D. thesis).

[16] Allen, I. (1987) op. cit.
Farrell, C. (1978) op. cit.

[17] Dallas, D. (1972) *Sex Education in School and Society* (Hove, King, Thorne & Stace).

[18] Wright, D. (1993) 'Constraints or cognition? Young men and safer heterosexual sex' in Aggleton, P., Davies, P. and Hart, G. (eds.) *Aids: Facing The Second Decade* (London, Falmer). Also Ford, N.(1991) op. cit.

[19] Taylor, N. and Brierley, D. (1992) 'The impact of the law on the development of a sex education programme at a Leicester comprehensive school', in *Pastoral Care*, March 1992; Peckham, S. (1992) op. cit.; Allen, I. (1987) op. cit.

[20] Delamont, S. (1990) *Sex Roles and the School* (London, Routledge).

[21] Lees, S. (1986) *Losing Out* (London, Heinemann) and Willis, P. (1977) *Learning to Labour: How Working Class Kids Get Working Class Jobs* (London, Saxon House).

[22] For further evidence on this point see Hilary Yewlett's chapter in this volume (Ch.9)

[23] Farrell, C. (1978) op. cit.; Allen, I. (1987) op cit.; Pugsley, L. (1993) op. cit.

[24] Delamont, S. (1990) op. cit.

[25] Rogers, R. (1989) *HIV and AIDS. What Every Tutor Needs to Know* (London, Longman).

Appendix 1
QUESTIONNAIRE: SEX EDUCATION (PUPILS)

AGE: YEARS   MONTHS
SEX: MALE [   ]   FEMALE [   ]
MOTHER'S OCCUPATION:
FATHER'S OCCUPATION:
NUMBER AND AGES OF OTHER CHILDREN IN THE FAMILY:
YOUR POSITION IN THE FAMILY:

1. Do you think sex education is:
    a. Useful   [   ]
    b. Essential   [   ]
    c. Waste of time   [   ]
    d. Don't know   [   ]

2. Where do you think sex education should be taught?
    a. At home   [   ]
    b. At school   [   ]
    c. In church   [   ]
    d. Combination of sources   [   ]
    e. Elsewhere   [   ] Please specify
    f. Don't know   [   ]

3. Where did you obtain your sex education?
    a. At home   [   ]
    b. From school lessons   [   ]
    c. From church   [   ]
    d. From friends   [   ]
    e. From the media TV/magazine   [   ]
    f. Combination of sources   [   ]
    g. Just picked it up   [   ]
    h. Don't know   [   ]

4. Do you think sex education lessons should be taught in school?
    a. More often   [   ]
    b. Less often   [   ]
    c. As they are   [   ]
    d. Not at all   [   ]
    e. Don't know   [   ]

5. Do you think sex education should be timetabled and examined to GCSE like English or Maths?
    a. Yes   [   ]
    b. No   [   ]
    c. Don't know   [   ]

6. Should sex education in school be taught?
    a. By the form teacher   [ ]
    b. By the science teacher   [ ]
    c. By a specialist teacher   [ ]
    d. By an outside 'expert'   [ ]
    e. By a priest   [ ]
    f. By a combination of people   [ ]
    g. Don't know   [ ]

7. Has the sex education you have received in school been
    a. Very relevant to your needs   [ ]
    b. Quite relevant   [ ]
    c. Not very relevant   [ ]
    d. Not at all relevant   [ ]
    e. Don't know   [ ]

8. Who would you ask for advice on sexual or personal matters?
    a. Parent   [ ]
    b. Teacher   [ ]
    c. Friend   [ ]
    d. Other   [ ] Specify
    e. No one   [ ]
    f. Don't know   [ ]

9. Who would you *not* want to discuss any personal or sexual matters with?
    a. Parent   [ ]
    b. Teacher   [ ]
    c. Friend   [ ]
    d. Other   [ ] Specify
    e. Happy to confide in anyone   [ ]

10. Is your present knowledge of sex
    a. As complete as you want   [ ]
    b. Less than you would like   [ ]
    c. Don't know   [ ]

11. Given the choice, which, if any, of the following would you want to receive lessons/more information on. (You may indicate more than one topic.)
    a. Contraception   [ ]
    b. HIV/Aids   [ ]
    c. Emotional issues   [ ]
    d. Physical issues   [ ]
    e. Other   [ ] Please specify
    f. None   [ ]

12. Would you prefer to have PSE lessons in single-sex groups for:
    a. All topics   [ ]
    b. Some topics   [ ] Specify
    c. Prefer mixed group   [ ]
    d. Don't know   [ ]

13. Has any information you have received to date altered your attitudes to pre-marital sex?
    a. Yes   [ ]
    b. No   [ ]
    c. Don't know   [ ]

If you answered b. or c. go to question 15.

14. If you answered Yes/a. to question 13, what information was it, where did it come from and how did it affect you. Please specify.

15. In what way, if any, would you like sex education lessons to be altered in school?
    a. More up to date   [ ]
    b. More detailed   [ ]
    c. More varied   [ ]
    d. Don't know   [ ]
    e. They are alright as they are [ ]

16. Some schools are considering installing condom machines in the sixth-form lavatories. Do you think this is:
    a. Essential in all schools [ ]
    b. A good idea   [ ]
    c. Not a good idea   [ ]
    d. Don't know   [ ]

17. If condom machines were installed in schools, in the sixth-form areas, should they be:
    a. In the boys' lavatory   [ ]
    b. In the girls' lavatory   [ ]
    c. In both lavatories   [ ]
    d. Elsewhere   [ ]
    e. They should not be in schools [ ]

18. Would a condom machine in a school
    a. Encourage more promiscuity   [ ]
    b. Encourage more responsibility [ ]

c. Just be a laugh   [ ]
d. Don't know   [ ]

19. There is far too much media attention given to sex-related matters.
    a. Strongly agree   [ ]
    b. Agree   [ ]
    c. Neutral   [ ]
    d. Disagree   [ ]
    e. Strongly disagree   [ ]

20. Whatever information/advice is given, teenagers will still behave the way they choose.
    a. Strongly agree   [ ]
    b. Agree   [ ]
    c. Neutral   [ ]
    d. Disagree   [ ]
    e. Strongly disagree   [ ]

21. Could YOU suggest any ways in which sex education could be taught, to make it more relevant/useful to young people? e.g., discussion groups, guest speakers.

Appendix 2
SEX EDUCATION: QUESTIONNAIRE FOR PARENTS

THESE QUESTIONS RELATE TO CHILDREN IN SECONDARY EDUCATION ONLY:

NUMBER OF CHILDREN:
                SEX:

TYPE OF SCHOOL: e.g. private school, church school. Please specify FOR EACH CHILD.

1. Is the teaching of sex education compulsory in all secondary schools?
    a. Yes   [ ]
    b. No   [ ]
    c. Don't know   [ ]

2. Do you think sex education should be taught in schools?
    a. Yes   [ ]
    b. No   [ ]
    c. Don't know   [ ]
If you answered No to question 2, go to question 4.

3. If Yes to question 2. Who should teach the subject?
   - a. The form teacher [ ]
   - b. A specialist teacher [ ]
   - c. An outside expert [ ]
   - d. A combination of teacher and expert [ ]
   - e. Priest or religious leader [ ]
   - f. Don't know [ ]
   - g. Other [ ] Please specify

4. Does your child's/children's school have a policy for sex education?
   - a. Yes a written policy [ ]
   - b. Yes, but not written down [ ]
   - c. No [ ]
   - d. Don't know [ ]

If you answered Yes/a. Have you seen a copy?

Yes [ ]   No   [ ]

5. Does your child/ren receive sex education in school? Please specify for each child.
   - a. Yes [ ]
   - b. No   [ ]
   - c. Don't know [ ]

6. Are you concerned that sex education might be taught
   - a. At too early an age [ ]
   - b. With the teacher's biased opinion [ ]
   - c. In a way objectionable to you [ ]
   - d. Not concerned at the teaching method [ ]
   - e. Other [ ] Please specify

7. Are there any particular topics you would like the school to cover in sex education classes?
   - a. Yes [ ] Please specify
   - b. No [ ]
   - c. Don't know [ ]

8. Are there any particular topics you would not wish to be covered?

   - a. Yes [ ] Please specify
   - b. No [ ]
   - c. Don't know [ ]

9. Some schools are proposing the introduction of condom machines in the sixth-form areas, do you think this is:

    a.   Encouraging promiscuous behaviour [ ]
    b.   Encouraging a responsible attitude [ ]
    c.   A waste of money [ ]
    d.   Just a trendy idea [ ]
    e.   Don't know [ ]

10. If your child's/children's school were to propose the introduction of condom machines in the sixth-form lavatories, would you:

    a.   Be in favour [ ]
    b.   Be against it [ ]
    c.   Not mind either way [ ]
    d.   Don't know [ ]

11. There is far too much media attention focused on sex-related matters.

    a.   Strongly agree [ ]
    b.   Agree [ ]
    c.   Neutral [ ]
    d.   Disagree [ ]
    e.   Strongly disagree [ ]

12. Whatever information/advice teenagers receive, they will behave as they choose.

    a.   Strongly agree [ ]
    b.   Agree [ ]
    c.   Neutral [ ]
    d.   Disagree [ ]
    e.   Strongly disagree [ ]

PLEASE INDICATE WITH A X IN THE BOX [ ] THE ANSWER YOU FEEL IS MOST APPROPRIATE.

ARE YOU NOW, OR HAVE YOU EVER BEEN, A SCHOOL GOVERNOR?

    YES [ ]   NO [ ]

AGE: 30–45   [ ]
        45–55   [ ]
        55+   [ ]

SEX: MALE [ ]   FEMALE [ ]

OCCUPATION: SELF

OCCUPATION: PARTNER

THANK YOU FOR TAKING THE TIME TO COMPLETE THIS QUESTIONNAIRE.

7

Take Our Daughters to Work: A positive action for some schoolgirls in Wales

JANE SALISBURY

Introduction

From behind his desk at the front of the class Mr Reers,[1] the careers teacher, carefully enunciates the title of the unit pupils are going to study today: 'What sort of person am I? Strengths, weaknesses, skills and abilities.' He asks the Year 10 class for hush several times, and continues when it's quiet:

> We've looked at the choices that face you next year. Now before we can make correct decisions we all need to know ourselves. So today we're going to do some *self-analysis*. You're going to read through these hand-outs [holds a deep bunch of photocopied notes in the air and proceeds to give them out as he explains] and you're going to answer honestly the questions. [Students flick through the handouts and teacher directs their attention to page 17 on *health*. He goes on to stress the importance of self-knowledge in relation to health, skills and abilities and he then gives *two* examples of occupations where health matters:]
> Imagine if I wanted to be a *Fireman*? What if I suffered from dizziness? [Chorus of voices saying things like: 'Sir you wouldn't be able to do the job' and 'Not safe Sir'.]
> That's right. You've all got the sense to see that a fireman can't have problems with dizziness or heights. Good.
> [Two boys in front of me are whispering about an episode of HTV's *Peak Practice* in which a fireman tried to hide the fact that he was ill with tinnitus and couldn't balance etc . . .] Teacher interrupts:
> Pay attention now because you've got to be perfectly realistic with yourselves. Let's take another example – What if I was *colour blind*? [Pauses whilst class think about this question. One boy adjacent to me whispers to his male seat mate, 'How do you know if you're colour blind?'

His mate shrugs shoulders and they don't ask this of their teacher.] Well you can't become a *policeman* if you are colour blind. So you can see that this *self-analysis* [emphasizes phrase] is very important indeed.
[Class are now reading the health questions and getting out pencil cases etc. Teacher looks at watch and flicks through the hand-out and directs pupils to begin.]
    I think we'd better make a start – there's a lot for you to think about here which will help you make an *informed decision* [emphasizes phrase].
              (Fieldnote extracts, Year 10 careers lesson, 16.2.95.)

Readers might be somewhat surprised to discover that the fieldnote extract presented here is not qualitative data collected in the 1970s, but describes a careers lesson I observed in a co-educational comprehensive school in south Wales at the beginning of 1995! The fieldnotes derive from a *single* careers lesson with *one* Year 10 class, and they capture the work of *one* teacher – as such it would be foolhardy to over-generalize from them. However, set against the school's own rigorous equal opportunities policy – a detailed ten-page script specifying the duties and responsibilities of deputies, heads of year, publication writers, work experience co-ordinators, and subject teachers – the careers teacher appeared to lack awareness.

It is agreed practice at this school that we will:
    As part of normal lesson preparation consider action necessary to counter any stereotyping of material.
    As part of normal lesson conduct, challenge any unfair actions, gestures, statements or words, reporting to Head of Department or Head of Year if necessary.
    Ensure pupils are aware of the wide range of traditional and non-traditional jobs which suit their particular skills and abilities.
              (Extracts from school policy document on equal opportunities)

The school in which this lesson took place had developed a detailed equal opportunities policy during 1990 and like other secondary schools in England and Wales the impetus to do so came from teacher interest groups, the criteria set out by the Training and Vocational Education Initiative (TVEI), and the local education authority (LEA).[2]

A number of us worked extremely hard to develop a policy with clear guidelines on its delivery, implementation and in particular we took pains to emphasize the *collective* responsibility [. . .] every pupil and every staff member ideally should be involved in working at the policy.
              (Female deputy headteacher and co-ordinator of equal opportunities)

It appears then, from the interview, documentary and observational data gathered at this south Wales comprehensive school, that Mr Reers, whose careers lesson opened this chapter, is working in a 'vacuum'. The hidden curriculum was operating in this lesson in which both occupational examples provided for pupils were gendered. A more 'inclusive' message might have been given to the class had the careers teacher used 'police officer', 'fire fighter', 'fire officer' or 'fire crew'.

The decision to open the chapter in this way was made for a number of reasons. I hoped to show that pupils at school are still exposed to lessons riddled with harmful and limiting messages. Further, I wanted to provide readers with a 'scene' from which they can make sense of the remaining sections of the chapter which explore a recent, national, positive action initiative for girls' careers education.

The empirical material presented in this chapter is drawn from a case study carried out as part of a large-scale research project on 'Educational Reforms and Gender Equality in Schools'.[3] In March 1994 the Equal Opportunities Commission (EOC) funded a research project to assess the development of gender equality in schools in England and Wales over the decade 1984–94.[4] The research design involved identifying important patterns and trends and discovering how the education reforms of the late 1980s and early 1990s had strengthened or interrupted previous trends and/or generated new ones. Data collection was organized at a number of different levels: meta-analysis of sets of statistical examination data for the period; questionnaire surveys to LEAs and samples of schools and case studies of policy and practices in eight selected LEAs. This chapter draws upon the data collected for a case study of one LEA in south Wales. Qualitative research methods including interviews, participant and non-participant observation and documentary analysis were employed over a six-month period in which the 'fieldwork' was carried out.[5]

'The preparation for adult life', already a matter of concern and policy-making for the 1990s[6] was adopted as one of the key themes for the EOC research project.[7] It is this theme which is explored here. How schools educate girls in employment and family life, how they approach careers advice and work experience are touched upon in the following pages.

A brief discussion of girls and women in Wales follows. Readers will then be introduced to the work of the charity 'Our Daughters' and their 'flagship initiative', the 'Take Our Daughters to Work' (TODTW, 1995) scheme. How this national project is interpreted in one Welsh county is then described. The voices and views of a number of key protagonists are used to portray the event. Later sections address ways in which schoolgirls in Wales can 'explore tomorrow's choices'.[8]

The section below provides brief details about girls' achievement and women's employment in Wales in order to contextualize and set the scene for the later empirical sections of the chapter.

Setting the scene: Girls' education and women's employment in Wales

Girls in Wales continue to achieve better results in a wider range of subjects than boys in public examinations – a situation reflecting the UK and Europe as a whole.[9] They are also more likely to participate in education beyond the age of sixteen, though boys' staying-on rates have increased in the last five years. A recent regional analysis has revealed substantial variations from one county to another; the staying-on rate for girls is highest in the rural counties of Wales (Dyfed, Powys and Gwynedd) and it is these three counties which have the lowest percentage of female school-leavers with no qualifications or graded results.[10] However, it is somewhat worrying to learn that unqualified female school-leavers are found in greater concentration in Wales than in any other UK region.[11]

Girls are leaving school with low career aspirations and expectations. They frequently view barriers to achievement in personal and individual terms, rarely referring to societal or cultural barriers.[12] Girls researched in the working-class valleys of south Wales displayed a certain 'fatalism' about their futures and felt that they had little autonomy or control. They anticipated 'broken' careers to accommodate caring for children and envisaged their future lives locally, thereby limiting education, training and careers to those geographically available.[13]

Data collected by the Careers Service in Wales indicate that girls' potential is not realized. They leave school with limited horizons compared to boys.[14] The majority of girls still enter sex-stereotyped female areas of employment and existing research has indicated that there is much awareness work to be done to combat these patterns.

Girls (and boys) in Wales need earlier careers education before gender stereotypes become too rigid; they need to be exposed to a wide range of career possibilities. Along with preparation for work, young people need to understand the changes in family structure and be prepared for family life in which traditional domestic identities are no longer as central for contemporary women.[15]

Recent research describing the position of women in the labour market in Wales has revealed that Wales is characterized by a particularly low rate of female economic activity (although this has been rising recently) and that women in the workforce tend to be in relatively low-paid, low-skilled and often part-time employment.[16] The Welsh workforce is highly segregated, both horizontally and vertically, with women working in a narrow range of industries and in the lower grades within these sectors. They comprise over two-thirds of all employees in personal and protective services, clerical and secretarial, sales and 'other occupations'. There are conflicting views about the belief that Wales is leading the UK out of the recession,[17] not least, as T. Rees writes, because it is clearly 'the case that gender segregation is more extreme in Wales than elsewhere'.[18]

Women at work in Wales are in a worse position than those in English regions. They are less likely to be in highly paid professional and technical posts. A study commissioned by HTV Wales illustrated the paucity of women in top jobs in Wales. The numbers of women in senior posts in both the public and private sectors in Wales is minute and an indication that the 'glass ceiling' – which women can feel but not see, and which prevents their route to the top – is double glazed. The proportion of women managers is much lower than in England and the proportion of women headteachers in Wales is actually declining.[19]

Numerous reasons are advanced to account for women's current position in the labour market in Wales,[20] and strategies to improve women's economic participation rates and involvement in education and training have been identified.[21] However, in a chapter as short as this there is little room to discuss these. Instead, the chapter takes one important and recent initiative aimed at school pupils – 'Take Our Daughters to Work' – and explores its enactment by employers, parents, teachers and schoolgirls in one Welsh county.

In particular, the remaining sections of the chapter will document girls' experiences drawing upon their accounts and those of careers teachers, organizers and employers. In examining the 'Take Our

Daughters to Work' initiative in one Welsh county, comparisons will be made with the 'Women's Training Roadshow' initiative, a two-day event which took place at the university college in Wales's capital city of Cardiff.[22] Discussion will focus on common problems and strengths, and highlight ways we can improve Welsh schoolgirls' willingness to invest in their human capital.

Take Our Daughters to Work Day: exploring tomorrow's choices

Last April over a 100,000 girls aged between 11 and 15 years old from schools across the UK spent a special day at their parents' or friends' workplaces. They joined scientists, fire-fighters, engineers, nursery nurses, doctors and veterinary surgeons – to name but a few – in their daily work in a wide variety of participating organizations.

('Take our Daughters to Work' leaflet, 1995)

This extract describes the national 'Take Our Daughters to Work' day held across the UK on 27 April 1994. The day is one of a number of projects being established by 'Our Daughters' charitable trust[23] whose aims are:

to promote the equality of women with men by the advancement of public education in:
• the role of women at work
• the opportunities for women at work
• the value of women in the workplace;
to advance the education of girls and boys about the opportunities for employment available to them.[24]

In their mission statement and publicity materials the charity stresses a commitment to working in partnership with families, schools, employers, advisory and professional organizations to improve the experiences of young women and men as they move through school and adolescence to become adult members of the workforce. The 'Take Our Daughters to Work' day (TODTW) has the endorsement of the Federation of Parent Teacher Associations (PTAs), the Careers Service and the Employment Department and is supported by many organizations and companies who also make donations to the charitable trust and who are concerned to broaden the ways in which women participate in the workforce.

The publicity leaflets draw upon a wide range of research to defend and justify the TODTW day. Research into girls' low self-esteem, peer-group pressure, classroom interaction, childhood and media socialization, examination performance and segregated/segmented labour market data are all used to show how conscious and unconscious processes limit the full expression of girls' abilities. The TODTW day is described as an attempt to 'challenge the inevitability of these processes'.[25] In giving girls the opportunity to view at first hand the daily working of a variety of careers, the initiative aims to alert them to the effects the choices they make can have on their futures.

The charity has outlined two ways in which the TODTW day can be organized and these are set out carefully in their handbooks for employers, teachers and students and their parents. Each of these three handbooks explain how the day can be initiated, choreographed and prepared for. An organization can invite their employees to bring their daughters, granddaughters, nieces or daughters of friends in to work with them for the day for planned activities. Alternatively it can contact a local school and formally invite groups of girls aged between eleven and fifteen years in to work. Similarly, schools are urged to link up with local firms and negotiate and help plan an event for girl pupils. The charity's literature encourages all approaches but points out that by targeting schools, employers might be giving girls who do not have an adult who can take them to work, a chance to see a workplace.

Every LEA and all UK schools with girls aged between eleven and fifteen are circulated with publicity fliers inviting their participation. A teachers' handbook with lesson plans, cross-curricular projects, quizzes and numerous preparatory activities is available by request. All handbooks explain the rationale for the initiative and are laced with quotations from large companies who have pledged support.

> Inviting girls into the workplace to see what goes on before they make vital educational choices is bold and enormously imaginative and the BBC is not going to be left behind.[26]

Media coverage of the 1994 TODTW event provided engaging reading and viewing for a mass audience. 'Thousands of girls missed school today!' was the ear-catching television news headline used throughout the evening of 27 April. The documentary footage and voice-overs captured the aims of the national initiative and examples of its enactment. Girls were shown wearing hard hats and wellingtons, recording in high-tech studios and alongside fire officers.

One father (filmed on a construction site) told cameras: 'It's good for girls to see what their fathers do!' Viewers were informed of the USA origins of the project and how 'in the USA over a million girls went to work last year'. A video-taped collage of edited cuttings from the 1994 event is now used to brief interested employers. Participant observation was conducted at a meeting of employers organized by a regional co-ordinator of Opportunity 2000 and TODTW, and viewing the video tape provided a focus of discussion. Those attending reviewed examples of good and bad practice, identifying some caveats for new recruits to the initiative. These are discussed in later sections of the chapter which follow a description of one Welsh county's work on the TODTW initiative.

A local response to a national initiative

In April 1994 over 150 girls in the county of 'M' in south Wales, went to work with members of their family, friends or in groups organized by their careers teachers in concert with the local TEC (Training and Enterprise Council), the LEA and various employers.

> We know that some schools – we think it's about eight – did not take part
> . . . whereas others arranged for over a quarter of their year 8 or year 9 girls
> to go to work . . . I'm afraid in 'M' [county] participation was very patchy.
> (Careers advisor)

Local companies and employers, who had targeted schools to work with, included Welsh Water, the BBC, the Welsh Office and County Hall. Groups like 'Women in Construction' organized places for thirty girls and a local 'business women's network' set up visits for at least fifteen girls aged fourteen and over who accompanied a variety of professional women from twelve different companies. The BBC, staunch supporters of the TODTW day, enabled a group of girls to make and edit their own programme which now forms part of a promotional video for the charity 'Our Daughters'.

> BBC Wales got girls working with three senior women – a presenter, an
> editor and a programme controller and they combined skills so that the
> girls created a programme . . . It was quite inspiring to see the confidence
> and dare I say 'professionalism' of the girls who all had great fun!
> (Regional co-ordinator for TODTW)

This section of the chapter reports on the girls' experience of the TODTW day and draws mainly upon questionnaire data that was somewhat fortuitously acquired. During the fieldwork for the EOC case study, I was offered a large brown envelope of eighty unanalysed questionnaires completed by Year 8 pupils following their day at work. The questionnaire data provide information for just over 53 per cent of those girls in the county of 'M' who it is estimated took part. However, as one careers advisor admitted,

> monitoring the numbers of girls who accompanied parents and friends to work was virtually impossible . . . in fact we believe that a lot more than 150 girls went but we have no hard evidence as schools didn't collect and return such data to us.

The questionnaire devised by 'Our Daughters' elicited no biographical data like age, subjects studied or parents' occupation, and therefore analysis is somewhat limited in terms of social class. Fortunately, age indicators were provided by the girls themselves who conscientiously entered their names and year group. Limitations aside, the data afford us insights into girls' views of the TODTW day as well as revealing significant data on their opinions about appropriate careers. A summary of key findings is presented below.

Twenty-five girls from the 'sample' of eighty stated that they would have more opportunities if they were boys.

> I'd definitely have more opportunity because most employers think that women are going to have time off to have kids.

> Yes, I would have more chances if I was a boy because people seem to be against women having powerful positions.

More optimistically, fifty-four girls reported that a male gender would not advantage them:

> If you have the ability and brains to do a job then your sex doesn't matter!

> Women can do the same things and better.

> I think that nowadays there are equal opportunities for boys and girls.

However egalitarian the girls' views, when asked 'Are there jobs you consider to be men's jobs and women's jobs?' forty-nine of them agreed that there were, with only twenty-eight stating that there were not. As examples they listed stereotypical gendered jobs as follows:

Men's jobs:		Women's jobs:	
Builder	Lawyer	Nurse	Teacher
Lorry driver	Doctor	Shop assistant	Cleaner
Electrician	Manager	Secretary	Hairdresser
Mechanic	Postman	Childminder	Waitress
Steel worker	Designer	Factory worker	Housewife
Football player	Milkman	Receptionist	Model

The occupational aspirations of the majority of these Year 8 schoolgirls were safely within the well-established realms of 'women's work'. Only a minority, nine out of eighty, were aiming for professional occupations of law, accountancy, medicine and teaching. The girls were asked, 'If you had a chance of taking up any career what would you choose and why?' Occupations listed and reasons given reflected both pecuniary and altruistic motives, for example:

I'd like to be a nursery teacher because I love helping children.

An accountant because its a well paid job.

Something to do with medicine because I want to help ill people.

A travel agent because you get loads of free holidays.

Fifteen girls left blank spaces for this open question. In contrast however, there was a 100 per cent response rate to a question asking girls to name a career they would not consider. This shows that although some girls were unsure or cautious about identifying a career, they had all come to a decision and could specify jobs they would not choose. The occupations listed and reasons given were illuminating, especially when read in conjunction with the girls' desired occupation.

Q: What occupation would you most dislike to be in and why?

A judge because some people really hate them [aspiring medic].

A mechanic because you get full of sticky oil [aspiring nursery nurse].

An MP because you might get assassinated [aspiring secretary].

A midwife because of all those screaming babies [aspiring lawyer].

A fireman because it's very dangerous [aspiring chef].

A vet because I love animals and wouldn't want to put them down [aspiring nurse].

A lorry driver because its a man's job! [aspiring hairdresser].

The comments demonstrate that these Year 8 girls, in their second year of comprehensive school, had already rejected certain occupations and had done so using limited negative factors. Occupational knowledge, however partial, is gleaned from family, school and media, well before people take up work. The media, particularly television, reinforce narrow gender-stereotyped work roles and contribute to the occupational socialization of children at an early age.[27]

Forty-two of the girls, just over 50 per cent of the sample, revealed that family was the biggest influence on their career choice. Only nine girls identified teachers as a strong influence. This was borne out by their responses to a question which asked them to identify someone whose career they would like to follow. Aunties, cousins and sisters dominated responses, but only two mothers, one father and one grandfather were cited as career role models.

Q: *Do you have someone whose career you would like to follow?*

My cousin – she's an RE teacher and I'd like to follow in her footsteps.

My auntie – she's a nurse.

My cousin's mum works in a travel agent in town called Thompsons . . . she uses the computer and changes money into different money.

My sister is training to do radiography.

My grandfather was a doctor in the Second World War!

Finally, of the eighty girls in the 'sample' all but three (who were unsure) stated an intention to remain in education after Year 11. Their anticipation of post-sixteen education and training might reflect their knowledge of an unaccommodating youth labour market or their awareness of the importance of credentials for women.[28] Several of them came to understand what qualifications they would need during their 'day at work' and it is to a discussion of their TODTW experiences that the section now turns.

In identifying 'things enjoyed most' and 'things which pleased' them most during their TODTW day, the girls' written responses showed more enthusiasm for those experiences which could be described as social or recreational rather than work specific. For example, over twenty girls referred to the refreshments they had been given:

The buffet was brilliant.

I enjoyed the slap-up meal and the computers.

I loved the yummy food and the tours.

Over half of the girls commented on the helpfulness and support of the staff they had accompanied.

They gave us so much attention and put in a lot of effort to make sure we enjoyed ourselves.

The people were fun and I'd like to go back there for work experience.

'Fun' has been identified as a necessary and key ingredient in any initiatives designed to reduce sex differentiation, and data from the schoolgirls reveals that the majority of them 'had great fun'.[29] Like the girls studied by Pilcher et al. who had participated in the Women's Training Roadshow, these girls seemed flattered that firms thought they justified such effort and expense.[30] Other research, for example Buswell's study of adolescents in Youth Training placements, indicates how important social relations are for young people.[31]

Only a few (12) individuals specified particular features of their day which referred to actual 'work' they had done. One girl, a would-be horse-riding instructor who had spent the day with a construction company, had enjoyed

building model towers and bridges and discussing the construction of show homes with a site manager.

She also stated however that she had not liked getting muddy and even though she had enjoyed and coped with the construction tasks and calculations given her, she considered 'building work and driving lorries to be men's work'. Another thirteen-year-old, a would-be geography or art teacher, spent the day with a print and design section of the City Council where to her surprise she was allowed to have a go at designing on the department's computer . . .

She stated that the most important things she had learned were:

> You have to get degrees in Art College.
>
> You don't have to be a man to do graphics work.
>
> It's hard to make a print negative.
>
> I would like to do this job.

A number of respondents like this girl acknowledged that they had witnessed a job which they would consider doing or a workplace they would like future employment in. Those girls who felt less positive about the occupations they had glimpsed can still be said to have 'explored tomorrow's choices' and gained insights into the world of work. The two girls who had accompanied their fathers to work were able to consider and reject lorry driving and building work more firmly on the basis of their TODTW experience. It is of interest to note however that these two girls were among the forty-nine who differentiated between men's and women's jobs. One of these, a would-be lifeguard, stated:

> Lorry driving is hard.
>
> The things delivered are heavy.
>
> Lorries kept breaking down.
>
> Men's work is harder.

With only two of the eighty girls having experienced the TODTW day with their parents, generalizations cannot be made, though the data suggest that some girls might learn the status quo from well-meaning parents and have their own theories of stereotypical occupations reinforced. 'Stereotyped beliefs about the differences in the technical and social abilities of men and women' are held by many employers, as G. Rees and his colleagues discovered. They reported that many of the south Wales employers they studied had fixed ideas about the 'gender-appropriateness of different jobs' and where men and women entered 'inappropriate' jobs, it was often the employer who guided them into other work.[32] A scheme which encourages school pupils into non-traditional work is unlikely to succeed unless, as Delamont has argued, it is 'aimed at males and females, employers and workers, teachers and taught, parents and children, advisors and advised'.[33] However, it is widely recognized that the difficulties of organizing 'effective' placements are paramount, as later sections of the chapter will reveal.

The TODTW day enabled these Year 8 secondary school girls to have some fun and to develop confidence in an adult setting. In some cases it provided opportunities for girls to demonstrate their abilities to hosting staff.

Q: The things that I am most pleased about are:

Being told that I worked really well.

Finding out that I was quite good at computer video design.

That I could deal with most phone calls efficiently.

I was nervous before but everyone was so polite and friendly I felt important and that made me work well.

These selected comments indicate that the girls enjoyed displaying skills and perhaps proving to themselves that they could manage certain work tasks.

Without doubt, the questionnaire data show that girls learned some important facts about work in their day away from school. Their responses to the stimulus question 'The most important things I learned were . . .' are revealing, as the examples here indicate.

Women can be environmental health officers as well as men.

School doesn't have to end when you leave school – you can study at work now.

Finding out that women can be welders as well as men.

Finding out that a woman can be a boss. Fiona Jones was the boss in Physiotherapy and it just shows that men aren't the only people who can have top jobs!

Although we should not over-generalize from the data yielded by eighty questionnaires from a county in south Wales, it appears that the main effect of the TODTW day was to make girls more aware of the range of jobs that women are able to do. Like the Women's Training Roadshow this initiative appears not to have changed girls' preferences but to have exposed them to wider career possibilities.[34]

Raising our daughters' horizons?

I took 3 girls into a meeting where a female chief executive directed and chaired an *all*-male board meeting of nine men. The girls were amazed at this woman's power and effectiveness. They all were 'wowed' by her salary as well [. . .] This was the best TODTW placement that I was involved in setting up. She *really* was a positive role model.

(Welsh Health Authority representative at Opportunity 2000 employers' briefing)

With so few 'women at the top'[35] the scenario described above where schoolgirls saw a woman wielding power, control and autonomy is likely to be rare. How can the TODTW experience be improved for its participants? This was the question asked of organizational representatives, attending a network meeting of Opportunity 2000 whose regional co-ordinator also organizes for the 'Our Daughters' charity. This section draws upon the narratives shared by those attending the regional meeting and identifies the strategies deemed successful by those representatives who had 'choreographed' the TODTW initiative in their own organizations in 1994.

Discussion centred on showing girls a variety of work settings and jobs along with ways of making the TODTW event memorable for them. Some organizers reported that they had put girls through rolling programmes. These included site tours and visits to departments, interview opportunities with staff, an introduction to equipment with time allocated for hands-on experience and an end-of-event discussion session.

Feedback from employees was mostly positive and it was felt that passing the girls around the staff was better than leaving individuals to shadow one colleague . . . we felt that neither the staff or the girls would want to be stuck in one situation for too long . . . for the younger girls this might be particularly daunting.

Where employees had brought their own daughters to work, less structured days had occurred though accounts indicated that parents had 'prepared' their daughters and mapped out some occupational experiences for them with willing colleagues. In contrast, where liaison with schools had produced larger groups of girls coming to 'work', their preparation was not always apparent.

Although the charity prepares free material with closely detailed activities for girls to undertake at work, informants revealed that many girls were ill-prepared. Some girls knew nothing of the reasons behind the 'girls only' event or what might be expected of them.

> It was obvious to us that some groups were ready to interview staff about their work and discover career histories and stuff but others came without a clue, no ideas, nothing to write with . . . it appeared that their teachers had done none of the valuable work to help girls get the best out of their day!

The personnel who had choreographed the 1994 TODTW event in their own organizations held firm views about girls' levels of preparation for the event.

> It becomes just a day out of school unless teachers do the necessary groundwork . . . I asked one girl *why* she was here and she said 'Cos I'm missing maths!'

It was evident from their discussions that these organizers were very familiar with the employers', teachers' and students' resource packs published by 'Our Daughters' charity.

> Ideally, a teacher could build a whole group of lessons around their pupils' experiences . . . girls could be fully briefed about what to find out, how to interview staff and what to do, then they'll go back to class with lots of materials they can present to their classmates.

Girls' preparation apart, a number of organizers felt that girls' horizons might be raised if their careers teachers were more enlightened. Referring to both work-experience placements and the TODTW event, two representatives complained that teachers had a limited awareness of the diversity of jobs undertaken in their organizations:

> Pupils are always surprised at the range of jobs in the Welsh Office because they are taught narrowly to think of civil service settings in purely clerical or administrative terms . . . careers teachers need updating, after all James Bond was a civil servant.

To assist teachers and their pupils, several companies were in the process of developing careers material and information packs so that girls could

> leave [the event] with something tangible to take back to class, share with their parents or deposit in the careers library at their school.

Welsh Water, one of the largest indigenous companies in Wales, had compiled twelve career stories written by women doing a variety of work for their organization. These included the 'potted biographies and career paths' of a research analyst, a countryside ranger, a geotechnical engineer and a managing director for customer services. The intention was to provide girls with 'role models on paper' as well as inform their teachers of the range of employment available to women in such a company.

Representatives shared other details of ways in which their companies were striving to make their TODTW event more valuable and memorable. Several companies were linking up with schools in their locality and making formal invitations to work-experience co-ordinators. The Patent Office, for example, was working closely with one school to provide stimulating activities for 'low-achieving girls'. A number of organizations had followed up the TODTW day with a 'Take our Employers to School' day and had further consolidated lessons learned in the workplace as well as facilitating employers' understanding of the contemporary curriculum.

For those representatives who had been involved in the initial 1994 day, the success of the TODTW initiative was seen to rest heavily upon the receptivity of the employees:

> The staff got quite animated and excited about the day – management think that it was a good motivator pulling teams together.

Educating the workforce before the event was seen as an essential and crucial preparatory stage. One organizer reported how a female colleague, who had missed the original briefing to employers,

> was very critical of the lack of ability of one of the fourteen-year-olds who spent some time with her. In fact, she wasn't sympathetic to the initiative at all . . . that's where the problem lay really.

Matching girls with 'suitable' employees and avoiding unsympathetic staff was seen as a method of ensuring that girls received time, attention and opportunities to ask questions and explore possibilities.

Assuring the quality of girls' experience in a large national initiative like TODTW is difficult. Though 'Our Daughters' charity issues a variety of resource packs for employers, teachers, students and pupils, it is unable to control or shape participants' experiences and cannot guarantee that 'appropriate messages' will reach girls.

Unintended consequences accompany most programmatic events. One girl spent her day with the Army and when asked how she spent her day revealed that 'making cups of tea . . . and doing a bit of cleaning' had filled up most of the time. Inevitably this fourteen-year-old felt that her time could have been far better organized.

Research into VISTA (women scientists and technologies project)[36] emphasized that role models are effective only if they are carefully briefed and prepared. The hosting Army staff referred to above certainly needed briefing so that the 'lessons' learned by placement girls are beneficial. Half-hearted attempts to challenge sex roles are damaging, as Guttentag and Bray have shown;[37] poorly planned or weak attempts undertaken by non-believers tend to reinforce conservatism in pupils. So how is an event such as TODTW viewed within the broader context of education and how, in particular, does it relate to or affect boys?

And what about the boys . . . ?

> There's a lot of backlash and people I've worked with for years say 'but what are you doing for the boys? You *can't* leave boys out!'
>
> (Health Authority representative)

In staff-room settings, planning meetings and other arenas, comments like the one presented above were made. Much of the discussion at the regional planning meeting for Opportunity 2000 representatives which I attended, focused on 'the boys'. As well as sharing stories of TODTW 1994, representatives talked at length about boys' 'exclusion' from the 'day out'.

> I'd be rich if I got a pound for every time one of our staff complained about the 'girls only' bit . . . A number of colleagues felt that it was divisive, so in response we are thinking about setting up a mixed event for both sexes.
>
> (Employee/organizer, Welsh Water)

'Our Daughters' publicity material and various handbooks explain that,

> TODTW is a special day for girls, the day also affords boys the opportunities to look at roles and relationships within the classroom setting.[38]

Oral accounts suggest however that many parents, teachers and boys feel that a 'special day in the classroom is a poor surrogate for a day in a workplace', however splendid the TODTW classroom activities!

> Look at it from the boys' perspective – its not much fun doing quizzes and role plays back in the classroom when half the class are out in the *real* world.
>
> (Female teacher)

The series of Women's National Commission (WNC) Training Roadshows described by Pilcher et al. were specifically aimed at girls and women. The role models, women engineers, taxidermists, plumbers etc., along with the displays, stalls, 'visitor's pack' and workshops were all designed to challenge female ideas about the labour market.[39] In contrast with this and with the majority of projects designed to change the sexual division of labour in the UK, 'Take Our Daughters to Work' is also aimed at boys. The charity's policy document *Encouraging Future Choices* has as its second major aim,

> to advance the education of girls and boys about the opportunities for employment available to them.[40]

Its board also recognize that there is much important work to be done to maximize boys' potential:

> Unless boys are supported in learning some traditionally 'female' skills they will be increasingly disadvantaged in the modern world.[41]

Youth labour markets in Wales are varied, with a dearth of jobs in rural areas and some of the worst labour-market problems being experienced by those living in the industrialized counties of Gwent, Clwyd and Mid Glamorgan.[42] One organizer recounted the anxiety that the women employees in her organization felt about their sons in this respect.

> In [place-name] women work and men don't. There's a lot of depression amongst the men. . . many of the mothers employed with us in the Health sector are worried about their sons because of the high male unemployment [and] the lack of primary industries for them.
>
> (Employee/organizer, Health Trust)

Discussion indicated that the TODTW initiative was seen by some as divisive and unfair, and, in areas with high male unemployment, as 'particularly insensitive to boys'. All participants in the regional planning meeting agreed that boys should have opportunities to undertake work experience in work settings untypical for their sex, especially in geographical areas like the one described above. The focus on females rather than males in projects designed to challenge sex roles is a directional issue that Delamont argues needs to be re-evaluated.[43]

Schools in different counties across Wales and their teachers and pupils, have different degrees of access to organizations who will host pupils on work experience. This point is further developed in the section below which addresses a number of other 'concerns' connected with the 'Take Our Daughters to Work' initiative.

Some voiced concerns

> What concerns me about the 'Our Daughters' initiative is the fact that some schools just don't bother [. . .] The sad thing is that it's often schools where girls need a diversity of experience and a widening of horizons!
> (Member of County TEC Women's Strategy Group)

Despite the fact that the registered charity 'Our Daughters' sent out publicity information and fact sheets to each LEA and every single school in the UK, uptake and involvement in the scheme was varied. Knowledge of the national TODTW day was and still is partial, and participation rates in the case-study LEA and across schools in Wales is very uneven. 'Mr Reers' whose careers lesson opened this chapter claimed to know nothing of this forthcoming event; more worryingly, he showed little interest in the details I jotted down for him! Careers advisers and regional co-ordinators are concerned that girls in different schools have unequal access to this positive action initiative. The concern and cynicism of one female careers teacher is captured below:

> If the publicity materials land in the lap of an uncommitted or unreconstructed male careers teacher then schools won't get to know of the initiative [. . .] There's no doubt that it takes a lot of organizing!
> (Careers teacher)

Other accounts elicited from both teachers and employers who had daughters of their own, indicate that the response at the school level is crucial. One mother, a senior manager from the Welsh Office, complained of the way her daughter's school ignored the event:

School did *nothing* towards it – My daughter had a miserable two nights catching up on homework and classwork. Only she and her friend were involved . . . the school seemed to know nothing about it.

(Welsh Office employee)

One head of Year 9 pupils, in a comprehensive school renowned for its 'leafy and affluent catchment area', recounted the consequences of her school's lack of involvement:

We had parents on the phone *all* day last year. They wanted to know why our school wasn't involved. The head had a lot of explaining to do because *our* parents like to be involved in everything that's going on.

(Head of Year 9, teacher)

Inevitably, this school, a front runner for a top position in the county league tables, subsequently made detailed action plans to involve parents and girls in the work-shadowing scheme for April 1995. For a school, the option whereby a parent, relative or family friend takes a 'daughter' to work is an easy and inexpensive way to do something about broadening girls' careers knowledge. Apart from the costs of circulating a letter of invitation to parents, the expenses are borne elsewhere. By not utilizing this fairly simple strategy, some headteachers or senior staff are perhaps indicating the low priority they attach to female careers advice and equal opportunities.

It would be unfair to lay criticism at 'unresponsive' schools and teachers however, without acknowledging how their work has intensified over the last eight years. A number of authors have described how the educational reforms of the late 1980s and early 1990s have impacted upon teachers' work contributing to stress.[44] Indeed the recent period has been characterized by extensive curriculum innovation. One empathetic advisory teacher pointed out that though 'equal opportunities and positive action strategies were important' they were only '*one* of the balls that schools are having to keep in the air!' Marketization, the effects of LMS (Local Management of Schools), league tables, and not least the National Curriculum, have all changed the work realities for teachers and managers in schools. Perhaps then, we can understand why some schools' annual development plans do not yet include a 'take our daughters to work' project.

A number of individuals, including organizers at the charity's head office, regional co-ordinators, teachers and careers officers, have expressed concern over the fact that schoolgirls in Wales have 'differential access' to this equal opportunities initiative. In some areas, schools are gravely disadvantaged in having little in the way of business or industry. Work experience co-ordinators struggle to 'place' their Year 10 and 11 pupils into local companies and are often unable to meet TVEI's target for pre-sixteen pupils to do two blocked weeks of work experience. In some areas, a number of schools are 'fishing in the same shallow pool of business and organizations' and competing with each other for pupil placements. This has resulted in TVEI 'relaxing' its rules and allowing schools to organize a scheme of day release for its pupils so that schools can 'share' their local organizations and distribute pupils.[45]

For schoolgirls in de-industrialized and particularly in rural areas of Wales the TODTW initiative is likely to be hampered by structural factors. Byrne argued that compared to girls in towns, those living in rural areas suffered more limiting gender role socialization and such girls were disadvantaged.[46] It is important then, to gauge the impact of the TODTW day in rural areas particularly, and perhaps plan careers resources for the classroom which *show* girls (and boys) a less traditional 'future of possibilities' to compensate for their missing experiential knowledge.[47]

Having briefly explained some concerns and dissatisfactions about the initial TODTW day of 1994, I will now turn to outline the way in which the south Wales county 'M' is planning future experiences for its 'daughters'.

Let's get it right: planning for national TODTW Day (28 April 1995)

The county, through its Education and Business Partnership (EBP) and Careers Service, targetted four comprehensive schools where 'girls might not get the chance to accompany professional parents to work'. The chosen schools from across the county were large comprehensives where socio-economic data indicate high levels of unemployment.

If your parents and family are out of work you can't tag along, can you . . .
(Careers teacher)

Its important for working-class girls to see the possibilities for work that exist for women – middle-class parents usually know them anyway.
(Careers Officer with responsibility for equal opportunities)

An assistant Education Officer at a planning meeting for the TODTW spoke of positive action plans to enable girls from Special Needs departments and schools to participate this year. Employers, for example, the BBC, the Welsh Office and the county council among others, were consulted about including the latter. Initial responses were favourable, and the 1995 TODTW event in the county of 'M' was planned to enable a wide range of 'differently abled' girls to attend work.

The county's Training and Enterprise Council (TEC) also facilitated the TODTW day and much of the planning and networking was undertaken by the women who form the 'Stay wide – keep moving' Women's Strategy Group. This all-women group consists of assistant education officers from the county, the careers service, a deputy headteacher, representatives from Opportunity 2000 and Chwarae Teg, the University of Wales, local training organizations and women representatives from a number of employers, for example, the BBC, borough council, the county council, an electricity company, a solicitors group and a management consultancy. This strategy group convenes under the auspices of the TEC to report on research and initiatives to enhance female participation in education training and employment. Four cluster groups formed to work on each of the following: education, family friendly issues, enterprise, and development.

The TEC via the 'Stay wide – keep moving' Women's Strategy Group identified the four schools from across the county, each of which was located within an urban regeneration area. Over ninety-eight local companies, who through the EBP offer work experience, were contacted. The group planned a large publicity campaign in the local press to launch the day. The convenor of the women's strategy group secured funding to carry out some research into the success of the project, and a small research team designed questionnaires and planned to conduct focus groups and interviews with schoolgirls after the event. The aim was to discover what girls learn from their work day and to identify ways forward to help them capitalize on their talents. County, Opportunity 2000 and TEC representatives, all agreed that the TODTW (1995) initiative would provide a wealth of data which like that of the Women's Training Roadshow should be documented and evaluated.[48]

We have remarkably little published work on positive action or school-based gender equality initiatives in Wales.[49] The useful collection edited by Burchell and Millman, which describes projects and policies to promote gender equality, has nothing from Northern Ireland, Scotland or Wales.[50] Similarly, volumes in the same series by Weiner and Wickham are also without Welsh data and are particularly Anglocentric.[51] Fortunately, for readers seeking such information on Wales, Daniel's paper reports on a number of projects in north Wales which have addressed, or are attempting to address, sex-role stereotyping and equal opportunities. She discusses in some detail one LEA's systematic promotion and monitoring of equality and describes valuable work on gender carried out by PGCE student teachers.[52] The report by Rees and Istance on women in post-compulsory education and training has also identified a number of positive action initiatives and filled a vast gap in the available literature in Wales.[53]

Concluding remarks

This chapter is a modest attempt to provide some insights into a recent and ongoing UK initiative and its enactment in one county in south Wales. It has highlighted some obstacles at a local and national level and shown how even in an industrialized county like 'M', girls' access to this positive action initiative is uneven. According to Rees, there are particular structural and economic factors impeding the success of positive action measures in Wales.[54] In the UK, 292 organizations have signed up to Opportunity 2000 and, to date, only thirty-one of these are in Wales. It is major national and international companies and large public and ex-public sector organizations which have shown most enthusiasm for positive action in the UK as a whole, and Wales has fewer of these. Small to medium enterprises (SMEs) dominate the Welsh economy and these, as Rees points out, do not have the flexibility or 'cultural inclination to embrace equal opportunities in such a thoroughgoing sense'.[55]

As this is being written TODTW co-ordinators for Wales are 'drumming up support' for the April 1995 event with interviews on local radio stations and seminars for employers. On 6 March 1995 'Our Daughters' London office reported that thirty-three organizations from across Wales had confirmed their involvement. In an 'era of mass work experience'[56] this is somewhat alarming. Considered alongside the current importance attached to work experience by government agencies, this is a worrying scenario. Two recent Welsh Office reports urge schools to 'encourage activities with employers' for all pupils over fourteen and have set criteria to promote more effective ways in which employers and schools can work together.[57] Many employers, as Delamont has argued, still do not have any interest in recruiting, training and retaining workers in non-traditional occupations, and many parents, teachers and careers staff have very stereotyped views about male and female behaviour.[58]

Barnes and his colleagues, in their evaluation of work experience schemes for TVEI, found that despite the high profile given to equal opportunities in the forty schools that they studied,

> there was little, if any, shift in the traditional patterns which determine the kinds of work students are selected for according to their gender.[59]

These authors argue that influential factors lie without the school.

The influence of childhood socialization on gender-related self-image will drive girls and boys towards traditional choices even when 'tasters' of non-traditional subjects and work are given.[60] Adolescents choosing unconventional jobs are under pressures from their own peers and adults and, as Cockburn's work shows, many of them have difficulty sustaining their choices.[61]

All projects which attempt to raise pupils' aspirations and which have the potential to modify attitudes and actions are valuable. Initiatives like TODTW are commendable because they attempt to chip away some of the wider societal influences on sex role stereotyping. Positive action measures like TODTW for schoolgirls all over Wales are especially urgent given that the situation of women in the Welsh workforce is worse than the British average.

A certain poignancy accompanied the closing remarks of a regional co-ordinator for TODTW as she reiterated the aims of the project to an audience of employers in south Wales. Though her words may not capture totally the contemporary situation of young women in Wales, it seems fitting to close this chapter with them.

> We women put our own full stops on our lives and we don't want our daughters to do that!

Notes

[1] Pseudonyms are used throughout the chapter to provide confidentiality and protect individual identities.

2 Arnot, M., David, M., and Weiner, G. (1996) *Educational Reforms and Gender Equality in Schools* (Manchester, Equal Opportunities Commission).

3 Arnot, M. et al. (1996) op. cit. Salisbury, J., et al. (in preparation) *Educational Reforms and Gender Equality in Schools: The Wales Report* (Manchester, Equal Opportunities Commission).

4 The research project 'Educational Reforms and Gender Equality in Schools', from which some of the data in the chapter derive was funded by the Equal Opportunities Commission. A number of women provided helpful insights during the fieldwork: Audrey Jones, Linda Humphries, Louise McCarron, along with co-researchers involved in other aspects of the EOC project – Sara Delamont, Lesley Pugsley and Mari James. Their support is gratefully acknowledged.

5 Spradley, J. P. (1979) *The Ethnographic Interview* (New York: Holt, Rhinehart and Winston). Spradley, J. P. (1980) *Participant Observation* (New York: Holt, Rhinehart and Winston). Delamont, S. (1992) *Fieldwork in Educational Settings: Methods, Pitfalls and Perspectives* (Lewes, Falmer Press).

6 Welsh Office (1995) *People and Prosperity: An Agenda for Action in Wales* (Cardiff, Welsh Office).

7 Arnot, M., et al. (1996) op. cit.

8 Our Daughters Charitable Trust (1995a) *Encouraging Future Choices* (London, Our Daughters Charitable Trust), 1.

9 Arnot, M., et al. (1996) op. cit.
Daniel, P. (1994) 'Promoting gender equality in schools' in Aaron, J., Rees, T., Betts, S. and Vincentelli, M. (eds.) *Our Sisters' Land: The Changing Identities of Women in Wales* (Cardiff, University of Wales Press).

10 Rees, T. and Istance, D. (1994) *Women in Post Compulsory Education and Training in Wales* (Manchester, Equal Opportunities Commission).

11 Central Statistics Office (1993) *Regional Trends 28* (London, HMSO) Table 5:7; Rees, T. and Istance, D. (1994) op. cit.; Welsh Office (1995) *People and Prosperity: An Agenda for Action in Wales* (Cardiff, Welsh Office).

12 Delamont, S. (1990) *Sex Roles and the School* (London, Routledge), 97; Pilcher, J., Delamont, S., Powell, G. and Rees, T. (1989a) 'Evaluating a careers convention: methods, results and implications', *Research Papers in Education*, Vol.4, 1, pp.57–76.

13 Pilcher, J. et al. (1989a). op. cit.; Rees, T. and Istance, D. (1994) op. cit.

14 Careers Service in Wales (1992) *Pupil Destination Statistics in Wales 1991* (Cardiff, Careers Service in Wales); Careers Service in Wales (1994) *Pupil Destination Statistics in Wales 1993* (Cardiff, Careers Service in Wales); Daniel, P. (1994) op. cit., 165.

15 Betts, S. (1994) 'The Changing Family in Wales' in Aaron, J , Rees, T., Betts, S., and Vincentelli, M. (eds.) op. cit., 27.

16 Rees, T. (1994) 'Women and Paid Work in Wales' in Aaron, J., Rees, T.,

Betts, S., Vincentelli, M. (eds.) op. cit.; Rees, C. and Willcox (1991) *Expanding the Role of Women in the South Wales Workforce* (Cardiff, Welsh Development Agency).

[17] Wales TUC (1993) *Tackling the Low Pay, No Jobs Economy* (Cardiff, Wales Trade Union Congress).

[18] Rees, T. (1994) op. cit., 95.

[19] Rees, T. and Fielder, S. (1991) *Women at the Top in Wales: A Report for HTV Wales 'Wales This Week'* (Cardiff, Social Research Unit, University of Wales College of Cardiff); Rees, T. and Fielder, S. (1992). 'Smashing the dark glass ceiling: women at the top in Wales', *Contemporary Wales: An Annual Review of Economic and Social Research* (University of Wales Press) Vol.5, 99–114.

[20] See for example, Rees, T. (1994) op. cit.

[21] Rees, T. and Istance, D. (1994) op. cit.

[22] Pilcher J., Delamont, S., Powell, G. and Rees, T. (1988) 'Women's training roadshows and the "Manipulation" of schoolgirls' career choices', *British Journal of Education and Work*. Vol.2, 2, 61–6.

[23] 'Our Daughters' was registered as a Charitable Trust (No. 1034226) in 1994.

[24] Our Daughters Charitable Trust (1995a) op. cit., 1.

[25] Ibid., 7.

[26] Our Daughters Charitable Trust (1995b) *Handbook for Teachers: Take Our Daughters to Work Day, Exploring Tomorrow's Choices* (London, Our Daughters Charitable Trust).

[27] Our Daughters Charitable Trust (1995a) op. cit., 3.

[28] Salisbury, J. (1994) 'Chasing credentials' in Aaron, J., Rees, T., Betts, S., Vincentelli, M. (eds.) op. cit. See also Startup and Dressel in this volume.

[29] Best, R. (1983) *We've All Got Scars* (Bloomington, Indiana University Press); Delamont, S. (1990) op. cit.

[30] Pilcher, J., Delamont, S., Powell, G., Rees, T. and Read, M. (1989b) 'Challenging Occupational Stereotypes: Women's Training Roadshows and Guidance at School Level', *British Journal of Guidance and Counselling*, Vol.17, 1, 59–67.

[31] Buswell, C. (1988) 'Flexible workers for flexible firms?' in Pollard, A., Purvis, J. and Walford, G. (eds.) *Education, Training and the New Vocationalism* (Milton Keynes, Open University Press).

[32] Rees, G., Williamson, H. and Winckler, V. (1989) 'The "new" Vocationalism' *Journal of Educational Policy*. Vol.4, 3, 227–44.

[33] Delamont, S. (1990) op. cit., 103.

[34] Pilcher, J. et al. (1988) op. cit.

[35] Rees, T. and Fielder, S. (1991) op. cit. Rees, T. and Fielder, S. (1992) op. cit.

[36] Whyte, J. (1985) *Beyond the Wendy House* (London, Longman).

[37] Guttentag, M. and Bray, H. (eds.) (1976) *Undoing Sex Stereotypes. Research and Resources for Educators* (New York, McGraw-Hill).

[38] Our Daughters Charitable Trust (1995b) op. cit., 1.

[39] Pilcher, J. et al. (1989b) op. cit.

[40] Our Daughters Charitable Trust (1995a) op. cit., 2.

[41] Our Daughters Charitable Trust (1995a) op. cit., 4.

[42] Rees, T. and Istance, D. (1994) op. cit.

[43] Delamont, S. (1990) op. cit., 100.

[44] Hargreaves, A. (1993) 'Time and teachers' work: an analysis of the intensification thesis' in Gomm, R. and Woods, P. (eds.) *Educational Research in Action* (Milton Keynes, Open University Press); Jephcote, M. and Williams, M. (1995) 'Defining the role of the school cross curricular co-ordinator' in Salisbury, J. and Delamont, S. (eds.) *Qualitative Studies in Education* (Aldershot, Avebury Press); Kyriacou, C. (1989) 'The nature and prevalence of teacher stress' in Cole, M. and Walker, S. (eds.) *Teaching and Stress* (Milton Keynes, Open University Press).

[45] Miller, A., Wall, A. G., and Jamieson, I. (1991) *Rethinking Work Experience* (London, Falmer).

[46] Byrne, E. (1978) *Women and Education* (London, Tavistock).

[47] Myers, K. (1992) *Genderwatch! After the Educational Reform Act* (Cambridge, Cambridge University Press).

[48] Pilcher, J. et al. (1988a) op. cit. Pilcher, J. et. al. (1989 a & b) op. cit. Pilcher, J., Delamont, S., Powell, G., Rees, T. and Read, M. (1990) *An Evaluative Study of Cardiff Women's Training Roadshow* (Cardiff, Welsh Office).

[49] Delamont, S. (1990) op. cit., 99.

[50] Burchell, H. and Millman, V. (eds.) (1989) *Changing Perspectives on Gender* (Milton Keynes, Open University Press).

[51] Weiner, G. (1985) *Just a Bunch of Girls* (Milton Keynes, Open University Press). Wickham, A. (1985) *Women and Training* (Milton Keynes, Open University Press).

[52] Daniel, P. (1994) op. cit.

[53] Rees, T. and Istance, D. (1994) op. cit.

[54] Rees, T. (1994) op. cit., 102.

[55] Ibid.

[56] Rikowski, G. (1992) 'Work experience schemes and participation' *British Journal of Education and Work* Vol.5, 1, 19–46.

[57] Welsh Office (1995a) *People and Prosperity: An Agenda for Action in Wales* (Cardiff, Welsh Office). Welsh Office (1995b) *A Bright Future: Getting the Best for Every Pupil at School in Wales* (Cardiff, Welsh Office).

[58] Delamont, S. (1990) op. cit., 1

[59] Barnes, D., Johnson, G. and Jenkins, S. (1989) 'Work Experience in TVEI 14–16' (University of Leeds School of Education, TVEI E17).

[60] Fuller, A. (1989) 'Promoting Equal Opportunities for Girls and Boys' (University of Lancaster, TVEI E20).

[61] Cockburn, C. (1987) *Two Track Training* (London, Macmillan).

PART THREE

*Gender and Socialization:
The Development of Identity*

8

Hey Wizardora, give us a kiss! – Assertion training for the playground

PATRICIA DANIEL

> There were these two boys from my class who kept following me around calling out: 'Hey Wizardora, give us a kiss!'[1] One of them was asking nicely.
> *So what did you do?*
> I said: 'All right, if you kiss Mrs Jones first'. They said: 'Ych â fi' and ran away. If they said it again, I said 'I told you I would if you kissed Mrs Jones first.' The other one says: 'Oh come on, he's asking nicely'. I say: 'No, no' and I just walk away.
> *Does that one really like you?*
> No he doesn't like me at all, he's just doing it to wind me up. But I don't get wound up so then they get tired and go away.
>
> (Dora)

This story reminded me of the rules for assertiveness: say the same thing three times firmly and without losing your temper.

My daughter Dora is just eight years old and she recently transferred to a new school where she managed to settle down quite quickly, despite minor problems like these. How did she become so assertive? Her ability to cope with the world around her surely must derive from her mother's contribution as a role model – a working woman, an academic who goes off with a briefcase and writes about equal opportunities in education. Or is it something to do with Dora's own individuality?

I have read the literature on gendering which discusses how differential treatment for girls and boys, beginning almost before birth, affects the aspirations and behaviour of little girls.[2] The 'early messages'[3] derived from girls' experience of different clothes, toys, language, family interactions and activities may affect both their self-image in terms of confidence *vis-à-vis* particular tasks and situations and the skills required to tackle them – the concept of what girls can or can't do being closely linked with what girls do or don't do. Five-year-olds, for example, display early gender-marking of activities as 'men's' and 'women's'.[4]

However, some researchers now argue that girls' behaviour is a conscious choice, particularly their tendency to form close collaborative relationships with their peers as opposed to placing a high priority, as boys often do, on claiming public space – physically as well as by demanding attention, volunteering answers and taking risks. This choice of girls can be 'interpreted as good and rational from a female perspective or experience and there is no need for a male reference'.[5]

The questions are, how can individuals transform for themselves the social representations around them as they develop[6] and – if it is true that the feminine and masculine dimensions are independent[7] – whether individuals can develop themselves as both co-operative (in the feminine dimension) and assertive (in the masculine dimension).

In previous research I have looked at what schools and training institutions are doing in Wales to promote gender equality.[8] In this present research project I wanted to hear from young girls themselves, to listen to their own perceptions of identity and influence rather than imposing an adult's analysis on their behaviour. These perceptions will of course be limited by the girls' developmental stage; their level of theoretical understanding and ability to articulate particular domains of gender identity and differentiation[9] – but I did not wish to prejudge this level.

My intention was therefore not to evaluate in any depth the school policy and practice as regards gender issues. The school is a backdrop for the experiences of the girls involved in the research. My study centred on a rural Welsh-medium primary school in a linguistically mixed catchment area of Gwynedd (80 per cent Welsh speaking, 20 per cent English speaking) with a prevailing atmosphere of quiet work and well-behaved, happy children. Despite its location in an area where traditionally the slate mines and the chapel have exerted a restrictive influence,[10] the school is lively and open-minded, it has a good reputation in catering for special educational needs and is involved in a development education project.

In contrast, Dora's previous school was situated in the bay area of Bangor, which is traditionally a seafaring community, with a mainly

English-speaking catchment, drawing in also a sizeable minority of children of overseas students and staff at the University of Wales.

What interested me particularly was the public space of the school playground, which to a great extent is the children's own domain, where large numbers of children of different ages are free to act and interact with minimal supervision from adults. The problems that can arise from bullying in this context have been well documented[11] as has the domination of the space by boys playing football.[12]

My questions of concern were as follows. How does my daughter occupy this space? How does she defend herself within it? And how does she open up the space for herself and others to grow as individuals? Who helps them do it? And what can we learn from this?

I employed a simple but enjoyable methodology – interviews with my daughter and her friends. My main source was Dora and this meant I was able to check details with her throughout the research period.[13] Her friends were chosen because they lived nearby and attended the same school. In addition I spoke to Dora's best friend from her previous school. I usually interviewed the girls with Dora present. The girls ranged from age six to nine, and were from families of different sizes and with different sibling patterns. The families varied in terms of parents' employment, level of formal education, income and life-style, but all the mothers were economically active in some manner inside or outside the home. Some of the families were Welsh-speaking, some bilingual and some English-speaking.

I followed up the interviews by observation at school, in the yard, at lunchtime and in the classroom, in order to check my perceptions against those of the girls. I also discussed the findings with the headteacher and members of staff.

The first thing I learned from the girls was that they were more than ready to talk about themselves and about their relationships with each other and with boys; they all held opinions and were often able to provide examples to support their points; they engaged in discussion and discovered areas of disagreement. The age range reflected the process identified by Tratner et al.[14] of moving away from the tendency for rigid gender-marking towards the beginning of flexibility and awareness of variety within and between sex groups.

The interviews with the girls centred around four main questions:

1. What games do you play?
2. Who do you play with?

3. How do you assert yourself?
4. What helps develop girls' confidence?

1. What games do you play?

Dora plays a variety of active non-competitive and apparently ungendered games 'on the yard'. These include 'Doctor, Doctor we're in a tangle'. (Everyone holds hands and tangles themselves up except for the doctor who has to untangle them. The last person to be untangled is the next doctor.) 'Sly Fox' (Y Blaidd Mawr) requires the skill to creep up behind the fox without being seen, if you can touch the fox and say 'Sly Fox', you can have your turn as the fox. One game with an arguably heterosexist theme involves forming a circle round two people and singing:

> Oh these two sailors sailed across the sea
> And if you want to marry one, they'd better choose me
> Wishy Washy Wishy Washy Wishy Washy Woo [twice].

The two sailors each pick a person from the circle and they dance round on the spot. Then the two new people stay in the circle for the next round.

The children use choosing rhymes like 'Dip dip dip, my blue ship' to decide, in an impartial manner, who is going to start the game. Another version with similar purpose is 'Mix around'; one child closes her eyes, the others sing 'Mix around, Mix around' and change position. 'Who will be on?' The chooser points without looking.

Clapping songs are also popular, for example:

> Mickey Mouse is dead
> He died last night in bed
> Cut his throat with a ten pound note
> And this is what he said
> Red white and blue
> My mother got the flu
> Achoo!
> Father went to Australia
> And met a kangaroo
> Boom de boom.

These songs tend to have fantasy or nonsense lyrics, rhyme and rhythm being more important than meaning. They are also useful for children to entertain themselves when they have to stand still: 'When we're standing in line (waiting to go into school or into lunch) we do 'Mickey Mouse is dead' or we play 'thumb fights'.

Most of these games are in English: the head corroborated the fact that games in Welsh have unfortunately dropped away.

When she joined the school Dora perceived that she had room to play:

> There's plenty of space on the yard because the really big boys aren't there. I don't know where the big boys are!

Later Dora discovered that the 'big boys' play football in a field at the back of the school, completely separated from the rest of the children.

The school is fortunate enough to have extensive grounds, including a separate playground for the reception class and grassy areas where children are allowed to play. But this only pertains in summer. When the field is wet, the boys are back on the yard.

What about other girls? I asked them: 'What's your favourite game?' Their answers generally reflect an equally active use of the yard.

> Footie. I play with Angharad and Gwenda and Iorwen [three girls] and the boys from our class.
>
> (Sian, age 8)

> Block One Two Three. It's like Hide and Seek. If you see the person you run back and say Block One Two Three.
>
> (Dian, age 8/9)

> Tick. We all play together, except the smallest class (they have their own playground).
>
> (Cadi, 6/7)

> Hide and Seek. Or running after the boys.
>
> (Brenda, age 6/7)

Others find alternative occupations:

> I don't always go on the yard. I go round the back where the small kids go. They've got climbing frames and a sand pit. The teachers don't mind. We play in the sandpit, there were little hedgehogs living there one year.
>
> (Rhian, age 9)

Observation at playtime confirmed a range of activities: hopscotch, running races (Sian), playing horses with a pair of friends roped together (Rhian), playing with a gameboy (a mixed group).

2. Who do you play with?

While there is a correlation in early life between type of activity and sex-group preference, Huston[15] suggests that, from age six, girls become less stereotyped about the games they are willing to play and boys become more so.

> Mostly girls play all these games – girls of different ages. Only the boys in our class [that is age 7–8] play the games. *Mainly boys play football, and the other games we all play.* [My italics.]
>
> (Dora)

Little girls do play football however, and although it still seems to be perceived as 'the boys' game', there is evidence that girls are challenging that view. At her previous school, Dora had had some problems with boys over playing football.

> The boys said, 'You can't play with us. Girls can't play football.' When I took my ball to school and we girls played, the boys tried to take over the ball. I said, 'You can't play with us.'
>
> (Dora)

> Paul kept asking to play but that was because he wanted to be captain.
>
> (Angharad)

> After you told the teacher, mum, she made sure they didn't bother us any more. Then the boys weren't allowed to bring their own balls, because they kept throwing them up on the roof. The girls can bring balls because they're not mucking about.
>
> (Dora)

Similar attitudes and conflicts prevail at the present school:

> The boys pick a few girls for their team (like three). [We assume this is not an impartial choice: author.] Some people when they're picked say no, but some people take the chance.
>
> (Dora)

> When the big boys are playing football, they let the little kids win.
>
> (Rhian)

I like playing with the boys [at football] but I won't play if no girls play [my three friends]. The boys say, 'Girls can't play football' but we just go and tackle everyone.

(Sian)

Dora and her friend Angharad used to play collaborative games with particular boys at her previous school:

There was the 'Jumping School' and then we played at Flying.

(Dora)

I still like playing with Lewis and Alun: they're nice boys.

(Angharad)

What's a nice boy?
They listen when you've got a suggestion. They play *mixed games*, like if you want to play tick and they want to play football, they say 'Let's play tick ball'. [My italics.]

(Angharad)

What do you mean by a bad boy?
They're mean and bossy, they kick you, they tell you what to do, they say 'You're fat'. *They want you to play their games.* [My italics.]

(Angharad)

At the new school, Dora has also found male friends to play mixed games.

We play Superpeople – Supergirl, Megagirl, Lucky Girl and Gareth is Super Dog. There's another boy, Rhys. Me and Rhys and a girl from his class play adventures, things from TV.

Of this last boy, Sian says:

He doesn't play football with the rest of us. He likes to play with girls.

The implication here is that the girls play football with the boys, not vice versa, because it is the boys' game and if a boy is not playing football, he must be playing 'girls' games'.

Some of Dora's friends demonstrated a very strong sex-group preference in play partners on the yard:

I don't play with boys.

(Rhian)

I don't play with boys.

(Brenda)

I never play with boys. I only play all girls.

(Dian)

Sometimes with boys. Kevin lets me play. But I prefer all girls.

(Cadi)

This may be a result of the fact that, as Angharad points out above, 'boys want you to play their games': same-sex grouping means girls play what they want to play. In fact, these girls sometimes play at chasing boys (away) or 'bashing the boys'.

Archer expresses concern about the restricted interactions which are a result of same sex-group preference and which may contribute to the construction of distinct social worlds.[16] However this does not take into account other areas of life where children have interaction with the other sex-group, both at home and at school, as will be discussed later in this chapter.

In addition, this strong identification with sex group membership, which is echoed in the chants which are sung by (all the) girls, on the yard or on coach trips, indicates an important source of confidence:

Boys are plastic
Girls are fantastic

or:

We are the champions we know what to do
Get all the boys and flush 'em down the loo!

While some girls play with some boys, many expressed a strong negative interest, at this stage, in boyfriends:

I'll never have a boyfriend. I don't like boys.

(Rhian)

Alternatively a fairly dominant role in the relationship was indicated:

She had a boyfriend but she dumped him.

(Dian)

The concept of 'boyfriend', while rather vague, is often used as a taunt and this may also affect some girls' attitudes about who to play with.

> I've got three boyfriends, but they don't like me.

(Brenda)

> If you're playing with a boy, everyone says he's your boyfriend.

(Angharad)

3. How do you assert yourself?

Lloyd and Duveen suggest that school is the arena of strategic action.[17] But confidence or a strong self-image is needed to assert yourself in a potentially difficult situation:

> There was an older girl singing:
> 'Wizardora, nothing surer
> She's the one who spoils your fun'.
> I just walked away, it's the best thing to do really because if you say something it just amuses them, so you just have to walk away.
> *How did you work out these strategies?*
> I just have an idea because if someone bothers you, you have to walk away. They don't go and do it on me any more, they say, 'Come on, let's go and get someone else to play tricks on – she's no fun.'

(Dora)

Dora suffered some harassment from older pupils and this is how she explained it:

> If someone new comes to the school they want to see if you're okay, they start bothering you (instead of asking if you want to play a game) – if they think you don't look right, they'll try and wind you up.

As she was now in a Welsh-medium environment, I was interested to know which language she used to defend herself.

> I always say something back in the same language they say to me. I always manage to say something, even in Welsh, for example when I'm wearing my balaclava and they say: 'Pwy sy' na? Ti wyt Nathan?' [Who's in there?

Is it Nathan?], I say 'Na'. If they lift off the balaclava to see who it is, I give a silly smile.

Taunts about boyfriends are also a method of trying to 'wind people up'. 'Mae Harri'n cariad i Dora' (Harry's Dora's boyfriend) or 'Mae Dora'n cariad i Harri' (the Welsh *cariad* is used for both boyfriend and girlfriend).

Other girls have had similar experiences and showed a similar ability to cope with the situation:

> I don't say anything, it's not worth bothering about, they're only playing.
> (Angharad)

> The boys run after me and say, 'Do you want to play with me?' They run after me and try giving me kisses. I just run away and go and play.
> (Sian)

> They swear and push me and that. I just walk away, I don't listen to them.
> (Dian)

Another form of harassment is when boys spoil girls' games, either intentionally or not.

> The boys would bother us when we were playing with skipping ropes, the boys were just chasing each other, they can't say, 'Excuse me', they just go through the rope.
> (Dora)

Similar events arise at the present school:

> It happens to me too. A boy was going through the skipping rope and tangling it up.
> (Cadi)

> The boys call the little kids names and kick their ball and take it away.
> (Rhian)

A lot of the complaints centre around the space boys take up with their own games:

> It's very dangerous, they [the boys] don't care, they take up all the space. Amanda tripped over the ball once.
> (Angharad)

They're a nuisance. On the yard you can't get past, they're in the way, playing football, cricket (even though there's a big field at the back).

(Rhian)

(This is particularly so when the field is wet. Observation showed that at least half the main yard is taken up with boys playing football – and the ball does hurt!)

What was important was that all the girls I interviewed try to sort out their problems themselves, even if it is a case of:

(a) Simply walking away.

(b) Saying, 'Don't do that. Stop it' (Cadi, Dora).

(c) A stronger method of verbal retaliation, for example with name calling:

Paul says 'Girls are stupid,' I say, 'Boys are Stupid *and dumb.*'

(Angharad)

(d) Physical defence:

They don't bother me, they're too scared of me because I give them a horsebite [this is a hard pinch between finger and thumb on the upper arm]. I don't let go. One of the boys did it to me – that's how I learnt it – and I did it back.

(Rhian)

Do you ask for help if someone is bothering you?

I try and sort it out myself.

(Sian)

I'd tell you if someone was calling names at me, but I wouldn't ask you to do anything about it.

(Dora)

So what do girls do about helping each other? One strategy is to tell the teacher.

The teacher tells the culprits off or 'just gives them a row'.

(Sian)

Does that work?

Not really, the boys just do the same thing again.

(Cadi)

It's not going to do any good. They just start doing it again.

(Dora)

Another strategy is direct action:

A big boy snatched the ball off Kate and we all ran after him but Kate just sat there watching.
I thought Kate was tough?
No, Kate just kicks, Kate just cries.

(Angharad)

Our friend Nancy is a tall one and she pushes them around if they bother us.

(Dian)

Yet another strategy is for a friend to speak up on your behalf.

Laura's a real good friend. When Meirion and Caradog are bothering me, she says: 'Dora's new at the school. She doesn't want people shouting at her.'

(Dora)

What's a good friend?
She always lets me play my game, she makes everything fair, she always helps with my Welsh if I'm stuck, and *if someone's being horrible she does something about it.* [My italics.]

(Dora)

Dora is emphatic about the need for verbal skills in asserting yourself: 'You have to talk them out of it.' She therefore sees it is important for girls to develop the ability to speak up for themselves: 'I'm teaching Josie how to be tough. I'm getting her to play games which will help her to get more tough.'

I wanted to find out how Dora had worked out the strategies she employs.

Where do you get your ideas from? Have you seen how to deal with problems like this on television?

Sort of, but you can't copy TV exactly because other kids watch the same programmes . . . anyway I don't like copying. For example, *Grange Hill*, but *it all comes to the same thing, being firm or being wimpish, don't just start crying or they'll carry on doing it* . . . I just got it from myself, I put all my ideas together . . . When I've been there a long time and everyone knows everything about me, everyone will be playing with me and no one will be messing me about.

4. What helps develop girls' confidence?

Three areas of experience were explored in the attempt to identify ways in which the girls had managed to develop the confidence they displayed: the activities they engaged in outside school, including the kind of interaction they enjoy; the positioning of their parents as regards their daughters' development; and finally the contribution of the school itself, which I discussed with both children and staff.

The children

Tastes in television programmes reflect an interest in adventure, proactive characters, dramatic plots – and humour:

> *Tin Tin, Children's Ward, Grange Hill, Kelly, Startrek, Get Your Own Back* and cartoons. *Biker Grove* has too much kissing.
>
> (Dora)[18]

> *Power Rangers* – they're always fighting though they don't always win. There are two women and four men, they're just friends, they do the same things.
>
> (Angharad)[19]

> *Funhouse*, quiz games, *Scooby Doo, Gladiators, You Bet.*
>
> (Sian)[20]

While all the girls, in contrast to boys, claimed reading as a major pastime at home, (thus conforming to national patterns) a similar taste for action and humour is revealed in their choice of books. 'Spooky' stories are particularly popular and there are many of them available at school.

> I've read nearly all the books in the school library. I like adventure ones, like the one about a haunted ark – a bag of flour fell over the man and he looked like a ghost!
>
> (Rhian)

I like the one about a robber inside a gorilla suit. He went to the circus on stilts and he was stealing a necklace, but he left footprints. A lady saw the robber and put handcuffs on his feet while he was still on the stilts.

(Cadi)

Millions of books: I like fairy tales, because they're exciting . . . I've got one about Polly and the wolf – he can't eat her, she turns and slaps him in the face and walks away.

(Angharad)

I like *Tin Tin*, *Famous Five* – because they're adventure books.
But all the main characters are boys in Tin Tin?
It doesn't matter – I imagine myself having the same adventures.

(Dora)

The importance of 'the girl in the adventure' is revealed in children's choice of a favourite character, even though they were not always able to explain the appeal.

Dorothy in *The Wizard of Oz* (but I don't know why).

(Cadi)[21]

George in *Famous Five* (she always gets her own way . . . she's always brave and wants to go adventuring even if the others don't).

(Dora)[22]

Mrs Hopkirk in *Randall and Hopkirk*.[23] Her husband is a detective ghost (she's nice, *she's always in the mystery*, she wants to get her husband back). [My italics.]

(Rhian)

Pippi Longstockings (she was funny, it was exciting).

(Sian)[24]

Beauty and the Beast: Belle knows what she wants to have and she goes to find it, she doesn't just talk about it.

(Dora)

However, Brenda had a different kind of role model:

The lady on the Philadelphia advert (she's funny).

(Brenda)

Brenda's mother had this interpretation:

Brenda thinks she's beautiful, she talks like you'd imagine a Cindy doll would talk, a fairy-like little voice.

(Joan)

A survey of play experiences at home reveals a range of activities, from Cindy dolls ('Cindies') to Meccano indoors and a similar range outdoors, showing a variety of interests both within and between individuals, in solitary and collaborative play. This indicates the development of skills and a self-image which is not highly gendered.

I listen to adventure stories on tape and act them out with my furry toys. My Sylvan family – I like putting them in their places and then I leave them.

(Dora)

And with your friends?

Inside we play Meccano, board games, tent and picnics (well, inside or outside), making magic potions (we didn't really taste it). Outside – bikes, roller skates, swings, football . . . exploring, finding things, me and Rhian see what's new down in the field, make secret places, dens, the gorse ones are still not known, we shout back when we hear someone shouting to someone else!

(Dora)

With your sisters and brothers?

At home I play with Hazel (younger sister) at explorers in the garden (finding hidden teddies) hunters in the bedroom (with water pistols). Outside – I love climbing rocks, getting to the top, racing.

(Angharad)

I play with my little brother Gavin. We play at house, shopping, football. I get on really well with him. He's funny. If I cry he gives me a big hug. I like practising football with my dad and Gavin.

(Sian)

I play with Karl [elder brother] on his megadrive. I tidy his room with him. No, he doesn't help me to tidy mine!

(Angharad)

We have cushion fights all together . . . I like playing chess and draughts with Gareth [her elder brother] because I usually win. Gareth's good at sewing.

(Rhian)

The parents

The mothers I interviewed were able to identify conscious decisions they had made and encouragement they had given relating to the development of their daughters' confidence and ability to assert themselves. These attitudes had changed with experience.

> We encourage them to have a go at anything. Because I know I lack confidence myself, I don't want them to be the same. I'm more stubborn than Dewi [her husband]. He's more likely to say 'Leave her', but I say 'You're going'. Like when she went to the orchestra – and she loved it. Every little bit gives them confidence.
>
> (Nia)

> I remember you made a conscious decision with Cadi [the younger daughter]. You used to tell Dian, 'You've got to share', but then realized she was being trampled on. With Cadi you've been more inclined to say, 'If you want something, go and get it.'
>
> (Dewi, Nia's husband)

> I always make a point of telling Rhian to think about what she wants to say before she speaks and to say it clearly – not whispering, but make sure she's heard. I also tell her she's a pretty girl, I try to build up her confidence, tell her she doesn't need make-up.
>
> (Joan)

(There is peer influence among nine to ten year olds to wear make-up and designer clothes for discos.)

Mothers were also able to identify other aspects of life with their daughters that might help develop confidence, although not specifically intended for that purpose.

> Getting the animals in – it helps not being afraid of animals (frogs, chickens . . .) Pottery – I do the youth clubs and Dewi does the schools; they see we're not frightened of doing group work. The youth club has really helped me [develop my confidence] a lot. Where Dewi works [a residential centre for adults with learning difficulties] we make a point of taking the girls in to meet the different residents. Some of them are very ill, they can be quite frightening, one comes up to the car and spits all over us. But they [the girls] see there are people worse off than us. Just the fact that Dewi works in a place like that, I think that helps.
>
> (Nia)

> Her dad [Dan] spends a lot of time with Rhian with animals – you can see Rhian sitting in a field full of sheep, Brenda would be screaming . . . Rhian's braver than I am with animals, I just put on a brave face in front of her [Joan helps out on the local farms]. Animals really like her. Another thing that helps is me working here at home, they see me switching to

different people all the time (and Dan) – that stops them being shy or coy – they can converse with all sorts of people . . .

(Joan)

Parents felt reasonably optimistic about the future for their daughters:

At school there are opportunities for the girls to do a range of things. For instance, Dian's class is doing woodwork, building houses. There are more options open for children these days. But I do think the village itself is very male-orientated – look at the new sports hall – there'll be rugby, cricket but no swimming.

(Nia)

The School

Although the county have not organized in-service training (INSET) specifically to discuss their equal opportunities guidelines, INSET courses on school subjects have addressed gender issues.[25]

The school staff are aware of the need to reconsider segregation by sex group and also the desirability of developing a range of skills among both girls and boys. They have discussed the need to involve girls more in asking and answering questions in class, for example in maths, and to encourage them generally to volunteer more (that is, to occupy more public space) and 'to make sure they get a fair chance at everything' (including fetching and carrying).

The children are organized into mixed-sex groups for classwork and similarly for PE

Otherwise the boys would go directly into an all-boys group.

(The Head)

According to the girls, this grouping may not always be effective in achieving the aim of inter-sex group collaboration:

We sit in mixed groups . . . the boys play tricks on the girls, like hiding the rubber, they're too busy doing that to work together; the girls help each other with the work.

(Dora)

However, the opportunity is there:

There are two nice boys in my class. They help me a lot. They help us with words. We help them as well.

(Dian)

The head had noted that in science, a subject which has taken on a high profile now in primary education,[26] the boys were still the keenest to *do* the experiments, but that it was the girls who were more perceptive, with their tendency to 'discuss more and explore the reasons why'. In other words, the collaborative trait can enable girls to achieve more highly in what have traditionally been seen as 'boys' subjects.

Even though the boys may take up more public space in class, the girls' perception of the boys' behaviour and performance strongly indicates a feeling of superiority over them:

As soon as the teacher steps out of the classroom, the boys put the music up and bash everything with a stick. The girls say: 'Mae Syr yn dod' [Sir's coming] and all the boys sit down and carry on writing. Even when the teacher is there, the boys are messing around, flicking rubbers. The boys do that much work (she indicates the top of the paper) and the girls are at the bottom of the page!

(Rhian)

Girls are better than boys. Boys do stupid pictures.

(Cadi)

We behave. Boys are a nuisance.

(Brenda)

Would you like to be a boy?
[Angharad gives a slow sweet smile and shake of the head.]
Girls can do more things . . . sewing, knitting, they have more patience . . .
And boys?
Boys are better at football.

(Angharad)

Is there perhaps a grudging admiration among the girls for what the boys do?

They put rubbers in their mouths. They flick their rubber on the ruler and ask Miss to go and get it.

(Dian)

Sometimes when the teacher asks a question, the boys say: 'Why Miss, don't you know the answer?'

(Dora)

However, in general the girls felt that they received the same treatment in class as the boys (except for what seemed to them the obvious fact that boys are naughtier and therefore get 'a row' and are sent out more often).

The school games afternoon used to be segregated but a new system of mixed games has been introduced, where everyone will have the chance to learn netball, football, rounders, basketball, rugby and cricket in rotation. Some girls are more enthusiastic about this change than others:

Rugby's my best, and cricket. I like rounders with the girls.

(Rhian)

The boys won't like playing netball and the girls won't like playing rugby.

(Dian)

I don't want to play football, I don't like it, because boys play it.

(Cadi)

It was interesting to hear Cadi's parents' response to this last comment:

In the summer Cadi loved playing at football here at home in the garden with me and Dian but she says she doesn't like it . . . *because it's a boys' game*. It's like when she's looking through catalogues, she says, 'No, they're boys' toys'. She's not got that from us, we don't say that.

(Dewi)

One explanation for this is the negative associations with football at school because of the boys' behaviour on the yard. Another is that Cadi is still in the phase of rigid sex-typing. It may be that, as Lloyd and Duveen suggest, teacher-organized activities can help children develop positive associations with less familiar (or other sex group) activities.[27] The following exchange shows Cadi's position moving when her older sister prompts her to consider her own abilities in the school Sports Day:

Girls are good at skipping. Boys are good at running.

(Cadi)

Girls are good at that as well.

(Dian)

Yes, in the sack race, first came Lucy, then me, then Bethan.

(Cadi)

This echoes changes of position among the staff:

I asked Mrs Parry to go to the science INSET on electricity because I didn't have time. She said, 'I can't even change a plug!' But she did go and she really enjoyed it.

(The Head)

Conclusion

This small-scale study provided grounds for a certain amount of optimism. Not only my own daughter but other young girls are developing the confidence to be themselves, the subject in their own lives, and to cope with problems when they arise. The interviewees reflected a range of gender identities (for example in their preferences for particular activities) and also different levels of flexibility towards variation in behaviour in and between the sex groups. They therefore displayed a range of strategies.

The girls are quite different personalities, they show confidence in different ways, [said one father about his daughters]. They might not have the assertiveness to take a stand when something happens, but they have the confidence to walk away and not be shaken up by it.

(Dan)

The study indicates the importance of social interaction, at home, with parents and siblings, and at school, with peers and teachers, in the development of this confidence. The focus of co-operation leading to confidence can be enhanced at school in teacher-organized activities. It is hoped that even this research itself may contribute in that it prompted the headteacher to say, 'I realized we don't actually sit down and talk to the children about how they feel.'

For it is not only individual development that is involved but also a transformation of social representations about gender within the wider community. As Dora says:

When a new person comes to school, I'll tell them. I'll turn everyone into independent people.

Notes

[1] 'Wizardora': British children's television series about a friendly good-looking witch (Wizardora) (Children's BBC).

[2] Chodorow, N. (1978) *The Reproduction of Mothering* (Los Angeles, University of California Press) and Gilligan, C. (1982) *In a Different Voice* (Harvard University Press).

[3] Goddard, A. (1989) *The Language Awareness Project, Years 4 and 5: Language and Gender Pack 1* (Lancaster, Framework Press).

[4] Smithers, A. and Zientek, P. (1991) *Gender, Primary Schools and the National Curriculum* (London, NASUWT and the Engineering Council).

[5] Wernersson, I. (1992) 'Gender differences in social interaction: Alternative explanations', paper presented at the First International Conference on Girls and Girlhood: Transitions and Dilemmas, 16–19 June 1992, Amsterdam, The Netherlands.

[6] Lloyd, B. and Duveen, G. (1990) 'A semiotic analysis of the development of social representations of gender', in Duveen, G. and Lloyd, B. (eds.) *Social Representations and the Development of Knowledge* (Cambridge, University of Cambridge Press). Lloyd and Duveen suggest that in learning to understand the world, the individual is not merely influenced in her development by the social representations around her – in this case, specifically representations of gender – but she can herself also influence those representations (microgenesis as opposed to ontogenesis). This transformation of social representations takes place through social interaction. See also Lloyd, B. and Duveen, G. (1992). *Gender Identities and Education. The Impact of Starting School* (Hemel Hempstead, Harvester Wheatsheaf).

[7] Bem, S. L. (1974) 'The measurement of psychological androgyny' in *Journal of Consulting and Clinical Psychology*, 45, 155–62. Bem rejects the traditionally held view that feminine and masculine characteristics are mutually exclusive (for example, the belief that a man can not have feminine characteristics such as caring without 'losing' his masculinity). If we see the feminine and masculine as two separate dimensions, then it is possible (and Bem suggests likely) that someone with strong feminine characteristics can also have strong masculine characteristics.

[8] Daniel, P. (1994) 'Promoting gender equality in schools', in Aaron, J., Rees, T., Betts, S. and Vincentelli, M. (eds.) (1994) *Our Sisters' Land. The Changing Identities of Women in Wales* (Cardiff, University of Wales Press).

[9] Huston, A. C. 'The development of sex-typing: Themes from recent research', *Developmental Review*. 5, 1–17.

[10] Clancy, J. P. (trans.) (1991) *The World of Kate Roberts. Selected Stories 1925–1981* (Philadelphia, Temple University Press/Cardiff, University of Wales Press).

11 See Blatchford, P. (1989) *Playtime in the Primary School: Problems and Improvements* (London, NFER Nelson) and Ross, C. and Ryan, A. (1990) *Can I Stay in Today Miss? – Improving the School Playground* (Stoke-on-Trent, Trentham).

12 Mahoney, P. (1985) *Schools for the Boys? Explorations in Feminism* (London, Hutchinson).

13 The research took place between November 1994 and March 1995. It was undertaken specifically for this volume.

14 Tratner, H. M., Helbing, N., Sahm, W. B. and Lohaus, A. (1989) 'Beginning awareness – rigidity – flexibility: a longitudinal analysis of sex-role stereotyping in 4 to 10 year old children'. Paper presented at the SRCD Conference, April 1989, Kansas City.

15 Huston, A. C. (1985) op. cit.

16 Archer, J. (1992) 'Childhood gender roles: social context and organisation', in H. McGurk (ed.) *Childhood Social Development* (Hove, Erlbaum).

17 Lloyd, B. and Duveen, G. (1992) op. cit.

18 *Tin Tin*: a British television cartoon series based on Hergé's adventure books. *Children's Ward*: a British children's serial based in a hospital (Children's BBC). *Grange Hill*: a British children's serial based around a city secondary school (Children's BBC). *Kelly*: British children's television series with Kelly the dog as the main character. *Startrek*: US science fiction series televised early evening in Britain. *Get Your Own Back* is a British children's television programme which provides the opportunity for children to 'get their own back' on an adult (this involves the adult in playing a lot of silly games and ending up in the 'gunge tank') (Children's BBC).

19 *Power Rangers*: US children's series, televised in Britain on ITV.

20 *Funhouse*: British children's television game show series shown on ITV. A pup named 'Scooby Doo': US cartoon about five children and a (scared) dog hunting ghosts, shown on British ITV. *Gladiators*: British television programme shown early evening, where viewers come in to challenge the resident team of athletes in various contests of physical prowess.

21 *The Wizard of Oz*: the film of the book by Frank Baum. Dorothy is the girl who leads a team to find the wizard and defeat the evil witch.

22 *Famous Five*: series of adventure books by Enid Blyton, involving four children and their dog. Georgina is George's full name.

23 *Randall and Hopkirk (Deceased)*: a US detective series televised in Britain.

24 *Pippi Longstockings*: British serialization of a book by Astrid Lindgren, televised on Sunday afternoon.

25 Gwynedd County Council (1992) *Equal Opportunities Guidelines. The Infants' Classroom* (Caernarfon, Gwynedd County Council).

26 Curriculum Council for Wales (1989) *A Framework for the Whole Curriculum 5–16 in Wales* (Cardiff, Curriculum Council for Wales).

27 Lloyd, B. and Duveen, G. (1992) op. cit.

9

The boys have taken over the playground

MARGARET SUTTON, SUSAN HUTSON AND
JACQUELINE THOMAS

Introduction

Sport remains a bastion of male culture in Wales and cultural forces
appear to combine with the structural organization of sports to
discourage and even exclude girls at all levels – on the school playing
field, in sports clubs, and even within the family. This chapter will
examine structural issues such as the provision of sport for girls as
well as cultural factors of gender identity and body image.

Much of the illustrative material is drawn from two episodes of
qualitative research carried out for the Sports Council of Wales
(1993/4). The survey was child-centred, based on in-depth interviews
with 106 girls and boys aged between ten and sixteen from north and
south Wales. These young people were encouraged to talk about their
experience of sport and leisure, so their 'voices' form an important
element in the study.

Children participate in sport in different venues – at school, sports
clubs, leisure centres, youth clubs as well as informally in parks, play-
grounds and in the streets. Previous research has confirmed popular
opinion that as children develop into adolescents participation in
sport, particularly for girls, diminishes.[1] Our conversations with
children also confirmed this, but it appeared that gender rather than
age was the over-riding factor in this disengagement. Indeed it was
clear to the girls, as well as to us, that boys dominate most sporting
venues. As one eleven-year-old girl said about playground activity:

> We [the girls] just walk around and talk. There is a netball court but the
> football is on it as well so we don't get a look in – the boys play football.

> The boys get there first and take our ball if we try to get on it. We complained to the teacher but he said there was nothing they could do.

As in the schoolyard, so in life – the boys have taken over the playground.

Nature v. culture in the gender match

> Boys are brought up to play football. Girls have to be taught how to play hockey and things. Boys just know.

It is easy to understand why this thirteen-year-old girl believed that for boys football is almost an innate rather than a learned skill. For boys, kicking a ball appears part of a natural progression, a stage of normal development – from controlling the head, sitting upright, crawling, walking, to controlling the ball. In the sporting arena such naturalistic explanations of ability or lack of ability may seem obvious.

Naturalistic views which continue to shape popular contemporary conceptions about the body suggest that the capabilities and constraints of human bodies not only define individuals but generate political, economic and social relations.[2] Inequalities in power relations are therefore not socially constructed and therefore potentially reversible but rather given or at least legitimated by the determining power of the human body. Thus, gender inequalities are the direct result of the superiority of men's 'strong' 'muscular' bodies over women's 'weak', 'delicate' bodies which are, moreover, constrained by their natural cycles of reproduction.

Biological explanations are often used as an ideological justification for inequality of opportunity in children's sport. Girls are defined as 'weak' and 'fragile' even though between the ages of ten to fourteen they may in fact be taller and stronger than their male contemporaries due to their earlier puberty.[3] When we asked the children whether there were any sports which should never be mixed, nearly half of both girls and boys regarded rugby as being unsuitable for girls because of their perceived 'weakness'. 'Rugby's too rough – big boys would hurt you', was the response of an eleven-year-old girl who was as big as any boy in her class. Many boys also offered biological reasons for girls' exclusion from rugby for example,

> After all, girls have babies and something might happen on the rugby field to hurt them – rounders would be all right though.

These prepubescent children had clear notions of what was appropriate sporting activity for girls and boys and they justified their responses with reference to biology. Although girls and boys differ in their height, weight and strength and the distribution of these features overlap between the sexes, the production of 'women' and 'men' as separate and unequal categories means that average differences are converted into absolute differences.[4] Thus a male PE teacher refused girls' requests for football lessons by saying 'girls don't know how to fall properly' (and presumably could not be taught).

Naturalistic views therefore generate ideas about what is appropriate sporting activity for males and females, rugby being perceived as 'too rough' for girls and netball 'too soft' for boys. If Berger's insight that 'men act and women appear'[5] is applied to sport it can be seen that those sports which are considered to be most appropriate for girls and women are characterized by a large element of display. For example, although sports like gymnastics, ice-skating and dance can be judged on technical merit, what is accomplished is essentially a pleasing performance or display.

Similarly in aerobics, which is one of the few sports performed by teenage girls after leaving school,[6] the aim is to achieve, maintain and display a perfect female body. This display element is enhanced by the fashion industry which provides attractive lycra sportswear. Moreover, the role models for this activity come not from the world of sport, but are rather fashion and film stars. Such perfect bodies represent goals which are impossible to reach. Chernin asks why women in the West are faced with a 'tyranny of slenderness' which restricts their social and physical growth and expression.[7] In contrast to men who are brought up to take pride in their bodies, women are socialized to dislike theirs and frequently become obsessed with the desire to reduce their size.

Should women or men stray into participation in gender-inappropriate sports or, for women, even serious competitive sport, they may well have their sexual orientation called into question. Such undertones are apparent in media descriptions of élite sportswomen. For example, Fatima Whitbread in her autobiography felt the need to emphasize her heterosexuality, thus answering unspoken questions.[8] Sportsmen, unlike women, are unlikely to be described with reference to their looks or reproductive capacities. Girls and women are thus restricted in embodying power in their physical selves. Large muscles remain unacceptable, and the fear of developing them puts many girls off PE.[9]

In contrast, sport for boys has been historically organized to reflect the development of muscular versions of masculinity.[10] Indeed, sport in general has been associated with masculinity often requiring a high degree of physical strength and more or less controlled levels of aggression or even violence.

Not only is sport a bastion of male culture in Wales but sport *is* rugby or football. Boys play these games. For them sport is about playing for a team, an activity which not only gives them status amongst their peers but also an entry into the world of men – where playing on the field, cheering on the terraces and socializing in the club bar reaffirm local, national and gender identity. For women, sport is more often an individual pursuit far from such wide social contexts.

An interview with Gethin, aged thirteen, illuminated this aspect of male sport. Gethin's brothers aged fifteen and eighteen were local rugby stars. His father also used to play competitively and was still actively involved in the local rugby club. Gethin was described privately by his mother as having 'two left feet'. Throughout the interview he claimed, quite inaccurately, to be a member of the school and rugby club teams. His mother explained that he fantasizes about being like his father and brothers and is too ashamed to admit that he is not a member of the team.

In an apparently similar situation, eleven-year-old Jessica's two elder sisters participate in a wide variety of sport to a high level. They called Jessica a 'couch potato' because she was not sporty and she herself used this label. One can suggest that although Jessica was teased about being a 'couch potato' such a label was not shameful for a girl. She was able to disclose it and even joke about it. However, in south Wales where rugby is an important element of male culture and even male identity, Gethin has a harder task in coping with the fact that he is the only male in the family who is not participating.

You can't hide your body in your satchel

Naturalistic views emphasize the link between male and female bodies and particular forms of social relations. They overlook how these relations themselves impinge upon the shape and development of bodies. In contrast, social constructionist theorists seek to explain how the significance of the body is determined ultimately by social influences which exist beyond the reach of individuals.[11] 'Culture' not 'nature' determines how we feel about our bodies and what we do with them.

Goffman has much of value to say about the relationship between the body, self-identity and social identity. Opposing naturalistic views which portray people's actions and identities as determined by their biological bodies, Goffman argues that individuals have the ability to control and monitor their bodily performances in order to facilitate social action.

According to Goffman, the meanings attributed to the body are determined by 'shared vocabularies of body idiom' which are not under the immediate control of individuals.[12] Body idiom which he considers to be the most important component of behaviour in public is a conventionalized form of non-verbal communication and includes such elements as dress, bearing, movements and physical and emotional expressions. As well as allowing us to classify information given off by others, these 'shared vocabularies' provide categories which label and grade other people hierarchically. Such classifications influence the ways in which individuals seek to manage and present their bodies.

The body for Goffman also plays an important mediating role between a person's self-identity and their social identity. The social meanings which are identified with particular bodily forms and performances tend to become internalized and hence influence both an individual's sense of self and feelings of self-worth. Goffman describes how in encounters with others people are required to act out specific social roles. He argues that if we are to be convincing in these roles we need to observe what Shilling refers to as the 'corporeal rules' which govern particular encounters.[13] However, social roles and corporeal rules may be contradictory, particularly when the rules of traditional gender-appropriate behaviour are broken and become confused. This is illustrated by a thirteen-year-old boy who found it impossible to assume simultaneously the roles of rugby player and a 'gentleman' during a mixed school match:

> I have played with girls and I don't know where you are supposed to put your hands when you tackle, so I just let them get away.

Such a mixture of biology, incompetence and embarrassment are hard obstacles to equality. Management of the body then is central to the smooth running of social encounters, to the management of social roles, and even to an individual's being accepted as a bona fide member of society. Because vocabularies of body idiom are used for self- classification as well as to classify others, this acceptance is vital to an individual's self-identity and self-worth.

According to Goffman, if a person's body management leads to them being categorized as a 'failed' member of society, the label will become internalized and incorporated into what then becomes a 'spoiled' self-identity. Goffman goes on to describe in his analysis of stigma and embarrassment how the relationship between self and social identity is mediated by the body. Embarrassment can be threatening to both self and social identities as it reveals a gap between *virtual social identity* and *actual social identity*. An individual's virtual identity is how they see themselves while their social identity is how others see them.[14]

Our virtual social identities are governed by the wish to present ourselves as 'normal' people worthy of playing a full part in society. Hence Gethin was embarrassed by the gap between his virtual social identity as a rugby star (albeit in his fantasies) and his actual social identity as an incompetent player, and he managed his resultant discomfort by lying. In contrast, Jessica was not embarrassed and consequently told the truth. There was no gap between her virtual and actual social identities as a 'couch potato'. In fact, few of the girls interviewed saw themselves as sportswomen. This exclusion from sport extended to their female relatives and even to the female sports teachers who despite being as active in sports as their male counterparts did not see themselves as sportswomen.

If one's virtual social identity reveals features which attract significant disapproval then one's virtual social identity is likely to experience a dramatic shift from being a normal and approved person to becoming a 'tainted, discounted one'.[15] Goffman has a particular interest in the stigmatization of disabled people because of the difficulties they face in being accepted as normal members of society. However, there are people who suffer a particular humiliation of stigma in relation to sport – namely those people considered to be overweight. PE lessons can be disastrous for overweight children, particularly girls, who in their interviews clearly perceived themselves as 'tainted'.

An important aspect of school sport is that it takes place in a very public arena. Sport requires a physical, public response from pupils. Consequently, it can generate feelings of personal inadequacy and public failure in the less able which is damaging to both their virtual and actual social identities. Furthermore, the source of inadequacy or failure – the body – cannot be hidden away in a desk or satchel like a failed geography project. It must remain permanently on display.

Adolescent girls are under particular pressure both socially and commercially to present the right body image, to wear the right clothes and to be the right size (eight or ten). Even in the junior school this is now a fact of life for girls. The age at which individuals first experience anxiety about their body shape and size appears to be getting younger, and research suggests that a substantial number of children as young as nine are unhappy about their bodies.[16] One eleven-year-old girl commented:

> It's important for girls to exercise to stay thin – the way they look is important. They get teased if they're fat. Body image is important for girls. A couple of girls in school get picked on because of their weight – also one boy – but girls get picked on more – there's more pressure to look good.

Not looking 'good', that is, thin, can lead to years of demoralizing taunting during sports lessons in the comprehensive school. Two fifteen-year-old girls report:

> They shout at me because I'm slow, 'Come on you fat bitch!' And lots of my friends feel the same – we're all fat and bad at it.

A thirteen-year-old says:

> I was in the netball and rounders teams once – I really enjoyed it! Then when I went to 'the comp' people made fun of me and I crumbled.

In the changing rooms, showers, gym and on the playing field these girls are in an extremely vulnerable position. It is hardly surprising that girls often 'crumbled'. Several reported that they had dropped out of school sports lessons completely, following humiliating remarks, often using considerable ingenuity to absent themselves from sessions in order to avoid comments, not only from their peers but also from PE teachers, such as, 'Come on girl – you could do with losing a few pounds.'

Looking good when one participates in sports was clearly important to both girls and boys, and sports kit was central to presenting the right image. However, the emphasis on *how* one looked good was very different for girls and boys and illuminated their respective roles – not only in the sporting arena but also in wider social life. Boys' concerns centred on wearing the *correct* kit – to be the same as their mates, to look like a team player. As one boy said: 'You have to have the *right* kit.' Girls, however, were more concerned with how they *looked* in the kit. A thirteen-year-old girl said, 'I really hate the school kit. The skirt makes my bum and thighs look enormous. I wish I could wear a track-suit.'

It was clear that the girls wished to present themselves as attractive *individuals*, not like the boys as one of the team. No boys qualified their answers with reference to their bodies. If boys were not selected to play in a team it was attributed to lack of skill. It was their ability rather than their bodies which had failed to make the grade. Berger's insight that 'men act and women appear'[17] is as relevant on the sports field as off it.

These influences are not only pervasive but also progressive, and children recognize the assumptions that underlie them – that men should be active and women should be passive.

The provision of sport is gendered and unequal

> Physical Education has a powerful role to play in developing physical self-confidence and feelings of security and of being at home in one's own body. At the moment it is far better at realising this role in the case of boys than girls.[18]

The links between sport, bodies and gender roles are central to participation but there are other reasons for gender differentiation in this area – namely the lack of provision for girls in school and in club sport.

Young people's experience of sport in school is of fundamental importance to their continued participation in later life and is also central to any attempt to overcome inequality of access to sport. Educationists have also argued that the importance of removing sexist discrimination within sport has broader relevance to the role of the school education system in eroding gender stereotypes in society. In the mid-1980s, Evans regarded the PE curriculum as a 'highly visible offender' in an area of teaching practice where gender stereotypes were more likely to be strengthened than challenged, often undermining efforts elsewhere in the school to encourage children to re-think traditional gender boundaries.[19] A decade later, our research shows that, despite a rhetoric from teachers and children about equality of opportunity and provision in sport, in fact girls still remain very much on the sidelines.

Gender issues in the teaching of PE in primary schools have received less attention than at the secondary level – 'perhaps because the more obvious divisions which operate at secondary level appear to be absent'.[20] Indeed, PE in the primary school occurs at a time when there are no physiological reasons to explain sex-related disparity in physical performance. In fact many girls will be bigger and stronger than boys at this stage. Despite this there are clear differences suggesting that cultural gender role expectations are already influential.[21] As outlined above, primary school children already identified particular sports as suitable for one sex rather than the other. However, their responses showed awareness that disparity in performance was not necessarily caused by innate differences between girls and boys but was affected by factors such as higher levels of skill resulting from practice.

There was a feeling that boys learn how to kick a ball as soon as they learn to stand, and boys certainly described their leisure time as being dominated by sport, especially football; in the street, the park, the school playground, developing skill in, and love of 'the game', a love affair which can be life-long. Many girls also spoke of playing football in this informal way. However, the skills and also attitudes of the boys are developed and matured in the male-only preserve of the community sports clubs where boys learn not only how to play but how to compete and, most importantly, how to win. This ethos of competition is in sharp contrast to that articulated in the primary schools where sport is presented as a fun activity to be enjoyed by all, irrespective of gender and ability.

Whilst nearly all the boys surveyed were or had been playing in clubs, under half of the girls had done so. Not only were girls less likely to belong to sports clubs, but the type of clubs they tended to join were different. Most boys belonged to football and rugby clubs whilst the girls' clubs represented *individual* sports such as gymnastics and trampolining activities with a strong element of display. Girls tend to join clubs at an early age, from five onwards, often dropping out around the age of eleven. The peak age for boys joining clubs was eight, but involvement can continue into adult life.

In many parts of Wales the social life of the community is centred around the rugby club which means that boys' clubs are linked to a central focus in the area's social life. As one thirteen-year-old boy said:

> People don't take enough interest in girls. Maesteg is a rugby town so it hasn't got much going for girls.

In such clubs, social activities are offered alongside sport, as well as the possibility of the highest accolade for Welshmen – to play for Wales. Girls' clubs on the other hand tend to be located in the local leisure centres and are not seen to require the same broad commitment. They are regarded as less 'serious'.

Women and girls are often involved in the male clubs in a stereotypically feminine manner – as 'support' for their men. In one family the fourteen-year-old son was recruited by a talent spotter of a major league football club. His father played for a community football club and coached at his seven-year-old son's junior club. The mother and sixteen-year-old daughter made tea and carried out secretarial work for all three clubs. They claimed that they did not have time for sport themselves but both felt that they had a duty to support the males in the family in their sporting activities which were perceived as being more 'important'. Thus in the adult world of social relations which underlie sport, young people are still receiving the message that men should be active and women passive and supportive.

Even in the 'fun' environment of the primary school the influence of male sports clubs is apparent. Despite the schools' declared commitment to mixed sport, in effect it occurred only at practice level. When it came to the serious business of matches, only the boys played. The boys often referred to the girls as 'useless' or 'rubbish' players. This remark from an eleven-year-old boy was typical: 'Girls – they're no good at games – they just get in the way.' The greater skill of the boys is hardly surprising; by the age of eleven many of them have established a history in the game – both in school and in the community.

Thus, even within the nurturing environment of the primary school where most of the teachers are women, boys are given greater opportunity to play school sports. Once in the comprehensive the more masculine competitive ethos of sport contributes to girls' even lesser participation and in many cases their eventual withdrawal from team games.

In the comprehensive, school trials mean that there is greater competition to get into teams: the emphasis has changed from the easy-going ethos of everyone getting a chance in the primary school to the serious work of developing talent in 'the best'. Much time and effort is invested in the game, particularly by boys and their specialist sports teachers. Competition in school is reinforced by competition in the club – for boys. Very few girls will have been exposed to these influences. The contrasting comments from two thirteen-year-olds illustrate typically different attitudes between boys and girls.

The boy says:

Winning is important. That's what it's all about.

The girl says:

If you're not on the team it doesn't matter at all.

Many of the children taking part in the survey agreed that they enjoyed team games. Those that did not were more often girls. Eleven-year-old Sarah and thirteen-year-old Tracy are typical. Both are overweight and said initially that they 'hated' team sports. However, Sarah admitted that she used to enjoy being in the rounders team but was now too embarrassed to play as the boys made fun of her breasts when she ran. Similarly, Tracy disclosed why she no longer enjoyed school sports: 'They only pick the good ones – if there was a "fatties" team it would be OK. I can't hope to compete.' This indicates that children are not put off by team games *per se* but by circumstances surrounding the game.

Many of the boys had belonged to a club rugby team since the age of six or seven. Even if these boys had not been playing 'seriously' this early start was seen as part of a *progression* which is taken as *natural* by their families, schools and clubs who hoped this would lead to excellence in the game.

In contrast, none of the girls had gained experience of team club sport under the age of eight. In junior school nearly twice as many boys as girls were team members. Despite this early handicap, when we asked the eleven-year-olds whether they would like to play in a team when they went to the comprehensive school, 75 per cent of the girls and 90 per cent of the boys replied that they would. Depressingly, amongst the thirteen-year-olds, only 40 per cent of girls compared to 75 per cent of boys were playing in a team. Many of the other girls would like to play but felt excluded. As two thirteen-year-olds said:

> If I was good at it I'd love to – I would even now if they had lower standards.

And:

> I was told I was too short to play netball in the first year – it put me off. I don't bother now.

By the age of thirteen it is apparent that many girls had lost hope of getting into a school team – but not through lack of interest or enjoyment. The girls expressed a feeling which was confirmed by a female PE teacher that by the end of Year 8 'it was already too late'. By the age of thirteen for girls the die is already cast on the sports field. One such girl commented regretfully:

> I would love to, but it's not possible now.

There does seem to be a critical period between the ages of seven and thirteen when children are neither too young or too old. What happens during these years is crucial for children's and particularly girls' continued involvement in sport.

Talking about sport

It is interesting to note the differences in the language used by the girls and boys when talking about their expectations concerning sport. For example eleven-year-old boys made positive statements. There was a confident assumption that they *would* continue to play rugby or football or cricket. There was no doubt at all. This response was typical:

> I've always been in the rugby team – of course I'll play for the Comp.'

When girls talk about their hopes for team sport in the comprehensive school the language they use is much more tentative, for example, 'I *hope* I can get in a team' or 'I'd *like* to play in a netball team again.'

The thirteen-year-old girls did not appear to have gained confidence in their future participation in sport and continued to use the same tentative language as the eleven-year-olds. For example: 'I'm *hoping* I will' and 'I *would really like* to.' These statements are in sharp contrast to the continued confident responses of the boys which illustrate very different expectations: 'I couldn't consider not playing' or 'I want to play for Wales.' The red caps proudly displayed in school foyers reinforce that this is an achievable ambition for many boys.

The language used by female and male sports teachers was predictable. '*Of course*' the males were sportsmen even if they no longer played. They gave accounts of past glories and present marginal involvement in school and clubs. A women teacher speaking of her own involvement in sport said: . . . '*I would like to*, if I had the time. It's difficult when you have a family.' The discourse of one specialist male teacher, though not typical, made one despair for the sporting careers of girls in Mid Glamorgan. Throughout an hour-long interview he talked only of football and rugby with not one reference to the girls whom he taught. When this was pointed out to him, he responded by saying that he thought the interview was about sport (and therefore about boys).

Together with schools and clubs, even the family colludes in making serious sport a male preserve. Nearly all the pupils reported playing sport with their families and spoke of the pleasure and encouragement which it gave them. However, it was clear that boys were expected to be better at sport than girls. When commenting on whether siblings were better or worse than them at sport it was clear that boys whatever their age were felt to be better at sport than girls. Whilst the majority of boys felt that their siblings were 'less good' than themselves, the majority of girls believed that their siblings were 'better'. Moreover, whilst all younger sisters were 'less good', over half the younger brothers were 'better'. This indicates that gender overrides the assumption that physique and sporting ability increase with age. The reason for this was apparent to many girls – boys have more opportunities. As one eleven-year-old girl said about her older brother: 'He's about the same [at sport] but he plays football and rugby for the school and the club so he gets more practice.'

Half the boys believed that being sporty made one more popular within the family. Girls did not feel like this which may reflect the fact that there is little expectation for girls to play sport but a greater expectation for boys to play and to play well. There were no references from the girls about family pride in their sporting achievements while such comments were common with boys. For example: 'It's nice when wins are reported in Assembly and even in the local newspaper. My Dad's very proud of me when I win.' This comment reminds us that boys can more easily enter the public arena through sporting achievements than girls for whom such positive reinforcement and linkage with local and national culture is rarely possible. In the next comment we have the sense of a sporting career which can only be open to a boy:

> It's good to play rugby because my brothers do and my father used to. He's proud of us. He wants us to play for Wales.

The fathers who were present during interviews were clearly proud of their sons' sporting achievements and were often anxious for them to elaborate on their answers. As one father said: 'Go on – tell her about the time you played at the Arms Park.' Few Welsh girls could be the recipient of such paternal pride.

Sport and leisure

While school sport was compulsory for the children in this study, many chose to play sport in their leisure time as well. Assumptions are often made about children, sport and physical activity. The first is that children become less physically active as they get older and that teenagers are especially inactive, particularly with the recent increase in television viewing and computer games. Second, it is believed that peer-group pressure, the demands of homework, interest in the opposite sex and other leisure activities pull young people away from sport as they get older. It was noticeable that differences in leisure patterns followed gender rather than age divisions.

Such a difference by gender can be seen in playground activity. In the junior school only a third of the eleven-year-old girls take part in any physical activity. Two-thirds reported that they would 'just hang about – talking and stuff'. The playground was dominated physically by the boys with nearly all of them playing football or mixing football with 'hanging about'. In the comprehensive schools *none* of the girls were taking part in physical activity and *all* described 'talking' as their primary activity. The boys however continue to dominate the yard with three-quarters of them still playing football. Not surprisingly the girls 'don't get a look in'.

When we asked the pupils what they did at weekends with their friends it was apparent that sport is a very significant leisure activity. However sport was mentioned four times as often by boys than by girls and clearly dominated their leisure time with football heading the list. This account by a thirteen-year-old boy is typical:

> I train down the rugby club and I go cycling. We also play football in the street or park.

If boys are playing so much football and other sports in their spare time then what are girls doing instead? 'Walking and talking' is the most commonly mentioned leisure activity for girls, together with 'going up my friend's house' and, for older girls, 'going round town, shopping'. The pupils recognized these differential leisure patterns and gave stereotypical accounts of boys' and girls' leisure. Boys' leisure was seen as more active, adventurous and outdoors whilst girl's leisure was seen as passive and spent indoors. This description of boys' leisure is typical: 'Boys are more adventurous than girls. Girls don't like to get dirty.' And girls' leisure is described as: 'Girls like to go shopping and go to each others' houses and gossip and watch *Neighbours* and stuff.'

When we asked about the leisure activities of older brothers and sisters the descriptions of older brothers often contained references to club sport and drinking: 'My brother plays a lot of football and rugby with his friends – he spends most of the weekend down the rugby club.' And: 'My older brother goes to the pub and drinks in the rugby club and goes to discos but he still plays rugby – he's got a girlfriend now.' Older sisters were often represented as being more home-based and studious: 'My sister is more studious – she stays in more – reads and does homework.' Many older sisters also went out in the evening to pubs and clubs, but the reasons for going were perceived as different. Older brothers went 'to meet his mates' and 'to get drunk' while girls went 'to find a boyfriend'.

It is commonly believed that as young people invest more time and effort into new relationships, less time and energy will be left for sport.[22] The majority of the children interviewed felt that going out with a boy or girl friend could interfere with sport. However, a third of the pupils thought that it would not make any difference, and, in this, they were generally referring to boys – for whom sport was 'serious'. This thirteen-year-old boy said:

> Some boys may, but if you're really serious you don't. My brother's got a girlfriend and he wouldn't let it interfere with his game.

Girls, however, had different priorities, and the majority felt that for them a date would be more important. One thirteen-year-old girl's observation was perceptive:

> It makes no difference to boys but it would to girls. With boys sport is a part of their lives and they would work their relationship around their football or whatever.

Adolescent girls' preoccupation with 'getting' a boyfriend can be dismissed as a frivolous goal, but research suggests that, for many, it is a goal that is also driven by emotional and economic necessity.[23] A successful partnership represents the entrance to adulthood and the fulfillment of wife and mother roles into which girls have been socialized from an early age. It is unsurprising therefore that,

> as the female teenager subculture appears to place great emphasis on catching and retaining a 'proper boyfriend', any factor, including enthusiastic participation in PE lessons and extra-curricular teams and clubs which leads to perceived loss of femininity will be avoided by those girls that regard this end as a major objective.[24]

PE is still the most segregated subject in the school curriculum and its organization remains embedded within gender ideologies of male bodily expansion and female bodily restriction. The anthropology of Mary Douglas has developed the idea of the body as a receptor of social meaning and a symbol of society. Douglas argued that the human body is the most readily available image for a social system and suggested that ideas about the body correspond closely to prevalent ideas about society.[25]

Traditional cultural practices related to gendered bodies seem to have been taken for granted by most of the young people in our study as part of the everyday reality of social life. In both sport and leisure, boys are encouraged to *expand* their bodies to 'pump it up' to be adventurous and to enjoy the *outdoors, social* elements of *team* sports. Many girls on the other hand were aware of the pressure to *restrict* and *diminish* their bodies in *individual, indoor* pursuits like diet and aerobics classes. They sought to achieve a socially approved, sexually desirable body, with the goal of 'getting' a boyfriend and hence being able to perpetuate the female role of homemaker and family *support*.

Conclusions

To understand the progressive disengagement of children from physical activity and why girls tend to disengage more than boys, together with the gendered 'choices' apparent in the range of their activities, it is important to realize that the answers will not be found solely in the world of the child but in the adult world of social relations. In a world where, increasingly, women are claiming equal opportunities with men, sport still remains largely closed to girls and women. Of course, a small number of women do play football and rugby, thus rejecting traditional gender expectations and challenging the male-dominated status quo, but such activity is often marginalized, trivialized and even ridiculed. Although sport is supposed to be taught equally to boys and girls in school, boys are more likely to play in school teams. Many boys envisage a career in sport which is not seen as a reality for girls. Specialist sports clubs, which in many parts of Wales dominate the social life of the community, involve boys from the age of eight years. Girls do not get this head start. Behind these differences in 'serious' sport participation lies the leisure world which, for boys, is dominated by sport – in particular by what Nick Hornby refers to as 'the *communal* ecstasy of football' which can be played anytime and anywhere.[26] Boys, it seems, are born with footballs – '. . . *boys just know*'.

Notes

[1] Coakley, J. and White, A. (1992) 'Making decisions: Gender and sport participation among British adolescents', in *Sociology of Sport Journal*, Vol.19, 1.

[2] For example, Laqueur, T. (1989) 'Amor veneris, vel dulcedo appeletur' in Feher M. et al. (eds.), *Fragments for a History of the Human Body* (Cambridge, MIT Press).

[3] Hadfield, J. (1976) *Childhood and Adolescence* (Harmondsworth, Penguin).

[4] Shilling, C. (1993) *The Body and Social Theory* (London, Sage).

[5] Berger, J. (1972) *Ways of Seeing* (Harmondsworth, Penguin).

6 Hutson S. et al. (1994) *Children's Participation in Sport: The Qualitative Interviews*, a report for the Sports Council of Wales.

7 Chernin, K. (1983) *Womansize: The Tyranny of Slenderness* (London, The Women's Press).

8 Whitbread, F. (1988) *Fatima: The Autobiography of Fatima Whitbread* (London, Pelham).

9 See Bryson, L. (1987) 'Sport and the maintenance of masculine hegemony' in *Women's Studies International Forum*, 10, 349–60.

10 Graydon, J. (1983) 'But it's more than a game. It's an institution' in 'Feminist perspectives on sport', *Feminist Review*, 13, 5–16 .

11 Goffman, E. (1968) *Stigma: Notes on the Management of Spoiled Identity* (Harmondsworth, Penguin) 35. Turner, B. (1984) *The Body and Society* (Oxford, Blackwell).

12 Goffman, E. (1963) *Behaviour in Public Places: Notes on the Social Organization of Gatherings* (New York, The Free Press).

13 Shilling, C. (1993) op. cit.

14 Goffman, E. (1968) op. cit., 12.

15 Ibid., 12.

16 See Hall, C. (1992) 'Girls aged nine "are obsessed by weight"', *Independent*, 10 April 1992.

17 Berger, J. (1972) op. cit.

18 Leaman, O. (1986) 'Physical Education and Sex Differentiation' in *British Journal of Physical Education*' Vol.17, 4, 123–4.

19 Evans, J. (1984) 'Muscles, sweat and showers – girls' conceptions of physical education and sport: A challenge for research and curriculum reform' in *Physical Education Review* Vol.7, 1, 12–18.

20 Williams, A. (1989) 'Equal opportunities and primary school physical education' in *British Journal of Physical Education* Vol.20, 177–9.

21 See Cooper, A. (1986) 'Gender and Primary School Physical Education' in *British Journal of Physical Education*, Vol.17, 4, 148.

22 See Coakley, J. and White, A. (1992) op. cit.

23 See Griffin C. et al. (1982) 'Women and Leisure' in Hargreaves J. (ed.) *Sport, Culture and Ideology* (London, Routledge & Kegan Paul).

24 See Cockerill, S. and Hardy, C. (1987) 'The attitudes of fourth year girls towards the secondary school PE curriculum' in *Bulletin of Physical Education*, Vol.23, 1, 6–12.

25 Douglas, M. (1970) *Natural Symbols: Explorations in Cosmology* (London, The Cresset Press).

26 Hornby, N. (1993) *Fever Pitch* (London, Victor Gollancz).

10

Marriage, family and career aspirations of adolescent girls

HILARY LLOYD YEWLETT

There's still a bit of prejudice against women doing anything they want to.
There's still a feeling about that they are the lower sex . . . *but it's gradually changing.* [My italics]   (Jane)

There really isn't any difference between men and women. Women are equal and they can do the job as well as any man.   (Frances)

These words of two fifteen-year-old Welsh schoolgirls introduce the main concerns of this chapter, namely, how do adolescent girls see and understand their place in society today? What expectations do they have for themselves and their futures? Do young Welsh women of today have wider horizons and bolder career aspirations than those of their mothers and grandmothers? Are they indeed modern-day 'daughters of the revolution'?[1]

This chapter is based on research which was conducted in two schools in east Swansea during the summer term of 1994. Thirty fifteen-year-old girls participated in two half-hour interviews. The girls were matched in terms of academic ability and social class. All but three of the girls were born in Swansea, the exceptions being born in Bangladesh, Dublin and London. The primary aim of the first interviews was to encourage the girls to talk freely about their lives in their own terms. To this end, questions were constructed around the following topics: parents, siblings, school and family life, leisure-time pursuits, religion, boyfriends, marriage and family, interests and ambitions. The second interviews were more sharply focused and more directive, following up areas of special interest to the girls. These proved to be, overwhelmingly: marriage, career and the role of women in today's society.[2]

Swansea was chosen as the location for this small-scale ethnographic research project because the researcher is both a graduate of, and a teacher at, the university there. Described by Dylan Thomas as 'an ugly, lovely town . . . crawling, sprawling, by a long and splendid curving shore',[3] Swansea is the second city of Wales, with a population of over 187,000. During the eighteenth and nineteenth centuries, it was one of the most important centres in the world for the manufacture of metal. Gwyn A. Williams comments graphically: 'For years, the real economic capital of Chile was Swansea, luxuriating in its nitrate clippers and Cape Horners.'[4] Peter Stead points out that 'it was copper that triggered off the development of Swansea as a modern urban centre'.[5] In 1974, the city became the administrative centre for the new county of West Glamorgan. Stead also observes that the key to Swansea's modern identity is to be found in the east, for the city 'provides a classic instance of the generalization that cities tend to generate their wealth in the east and then locate their smarter suburbs in the west'.[6]

East Swansea is still a predominantly working-class area. In June 1994, the unemployment rate for West Glamorgan was 9.2 per cent, the rate in the principality as a whole also being 9.2 per cent. The rate for Great Britain at that time was 9.1 per cent (Welsh Office Statistics). Research has repeatedly shown that there is a very high correlation between one's social class and one's level of educational attainment.[7] It was for this reason that the research was carried out in central Swansea and the suburb of Morriston, where unemployment rates remain high. However, religion was also one of the research variables[8] and though the Catholic school, where some of the fieldwork was conducted, lies to the east of the city, its pupils are drawn from a wide catchment area. The socio-economic background of these pupils is consequently more diverse than that of those pupils who attend the inner-city school.

The Catholic school (Cardinal Smith) has recently opted out of local-authority control and, as it now has power over its own budget, some of its resources have been used to make the environment more attractive to work in. The staff room, for example, resembles a comfortable hotel lounge and the gymnasium has much of the equipment that is associated with a sophisticated leisure centre. The inner-city school (Morgans) has the threat of closure hanging over it and, although areas are attractively painted, with parts being double glazed in an attempt to eliminate the noise of traffic, this once famous, former grammar school which numbered Sir Harry Secombe among its old boys, is old and no amount of paint will disguise its decaying fabric.

The chapter draws heavily on transcripted conversations and allows the girls to speak for themselves – about their families, their experiences at school, including gender divisions and sexual discrimination, their expectations of work and their views on marriage.

School, home, leisure and gender

Because the interviews were conducted during school time and on school premises, the interviewer sought to put the girls at their ease by talking, initially, about that common environment. The inner-city school 'Morgans', has the reputation of being a 'second chance' school and the girls who have moved there from other secondary schools in Swansea do not seem to regret the change.

> I was in – –. It's just not a good school at all. Everybody boasts about it. But it's not a good school. I learned more in six months here than what I did in a year in – –. [Nervous laugh and some reluctance to tell me why she left her previous school.] My mother wasn't happy with me there. It's such a big school. In a smaller school there's more opportunities, in a way. Although there isn't a sixth form, we can go on to college, and not everyone in – – went on to sixth form. I've been here two years and I love it. We've moved down the Marina now so it's easy for me to get here. I don't regret the change.
> (Andrea)

Rees and Rees allege that there is some considerable evidence to suggest that an academically élitist ethos, more conventionally associated with the grammar schools, pervades the comprehensives in Wales.[9] Certainly, before comprehensive re-organization, – –, situated as it is in the more affluent suburbs of west Swansea, enjoyed a high academic reputation, which unlike Morgans, it has not entirely cast off.

Nevertheless, those girls who attend Morgans clearly take pleasure in the experience.

> I was accepted at – –, but all my friends were coming here, so I decided to come too. I don't regret my decision.
> (Joan)

The girls of Morgans were most concerned to convince me that the 'bad' reputation of their school was unfounded. Many of them made observations similar to these:

> Sometimes, with exams and stuff, we do get a bad reputation, but we had a girl last year who had nearly all 'A's and 'B's in her GCSEs. Nobody outside got to hear of that. Other schools are always being put forward as the highest, but we just get put down for the bad things we do. The good things we do don't get published. (Julie)

> This is a good school. It's small. You know everybody and you get to know the teachers better. It did have a bad reputation, but it's getting better. They've tried to improve things with double glazing, new computers and a lovely new library. Yes, we did have a bad name because of past people, but it's picking up now. I prefer a small school because you get to know everybody. I know every teacher. In some schools, they don't even know half the teachers. This place is small, nice and friendly. (Kate)

Comments such as these suggested that the staff at Morgans worked very hard to provide the pupils with quality education, despite their unlovely surroundings.

Cardinal Smith has recently become a grant-maintained school and it now has much more lavish facilities than it had when it was in the care of the local authority. The girls did not comment about these changes very much, however. They were much more concerned than were the girls at Morgans about what they perceived to be the strictness of the regime:

> This school is strict. About uniforms and everything. They go over the top about coats, but I suppose it's because they don't want to differentiate. They are strict about homework too. (Mary)

> This school reckons it practises equality of opportunity, but it won't allow girls to wear trousers. Girls in some other schools do. (Joyce)

In both schools, the girls were aware of gender bias in some classrooms:

> Our first CDT teacher preferred the boys. He didn't like the girls at all. He used to say 'You shouldn't be in here anyway, so don't bother to do anything.' He wouldn't even let us make a key ring. (Joan, Morgans)

> Some of the teachers do discriminate between boys and girls in class. Our

science teacher used to ask all the boys questions. He was more friendly towards them than us. The good teachers help anyone who is trying hard – boy or girl. (Carole, Cardinal Smith)

The women teachers treat us fairly. Most of the men do too. But there's one teacher, a man, who automatically thinks we're dull – all of us. He has a bad attitude when he's teaching. He just talks to the boys about sport and ignores the girls, unless he's flirting with them. (Jean, Cardinal Smith)

Delamont has commented on the sexual stereotyping in some teaching in Welsh schools.[10] The girls interviewed in this study were aware that such stereotyping existed not only in the world of school but also in the world of work:

I don't think that catering will attract as many men as women, because the attitude 'Oh, you can't be a cook, you're a boy' still occurs. There's three boys in my cookery class. They are better cooks than some of the girls, but I don't think they want to do cookery as a career. (Gail, Morgans)

Isn't it interesting the way jobs are described? Sometimes they call a woman a cook and a man a chef. Do you think it's important, the way people label jobs?

Yes. Chef seems to be higher than a cook. There are still men's jobs and women's jobs. They may be similar jobs but the men's jobs seem to have titles that make the work look better and more important. More glamorous – with more status and more money. We don't talk about this much in school. (Gail, Morgans)

Our cookery teacher is a woman. Our CDT teacher is a man. There are seven boys and three girls in the cookery class. Our teacher tends to give the boys more help, because the boys can look at her dumb when she asks them to do something. (Alma, Cardinal Smith)

Some of the girls were aware that sexual discrimination can sometimes affect boys, as well as girls.

Girls and boys have got more equal life chances now, but there is still discrimination in some areas. Child-minding is not an exclusively female job, but men wouldn't enjoy changing dirty nappies. (Angela, Cardinal Smith)

Men are just as good as women with kids, but they are more into care than playing around with babies. My brother is a good father. He takes care of his kids. Men are supposed to be tough, so the image of being a nursery nurse is not appealing to them. They'd get a lot of stick from their mates if they said they wanted to be something like that.   (Frances, Cardinal Smith)

It's not as bad as it used to be. Some fathers are good with babies now. My mother says that my father was very good with me, because I'm the youngest.   (Jane, Morgans)

Within their families, work was not necessarily divided along gender lines. It depended on the relationship between the partners:

My stepfather tends to do more of the housework than my mother. He buys and sells second-hand cars, so he's often at home. He does most of the cooking too, but then, he's a qualified chef. If he's bored in the house, he cleans. Strange, very strange! [Said with wry humour.] He likes to live in a tidy atmosphere. He doesn't like messy places and if something's untidy, he won't go into the room until it's tidied up. He'll even clean up someone else's mess, if there's no one else in the house to do it. But he expects me to clean up my own mess. My mother does her fair share.   (Helen, Morgans)

Ruddock has also noted the beginnings of some different basis of sharing in the home,[11] but despite these indications of change, the majority of the Swansea girls' mothers appeared to end up doing 'their fair (?) share' of the housework.

Both my parents work, but my mother ends up doing most of the things around the house.   (Anna, Cardinal Smith)

My father works nights on the taxis. My mother works part-time in a local shop. She carries the major responsibility for running the home.
(Andrea, Morgans)

My mother does all the housework. My father just sits there. He hasn't got a job. In my culture [Asian], traditionally, men do less work at home than women. Things might change in the future. Not now, but later on.
(Radha, Morgans)

Life is still much harder for girls than boys. I do much more work around the house than my brother. With school, and all, it's a lot.
(Anna, Cardinal Smith)

Many of the girls have part-time, paid employment after school hours, working mainly at the weekends as waitresses in cafés or hotels. Some of them work long hours for little pay:

> I've got a part-time job in R's in Morriston. It's a fish bar and a restaurant. I work there Tuesdays, Fridays and Saturdays. Tuesdays and Fridays from 4.30 to 8.30; Saturdays 11.00 to 7.00. I'm paid £2 an hour.
>
> (Angela, Cardinal Smith)

Clare (Cardinal Smith) works from necessity:

> My father is not in work. Neither is my mother. I've got three brothers: thirteen, twelve and nine. My sister is ten. They help me. I get £4 for delivering papers.

Only Elsa (Cardinal Smith) sees her part-time work as being of help to her in her chosen future career:

> I've always liked hairdressing and I work Saturdays in a hairdressers. I've got loads of leaflets at home about being a hairdresser. My boss gave them to me. I wash hair, put in perms, help around. I like it. It's brilliant. The boss is training me as well, so that's even better. I've learned about the care of the hair. I learn to X-Ray hair too. I work from 9 till 3 and I get a bonus if I stay on after 3. We're all moving to London next year. My Mum has promised to put me with Vidal Sassoon then.

Few of the girls, however, are as single-minded in their pursuit of leisure activities. Like McRobbie's,[12] these girls take pleasure in hanging round in groups.

> I go out every night, except Thursdays, when I play netball. 'Out' means up my friend's house, down the Marina, or hanging round the streets.
>
> (Gwyneth, Morgans)

> I go baby-sitting or we hang around the streets. Hanging round the streets is fun.
>
> (Susan, Cardinal Smith)

> I either stay in and do homework, or I just walk about the streets. I go down Caswell [Bay] in the summer.
>
> (Helen, Morgans)

Several of the girls' parents own caravans on the Gower peninsula or in west Wales. When circumstances permit, they spend weekends there as a family. The part-time closure of a youth club near Morgans school, in the city centre, has meant the loss of a much-valued facility for some.

> The Youth Club used to be open four nights a week, but the Council has reduced the hours and now it's only two nights a week. That's boring, because we haven't got anywhere else to go.
>
> (Kate, Morgans)

Neither the leisure centre in central Swansea, nor the multi-purpose sports complex at Morfa stadium to the east, holds any attractions for these girls. For some, the entrance fee is beyond their means.

Marriage and career

Unlike the girls studied by Willis and cited by Delamont, the girls interviewed in this study were not blinded by 'the rosy glow of romance to the realities of the labour market'.[13] Many of them either did not believe in the institution of marriage or did not regard it as a life-long commitment to one partner. Some of them, clearly, had been badly hurt by the break-up of their parents' marriages:

> My mother and father are divorced. My mother married again and divorced again. She shames me [embarrassed laugh].
>
> (Clare, Cardinal Smith)

> It's my stepfather's Italian surname. My real name is H–. But I don't know where my real father is. I haven't seen him since I was one. I've got one real brother. After my parents divorced, my mother met an Italian. They had three children together, so we're five. I don't get on with my stepfather . . . He's not too happy with me, but I don't care. He's more concerned about his own son who's in this school.   (Susan, Cardinal Smith)

> My parents are divorced. I have a stepfather. I don't see my father. I don't want to have any contact with him. He's not a nice type. My mother doesn't like me to talk about him. She took me away from him when I was very young. She did the right thing, I believe, and I really don't want to know.   (Carol, Morgans)

> My mother's on the social. My Nana gets us what my mother can't. We're taking my father to court for maintenance. He thinks more of his second marriage than he does of his children. No, he hasn't got any children with his second wife [sounds bitter].   (Alma, Cardinal Smith)

I'm cautious about marriage, because of what my parents went through. They're divorced now. (Donna, Cardinal Smith)

Even if the girls' parents are still married to each other, they see their older siblings rejecting the institution of matrimony as a way of life:

My brother's in the RAF. He's got a little girl who's three. He's not married. (Kim, Morgans)

My oldest sister is training to be a junior school teacher. She lives in a flat in Townhill. She's got a little girl, aged two. She's not married. (Joan, Morgans)

One of my sisters has a baby. She's just got engaged. (Angela, Cardinal Smith)

Most of the girls themselves have boyfriends, though none seems to be in a serious relationship.

I've got three boyfriends. They don't know about one another. Why shouldn't I have fun like that? Boys have always done it to girls. (Gwyneth, Morgans)

I've got two boyfriends. They don't know about each other. One's ugly and one is handsome. One's got personality and one hasn't. The handsome one with the horrible personality buys me stuff. The one from the other school takes me on his motorbike everywhere. The one in this school just takes me up his house. They don't know about one another and I'm not serious about either of them. (Joy, Cardinal Smith)

My boyfriend is eighteen. He's a right criminal. He got sent down for GBH. It was his first offence. He didn't like it in prison. So far, he hasn't done anything else wrong. If he did, I'd dump him. (Jane, Morgans)

I've got a boyfriend. He's on the dole. He can't get any work, even though he did a painting and decorating course at the Tech. (Andrea, Morgans)

Morgan has shown how, since the Second World War, the traditional way of life for Welsh women – housework and chapel on Sunday – has changed irrevocably.[14] Wales is no longer a puritanical, Sabbatarian land. The impact of the chapels on social life has almost totally diminished. That the chapel ethos no longer has much impact upon moral values in relation to marriage is clear in these girls' views about the institution:

> I'm not going to get married. It's too much hassle. I might live with a fellow, though. You wouldn't have to pay a solicitor for the divorce then.
>
> (Jane, Morgans)

> I don't know if I'll get married. I know people say it's immoral, but I'd have to live with someone first, before I could marry them. Someone said to me the other day 'You can't do that!' Why can't I do that? I don't think people take much note of religion today. There's so many divorces. It's better to live with someone and make sure, before you get a certificate and a ring. But marriage doesn't stop people these days having affairs anyway. It's the principle of marriage too, in a way. If you were just living with him, he could walk out any time. Marriage is more of a commitment. I would walk out on someone, if he'd done something really bad. You'd need a career, though, if you were going to pack your bags and go. You couldn't go without a penny behind you. So, a career has got to come first.
>
> (Gwyneth, Morgans)

None of these girls sees marriage as an alternative to having a career of one's own:

> I'll get married one day. I wouldn't give up work when I get married. I want to have my own career, earn my own money and not have to rely on my husband. If he was sacked, where would we be? I wouldn't mind staying in the house all day, living in the lap of luxury, but some things you just can't do! [laughs]
>
> (Kate, Morgans]

> In my culture, girls have to be married. That's their destiny – to get married and have children. I don't like arranged marriages. I don't like to be picked out like you'd pick a new car. But not many arranged marriages end in divorce. I'd continue my career after marriage, and I wouldn't marry any man who'd try to stop me.
>
> (Radha, Morgans)

Even at Cardinal Smith, where one would expect the spiritual power of the Church to prevail, the girls look forward to maintaining their economic independence within marriage.

> I'll get married one day. Maybe in my twenties. I don't know about children yet. I don't want to have them too young. I wouldn't give up work if I got married. I want to be independent. I'd never take money from my man.
>
> (Susan, Cardinal Smith)

If I married, I'd want my husband to have his career and I'd like to have mine. We don't talk about this much in school, though we did once. The boys thought the girls should stay at home. They believe that is what should happen. If I had a husband who expected that from me, he could sling his hook straight away. (Carol, Cardinal Smith)

The suggestion here is that boys still need to be educated to accept the changes in domestic roles and responsibilities that will come about as a result of these girls achieving financial emancipation. Some of the boys are still seen to be victims of sex-role stereotyping and clinging to out-dated myths regarding women. Ruddock suggests that 'the way that the school manages its advice about futures is pivotal', and that gender equality should be raised as a whole-school issue.[15]

The girls at Cardinal Smith are taught the conventional Catholic view of marriage, though not all of them accept their church's teaching:

We are taught that marriage is for life, but it doesn't work out like that now. Life can be tougher for women than for men. As a woman, if you've got kids and you're divorced, you're stuck with the kids. The men just go off and find someone else and it's just the mother that does everything for the kids. (Clare, Cardinal Smith)

What about sex before marriage?

The teaching about sex and contraception is as it has always been. We have booklets about it. They don't actually say: 'Right then, you're not allowed to have sex before you are married', but they work around to it, so we know clearly that that is the church's teaching. It was our parents' decision to send us to this school, but that doesn't mean that we agree with everything in our religion. (Clare, Cardinal Smith)

The church believes that if you are pregnant, then you should get married straight away. I don't think it's wrong to have sex before marriage, though not with anyone. In Year 9 there's a girl who's pregnant and they pick on her, so she doesn't come to school. They don't make fun of the men, do they? It's always the girl. (Barbara, Cardinal Smith)

Traditional views of female sexuality seem to be perpetuated, not only at Cardinal Smith, but also in the teenage culture of which these girls are part.

> Boys only want you for one thing. A few might really like you. If a girl has sex with a boy, then she gets called a slag, but if a boy has sex with a girl, then he's thought to be quite a lad. Of course it's not fair. But we can't do anything about it. Even if you tell a boy 'No', he'll go back and tell his friends that you did have sex with him, and your reputation will spread around the school. It isn't just true in this school. It's what boys and girls say down the precinct and in the discos.　　　　　(Alma, Cardinal Smith)

As Lees points out: 'Defining girls in terms of their sexual reputation rather than their attributes and potentialities is a crucial mechanism of ensuring their subordination to boys.'[16] Not all of the girls interviewed were sufficiently confident to challenge the boys' boasting, though some of them, like the girls in Lees' sample, develop a vocabularly of their own to put the boys down.

All of the girls planned to work outside the home. In contrast to the Canadians interviewed by Gaskell,[17] the Welsh girls taking part in this study saw working for pay as an important personal right as well as an economic necessity. That much, at least, has changed in twenty years.

> If you leave school without qualifications, you are unlikely to get a job and you'll end up on the dole for most of your life. That's not something I want. I want to have a job that I enjoy and a good salary, so that I can have my own house.　　　　　(Jane, Morgans)

> I'd like to go on to college and do 'A' levels. My parents are happy for me to do that. Then I'd like to get a good job – not teaching! I like to be in charge, so it would have to be a job where I can have my say. If I want something, then I'm determined to do it and I work until I get it.
> 　　　　　(Glenda, Morgans)

Many of the young women interviewed explicitly reject the old expectations of wife and mother. All their own mothers are working or are actively seeking employment. For many, it is financial pressure that obliges them to work. Nevertheless, these girls have learned from their mothers that work outside the home is more interesting and rewarding then 'boring old housework', but, the kind of paid work they are aiming for reflects, in the main, their social class origins. None of the girls interviewed came from professional families and only one of them aspires to enter the professions. Even she is torn between becoming an air hostess and a lawyer.

I want to be an air hostess when I leave school. I like flying and catering. I fly every year to Italy on holidays. I've wanted to be an air hostess since I was in junior school. I'd like to fly all over the world. We've just filled in some career aptitude questionnaires in school. I'm suited to social work, it appears! I wouldn't mind being a lawyer, either.   (Frances, Cardinal Smith)

Two girls envisaged their futures in the precarious world of the theatre. Neither of them was aware of how useful it would be to them to speak Welsh. Welsh-speaking actors are at a premium in the principality. However, both girls were realistic about the difficulties of achieving success in the theatre. Even so, they seemed determined to pursue their chosen career:

My favourite subjects are drama and English. After GCSE, I want to go to Drama School. Very hard. Very competitive. My mother [parents are divorced] is writing to find out if there are any drama clubs outside school for me to go to, so that I can have extra practice. They've got drama classes in the Grand Theatre, but I've never been there. I like singing and dancing . . . no, I don't mind people looking at me. I've never been shy of performing in front of other people. I was in loads of plays in primary school. I've been in all the musicals in this school. They're really good.

(Sandra, Cardinal Smith)

I want to do something in the theatre. Anything I can get. Sweeping the stage if I have to. I've just had my exam. I had an A for drama. My parents are OK about my career choice, but they tell me to make sure that I have something to fall back on. I was thinking of journalism if I can't get into the theatre. I couldn't get to do work experience in the theatre. They wouldn't take me in the Grand or the Taliesin. We tried the BBC and S4C [Welsh TV] too. I'm trying to get a placement in the Sherman Theatre [Cardiff] but you've got to book ages in advance.

(Gwyneth, Morgans)

Work experience is something that is made available to all pupils in comprehensive schools in Swansea, at the appropriate stage in their school careers. The girls at Cardinal Smith had not yet had this experience, whereas the girls at Morgans had. Its impact upon them was very positive, even though many of them were given experience of traditionally female jobs. Several had worked in restaurants, some had been to Marks and Spencer, others had been to nursery schools.

Whereas all agreed that 'things are changing now, child care is not an exclusively female job', several of the girls saw the professional care of children as a rewarding career.

> I'm thinking of doing something with children. I might become a nanny. I do baby-sit quite a lot. My Mum's friend has got a little daughter, three. I try to take her out a lot. I get on well with her and it gives her parents a break. I went to an infants' school for work experience. Apart from the children pulling my hair, it was alright. After my GCSEs, I'll probably go to Tech, and do the NNEB [nursery nurse course] there.   (Jane, Morgans)

In Jane's second interview, she expressed some reservations about her choice of career. She made plain why her second choice was more tentative:

> If I don't become a nanny, I'd like to be something like a mechanic. The only thing is sexual discrimination. There was a case about it in the papers. I like to get messy, so I wouldn't mind doing it. It would probably take me a bit of time to learn where things went. We don't do anything about mechanics at school.

Andrea (Morgans) had no doubt about her choice of career:

> I want to work with young children, anything like that. I went on work experience to a local junior school. I went in all the classes. I liked the nursery and six and seven year olds best.

Joan (Morgans) was torn between two traditionally female jobs:

> I'd like to be a nursery teacher or maybe work in an office, like a secretary. I'm in between at the moment.

At Cardinal Smith too, the appeal of nursery school teaching and office work is equally strong, though one of the girls did want to do something slightly out of the ordinary:

> For ages I've wanted to be a vet, but I don't think I'm brainy enough. My mother said 'Become a policewoman and train dogs.' It's a good idea because dogs are what I like best. I'm going to visit the Police at Bridgend shortly to find out more.   (Carol, Cardinal Smith)

Other aspirations ran along more traditional lines.

> I'd like to work in a hotel or a hospital. I went to a hotel for work

experience. It was brilliant. Since then, I've become really interested in catering, and I'm going to do catering at the Tech.

(Joy, Cardinal Smith)

Doreen (Morgans) with her droll sense of humour, once had thoughts about taking up her mother's line of work;

My mother wants me to go to Tech, but I don't want to. She was going to fix me up in her work, but I can't sew a button on. We've had sewing lessons. Mrs Hemming [unware of the pun] gave them to us, but only on paper. You put your foot on the pedal and you were away! I couldn't follow the tracks on the paper. Mine were all over the place! I went to B & Q for my work experience. It's quite nice up there. I wanted to be a fire fighter once, but I can't stand heights. And you've got to be fit. I'd be dead by the time I was twenty-six. A woman came up the school once and she was showing me everything. That's what got me interested. Then, I thought, 'No, never mind.' I'm scared of heights. You got to go up in a building. No thanks! Going up on that ladder? Trying to save someone? I'd die – just looking down, I would!

After hearing the girls' radical views on marriage, their career aspirations came as something of a disappointment. It seemed that many of the girls interviewed aspired to careers that were likely to reproduce not only their class position, but also their subservient gender position. Yet, as Gaskell points out:

Expectations and decisions at this age are not binding. The ways these young people anticipate and plan for life may not last and certainly will not take into account all the contingencies that will shape their behaviour over the years. *However, the way they anticipate the future affects what the future will bring them'*.[18] [My italics.]

It may be, however, that they are more hard-headed and realistic about the job market than one gives them credit for being. Jane (Morgans) sees the situation thus:

There's still a bit of prejudice against women doing anything they want. There's still a feeling about that women are the lower sex and some men still think women should be chained to the kitchen sink, but it's gradually changing.

Let Frances (Cardinal Smith) have the last word:

There isn't really any difference between men and women. Some men expect women not to do certain kinds of jobs and then they criticize women for doing them, saying that they perform them badly. Yet, if you want something badly enough, you've just got to go for it and fight everybody all the way, until you *do* get what you want, because if you want it badly enough, then you *will* do it. Women are equal and they can do the job as well as any man.

As Muir protests, 'how long must women still have to work twice as hard in order to be considered half as good as their male colleagues?'[19] With the closure of the pits, the stereotyped image of the Welsh miner has begun to disappear. Wales is now in the grip of a new industrial revolution which will transform patterns of employment in the next century. With the transformation will surely come better career prospects for women and, one hopes, an end forever to the myth that a woman is 'less equal' than a man.

The girls in east Swansea are right: women can do most jobs just as well as men. Those women 'called up' for work during the Second World War proved that. Those were years of social fracture. What many fail to realize, however, is that the fissure is permanent – the words of these young women attest to this. They provide evidence of changing attitudes and changing roles. The girls in this study question traditional sexual stereotypes in a lively and courageous manner. They desire personal and economic independence and do not view marriage as a viable alternative to a career. The views they express indicate fundamental shifts in the perception of marriage and its role for women.[20] These girls do not intend to relate to the world solely in terms of their relationship to men and children. They crave a much greater independence through work, albeit mostly of a traditional female kind. Perhaps the current deep economic recession has restricted their job opportunities and aspirations[21] but these Welsh daughters nevertheless provide us with grounds for much optimism for the future as they seek to strengthen and speed the development of women's hard-won emancipation.

Notes

[1] See Betts, S. (1994) 'The Changing Family in Wales' in Aaron, J., Rees, T., Betts, S. and Vincentelli, M. *Our Sisters' Land, The Changing Identities of Women in Wales* (Cardiff, University of Wales Press).

Marriage, family and career aspirations of adolescent girls 257

2 The motivation for this research came from two recently published books – Wilson, M. (ed.) (1991) *Girls and Young Women in Education: A European Perspective* (Oxford, Pergamon Press) and Gaskell, S. J. (1992) *Gender Matters from School to Work* (Milton Keynes, Open University Press). Wilson deals with the problem of girls' education and work from a European perspective, whereas Gaskell delineates Canadian girls' experience. As a young woman, I studied and taught in two European countries, France and Sweden. As a mature academic I have visited Canada more than once. Now, as an established teacher in the University of Wales, I was curious to discover if the experience and hopes of Welsh girls mirrored those of their European and North American counterparts. Qualitative research appealed to me because it has something in common with the technique of the novelist (I am an English teacher) who also has an insatiable curiosity about human behaviour, even if she uses different methods to record it. This study used life history interviews. The elicitation of structured autobiographies for the purposes of social research is one of the central methods employed by ethnographers, see Hammersley, M. and Atkinson, P. (1993) *Ethnography: Principles in Practice* (London, Tavistock).

3 Thomas, D. (1954) *Quite Early One Morning* (London, Dent), 1.

4 Williams, G. A. (1985) *When was Wales?* (Harmondsworth, Penguin), 222.

5 Stead, P. (1992) *Swansea* (Swansea, Christopher Davies), 7.

6 Stead, P. (1992) op.cit., 9.

7 Halsey, A. H., Heath, A. F. and Ridge, J. (1980) *Origins and Destinations: Family, Class and Education in Modern Britain* (Oxford, Clarendon Press); Jonsson, J. O. and Mills, C. (1993) 'Class and Educational Attainment in Historical Perspective: a Swedish-English comparison'. *British Journal of Sociology*, Vol.44, 2, 213–49.

8 A Catholic background did not affect the girls' career aspirations, nor did it influence their attitudes to marriage and family life.

9 Rees, G., and Rees, T. L. (eds.) (1980) *Poverty and Social Inequality in Wales* (London, Croom Helm) 83.

10 Delamont, S. (1990) *Sex Roles and the School* (2nd edn.) (London, Routledge).

11 Ruddock, J. (1994) *Developing a Gender Policy in Secondary Schools* (Buckingham, Open University Press).

12 McRobbie, A. (1991) *Feminism and Youth Culture* (London, Macmillan).

13 Delamont, S. (1990) op. cit., 54.

14 Morgan, K. O. (1981) *Rebirth of a Nation: Wales 1880–1980* (Oxford, Oxford University Press and Cardiff, University of Wales Press).

15 Ruddock, J. (1994) op. cit., 111.

16 Lees, S. (1993) *Sugar and Spice* (Harmondsworth, Penguin).

17 Gaskell, S. J. (1992) op. cit.

18 Gaskell, S. J. (1992) op. cit., 73.

19 Muir, E. (1994) 'The Highest Honour' in Aaron, J. Rees, T., Betts, S., and

Vincentelli, M. (eds.) *Our Sisters' Land: The Changing Identities of Women in Wales.* (Cardiff, University of Wales Press).

[20] See McCrindle, J. and Rowbottom, S. (eds.) (1977) *Dutiful Daughters* (Harmondsworth, Penguin).

[21] See Coote, A. and Campbell, B. (1982) *Sweet Freedom* (London, Pan Books).

Index